MARINE
INVERTEBRATES

The POCKETEXPERT™ Guide Series
for Aquarists and Underwater Naturalists

Front cover: Elegant sea star (*Fromia monilis*), page 370
Photograph by Denise Nielsen Tackett

Back cover photographs:
Janine Cairns Michael (top); Scott W. Michael (center and bottom)

Produced and distributed by:
T.F.H. Publications, Inc.
One TFH Plaza
Third and Union Avenues
Neptune City, NJ 07753
www.tfhpublications.com

MARINE INVERTEBRATES

500+ ESSENTIAL-TO-KNOW AQUARIUM SPECIES

TEXT BY

RONALD L. SHIMEK, PH.D.

MICROCOSM

tfh

PROFESSIONAL SERIES™

T.F.H. Publications
One T.F.H. Plaza
Third and Union Avenues
Neptune City, NJ 07753
www.tfhpublications.com

ISBN 1-890087-66-1

**Library of Congress Cataloging-in-Publication Data
available on request**

Designed by Alice Z. Lawrence and Alesia Depot

Co-published by
Microcosm Ltd.
P.O. Box 550
Charlotte, VT 05445
www.microcosm-books.com

To my wife, partner, and best friend,
Roxie Fredrickson, whose support and reasoned criticisms
have really made my tertiary career as a reef aquarist and
marine aquarium writer possible.

ACKNOWLEDGMENTS

THE INFORMATION IN THIS BOOK IS THE RESULT OF MANY years of observing invertebrates in the wild and in aquariums, as well as many years of answering questions about odd and interesting animals. I thank John Link, of the Reef Central BBS, for providing me with a forum in which I have been able to discuss animal care with reef aquarists. The input of aquarists was invaluable in the choice of animals or groups of animals discussed in this text. Every animal discussed herein has been seen in a reef tank.

Additionally, the information here is the result of a career of invertebrate zoology, with my initial training from Drs. Harold Picton at Montana State University, Alan Kohn, Paul Illg and Eugene Kozloff, all of the University of Washington). These gentlemen all had a breadth and depth of experience that greatly benefited a student in their tutelage. My own experiences, gained first as a student, then as a researcher and instructor, as well as from discussions with my colleagues at the Friday Harbor Laboratories, the Marine Biological Laboratory in Woods Hole, Massachusetts, the Bamfield Marine Science Centre, and the Harbor Branch Oceanographic Institution, also provided much of the data utilized in this book.

I thank my editors—Alice Lawrence, Alesia Depot, James Lawrence, Larry Jackson, and particularly Kathleen Wood—for their efforts in turning my work into a finished product. A lot of changes from various sources may occur during the production of a book such as this. However, any errors that have crept into the text are my responsibility and not anyone else's.

—*Ron Shimek*
Wilsall, Montana

Contents

IF YOU READ NOTHING ELSE, I HOPE YOU WILL READ THIS SECTION. It will save you considerable grief as you try to use this book.

Problems with Identifications

Many invertebrate animals are difficult to identify without either specialized training, scientific references, or specialized equipment. This is unfortunate, but it is a fact of life and we have to live with it. In this book, I will discuss the animals as precisely as I can. In many cases, the animals are sufficiently distinctive as to allow a discussion of particular species. This is particularly true in such well-known groups as the mollusks, arthropods, and echinoderms.

In many other common groups, such as sponges, hydroids, and annelid worms, the characteristics necessary for specific identification are generally microscopic or internal, and thus beyond the reach of the average hobbyist. For example, sponge identification is generally done by dissolving sections of the animal and microscopically examining the remaining internal hard structures. Few aquarists would want to destroy their animals to identify them. Consequently, for such animals, I will discuss only the general groups.

The "Scientific Name" and Nomenclature

Hobbyists, particularly advanced hobbyists, often want to know the so-called "scientific names" for the animals they keep. There are numerous reasons to want to do this, but primarily this is done to allow the hobbyist to find additional information on the care of the

Indo-Pacific reef scene with a profusion of sponges, gorgonians, stony corals, soft corals, and other life forms.

particular organism. This is an admirable goal. Unfortunately, it is also one fraught with problems and errors. Most of these errors have to do with the use of the "scientific name."

A little background about these scientific names is necessary. The scientific name of an animal is in two parts, and because of this duplex nature, it is termed a binomial, literally a word that means "two names." The first part, always capitalized, is the name of the genus. The second part, never capitalized, is the name of the species. These names are written in a derivative form of Latin, which is, of course, a foreign language. Because of this, by convention, the names are often italicized when printed or underlined when written.

However, other names also go with the specific and generic names. Biologists group similar organisms together, and these are considered to be many levels of similarity. Consequently, a hierarchy of names exists. Ranging from the least similar to the most similar, the basic levels in the hierarchy are:

Kingdom
Phylum (plural = phyla)
Class
Order
Family
Genus (plural = genera)
Species

The fundamental biological unit, the species, is the smallest level in this hierarchy and is considered to be a group of all animals that can, in nature, sexually reproduce with one another and give rise to fertile offspring. Similar species are grouped into a genus, and similar genera are grouped into a family. Likewise, similar families are grouped into orders, orders into classes, and classes into phyla. All

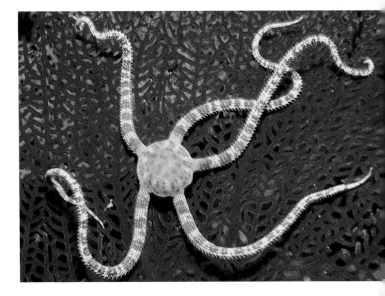

Ophioderma rubicundum (ruby brittle star) on a sea fan in the Cayman Islands.

animal phyla are in the animal kingdom, the most inclusive group in the hierarchy. A point worth remembering is that except for the "species," all of these groups are arbitrary and may be changed or challenged by various specialists, depending on their interpretation of, or new knowledge about, relationships.

This description of binomial nomenclature is of its *ideal* use in scientific literature and research. The *reality* of its use within the aquarium trade and hobby is something else again. Before a specific name can be accurately applied to a given animal, it has to be carefully examined by someone who knows what they are looking for and at. In most cases in the aquarium hobby, where scientific names are applied, this has never been done. Generally, a photograph is

Tridacna maxima (maxima clam): difficult to identify by photographs alone.

compared to the organism and the presumptive "scientific name" is determined. For a few distinctive invertebrate animals and some fishes, this method will work well. For most invertebrates, this process is, at best, deeply flawed. At its worst, it provides a false sense of security about the validity of the identification. For many animals, this is no big deal. For animals that are potentially dangerous to either the aquarist or other denizens of the aquarium, misidentification may be a very important point, indeed. Some sea urchins, snails, and cnidarians, for example, have the capability of killing humans. I have seen misidentified examples of some of these animals for sale in dealers' tanks. Fortunately, no hobbyist has yet died of cardiac arrest from handling a misidentified sea urchin or snail, but it really is only a matter of time before this occurs.

Obviously, the scientific names applied to an animal in a dealer's tank or on a mail-order list should *always* be considered to be suspect. Given such a situation, what can the hobbyist do to get accurate identifications? First, compare with a number of different references. Don't neglect using scientific descriptions as well; there is nothing magical or devious about these. You really *can* take a bit of effort to look up the creature in the scientific literature, and compare descriptions of it to your organism.

Look at pictures in hobbyist publications, but remember they may be misidentified as well. Many of the identifications given in hobbyist publications are doubtful. Examine the authors' credentials for identification of the animals they are selling or discussing. See if they say that the identification of the animals they are describing or picturing have been verified by some real taxonomic authority. I have taken a conservative approach in this book with regard to names, and many hobbyists will find this frustrating. At the same time, I am a professional taxonomist—I really do identify organisms for hire—and believe me, if I can't come to a conclusion on the basis of a photograph or other data that are available, neither can the average hobbyist.

There is a further complication in the identification of aquarium animals. In many cases, we have no way of knowing where the animals originated geographically. Even if dealers tell us where the animals in a shipment come from, those animals are often placed in tanks where cross-colonization from other sources may occur. Many scientific species descriptions are written discussing how a given species differs from its nearest *local* neighbors. Species living in distant parts of the world may often look surprisingly similar. Without knowing areas of collection, certain animals, particularly corals,

Lysmata amboinensis (scarlet cleaner shrimp) with *Nemenzophyllia* sp. (fox coral).

hydroids, sponges, and some echinoderms, simply cannot be identified to the species level.

For those animals you can't identify with certainty, there is certainly nothing wrong with using common names—after all, a scientific name incorrectly applied is nothing but a different "common name." When I illustrate an organism that you cannot definitely identify with a photograph, that organism or group of organisms will be referred to by some name other than a specific one.

Conditions of Maintenance

Tropical reef animals have a particular, and reasonably precise, set of conditions in which they will do best. Relatively few of the animals we keep are found at conditions outside these normal ranges, and relatively few of them do well at conditions outside these ranges. Because of this, a word about marine animal distributions is in order. Marine animals often have a larval dispersal phase that lives, swims in, or is distributed in the plankton. Because of this, they have the potential of spreading very widely.

Most animals have a range of conditions under which they may survive. For example, some corals can survive from temperatures of 68°F (20°C) to 90°F (32°C), and they are often found in areas where the temperatures reach the extremes or are predominantly shifted to either the colder or the hotter parts of their range. Animals living in such marginal environments are not thriving, they are simply surviving. The larvae that gave rise to these adults settled out of the plankton at such a site because other cues were acceptable. Once there, the animal is essentially stuck—literally, as it cannot get up and move. In the marginal environments, animals such as corals survive, but they reproduce poorly, if at all, and they grow slowly.

Most coral reefs have temperatures that range between 78°F (26°C) and about 86°F (30°C). The average temperature of about one thousand coral reefs spread throughout the world is about 81°F (27°C). Virtually all coral reef animals will do best within this range, and I consider the temperature range of 81 to 84°F (27 to 29°C) as the optimal and *normal* temperature to maintain all reef animals. There is a similar range for acceptable salinity, but it is a narrow band, around 35 to 36 parts per thousand (ppt). At normal reef temperatures, this is a specific gravity of about 1.025 to 1.026.

On coral reefs, the pH will vary from about 8.0 to about 8.5 depending on the time of day and current patterns. The stability of pH on a reef and in aquariums is due to the stability-enhancing

effects of dissolved calcium and carbon dioxide. These materials are assessed in aquariums by the monitoring of both calcium and alkalinity. Depending upon the animals kept in a given tank, it will be necessary to supplement these materials regularly. This will replace the critically important dissolved calcium and will ensure that the pH remains within a normal range.

Lighting is more variable and dependent upon habitat. This will be discussed within the context of each animal group. Unless otherwise noted, the basic conditions for all animals discussed in the book are listed in the paragraphs above. To provide a quick method of assessing suitability of the animals discussed in this guide, I have used two, very subjective, indices.

Aquarium Suitability

This indicates whether an animal is suitable for a reef tank, or not suitable at all. Note that animals may be easy to keep, but not suitable for captivity for a number of reasons. As an example, the textile cone shell, *Conus textile*, is quite easy to keep in an aquarium. It also can sting and kill people. I consider this an attribute that disqualifies the animal as a "good" aquarium pet.

Reef Aquarium Compatibility

This category assesses the ability of the organism to survive in reef aquarium conditions. Many animals, such as the beautiful *Dendronephthya* species, would be suitable for reef aquariums, if only we knew how to keep them alive in the tank. However, as we cannot maintain the animals, they should be left on the reef, and are given a poor compatibility rating.

Orange cup corals (*Tubastraea* spp.) and feather stars (Crinoidea).

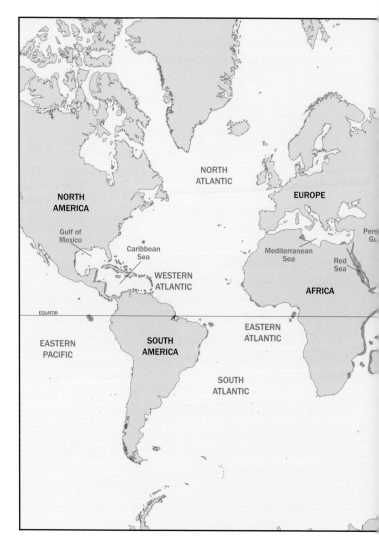

NORTH
ATLANTIC

NORTH
AMERICA

EUROPE

Gulf of
Mexico

Pers
Gu

Caribbean
Sea

Mediterranean
Sea

Red
Sea

WESTERN
ATLANTIC

AFRICA

EQUATOR

EASTERN
ATLANTIC

EASTERN
PACIFIC

SOUTH
AMERICA

SOUTH
ATLANTIC

Mercator Projection, Compiled by Microcosm Ltd.
References: Defense Mapping Agency, World Resources Institute,
International Union for Conservation of Nature and Natural Resources

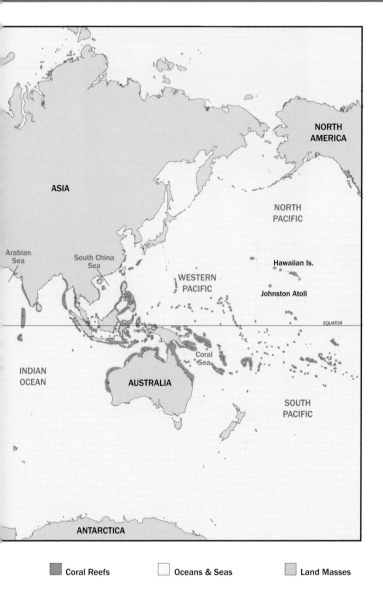

NORTH
AMERICA

ASIA

NORTH
PACIFIC

Arabian
Sea

South China
Sea

Hawaiian Is.

WESTERN
PACIFIC

Johnston Atoll

EQUATOR

INDIAN
OCEAN

Coral
Sea

AUSTRALIA

SOUTH
PACIFIC

ANTARCTICA

Coral Reefs   Oceans & Seas   Land Masses

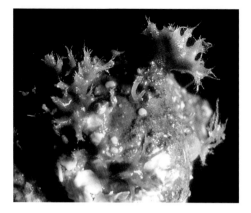

Homotrema rubrum
Red tree foram

Maximum Size: 0.25 to 0.5 in. (6 to 13 mm) in height and in diameter.
Range: Tropical seas.
Minimum Aquarium Size: Nano tanks, 1 gal. (3.6 L) or less.
Lighting: Immaterial.
Foods & Feeding: Eats suspended particulate material captured from the aquarium water.
Aquarium Suitability/Reef Aquarium Compatibility: Good animal for reef tanks. Decorative and harmless. No real care necessary.
Captive Care: This foram needs normal reef salinity and temperatures but is somewhat tolerant of both high and low salinities outside the normal range. A common hitchhiker on live rock, *Homotrema rubrum* is the only foraminiferan easily identified by hobbyists. It looks like a small red or pink crystal composed of spikes or branches and is usually found growing off rock, glass, or sediment particle surfaces. Often fine threadlike pseudopodia can be seen extending from the tips of its branches. It is harmless and is probably a food item for some grazers, such as keyhole limpets or perhaps sea urchins. Bottom-nipping fishes may also eat these forams.

Branching sponge, possibly *Higginsia* sp., may survive in an aquarium: vexing to identify, sponges are challenging to keep, with mandatory filter-feeding needs.

Introduction to Sponges

Sponges are classified in the Phylum Porifera, a group where specific identifications of all but a few forms are impossible without examination of the internal skeletal structures. Some sponges have a defined shape and adult size, and these may often be identified from photographs. Most sponges, however, tend to grow without a defined shape or size, making them hard to describe unambiguously.

Scientists who study sponges use internal structures, called spicules, to define sponge species and to assign the sponges to various groups. Spicules are mineralized internal skeletal bodies that are secreted by the sponge cells. The spicules may be either calcium carbonate or silica. And in a few cases, just to make life interesting, spicules are lacking and the sponge has a wholly proteinaceous skeleton. The spicules range in size from a few millionths of a meter to several centimeters in length. The majority are probably from 0.01 to about 0.5 mm long.

There are several dozen types of spicules, and often several types are found in a given sponge. Identification of sponges to the species

Short of dissection and microscopic examination by an expert, many sponges that arrive in aquariums on live rock cannot be identified with certainty.

level often requires examination and measurement of the spicules, as well as a determination of their relative abundance. This generally involves a lot of microscopy, and requires equipment that most hobbyists lack. The bottom line: You generally can't determine the exact species of most sponges using photographs. Be satisfied with an approximate or common name.

Introduction to Calcareous Sponges

Calcareous sponges, in the Class Calcarea, have a body of spongy fibers supported by spicules made of calcium carbonate (rather than silica, as is found in the demosponges, starting on page 24). Most of the time, calcareous sponges occur in our systems accidentally; they come in on live rock or as larvae. Their maximum sizes are generally smaller than most demosponges.

SYCON SP.

Clathrina spp., *Leucosolenia* spp., *Scypha* spp., *Sycon* spp.
Tubular calcareous sponges

Maximum Size: 5 in. (13 cm) in height and in diameter; most much smaller. Seldom over 1 in. (2.5 cm) in height in captivity.

Range: Found in all seas, but many tropical species are found in the Indo-Pacific, relatively fewer in the Caribbean.

Minimum Aquarium Size: Nano tanks, 1 gal. (3.8 L) or less.

Lighting: Immaterial for most.

Foods & Feeding: Eat small particulate material suspended in the water and will do well in well-fed tanks or tanks with a good population of sediment infauna.

Aquarium Suitability/Reef Aquarium Compatibility: Harmless addition to tank biodiversity.

Captive Care: Introduced to reef tanks on live rock. Small sponges made of white, tan, or yellow interconnected tubes. Color may vary within the same species (even within the same specimen). Water is pumped through very small passages in the walls of the tubes and out the ends; particulate materials are captured by cells lining the passages. Organism is typically a single cylinder or an amorphous mass of tubes. Tube walls are thin; may look like stiff tissue paper.

A young barrel sponge that in the wild might live for a century or more and grow large enough to hold an adult human in its central chamber.

Introduction to Demosponges

The sponges of most interest to aquarists are all in the Class Demospongiae. (The third sponge class, Hexactinellida, is primarily deep water and will not be found in coral reef areas or imported for aquarium use.) Demosponges are characterized by spicules made of silicon dioxide or silica. Silica is the major constituent of glass, and as you might expect, relatively few animals can metabolically utilize this material. Sponges can, however, and they use it to their advantage as a structural and defensive material. Demosponges are typically larger than calcareous ones, and may be very large indeed; some in the Antarctic are about the size of small houses.

Demosponges are found in all seas and in freshwater environments. They are typically much more structurally complex than calcareous sponges, yet most of them feed on the same sorts of micro-particulate foods.

They are found in virtually all colors, but not all of them are suitable for the home aquarium. In nature, bright colors are often used to advertise to various visually based predators, such as fishes or crabs, that the bearer is distasteful or poisonous. Many beautiful sponges are exceptionally toxic and have no place in the home aquarium.

Fortunately, many others are fine, and sponges add a component of color and structure to a system that is normal to a reef, but often lacking in home aquariums. Sponges are not equally abundant or dominant on all reefs, and are much more evident and large in the Caribbean than in the Indo-Pacific. Consequently, most of our large demosponges are collected from the Caribbean.

Demosponges are often purchased (rather than accidentally introduced to tanks like calcareous sponges), and it is important that several precautions be taken to ensure their continued health. Air should *never* be allowed to touch the surface of the sponges. Sponges are perforated by millions of microscopic canals that are used in feeding and respiration. Any air bubble getting into contact with these canals will be drawn in by capillary action and will plug the canal. This will kill the cells surrounding that bubble. These cells will rot, causing more gas, which causes more bubbles that spread outward in a gassy sphere of mortality. Eventually, the whole sponge will die. Most sponges are from areas where large bubbles never occur naturally, and they have no physiological or mechanical means to remove the bubbles from their canals. Always transfer sponges totally submerged.

A curious hobbyist can confirm whether a sponge is a demosponge or a calcareous sponge by removing a sample of the sponge (about 1-2 mm) with forceps. DO NOT use your fingers. (The sponge will regenerate the damaged area.) Completely dissolve the sample in chlorine bleach. Pour off the bleach, add freshwater, and rinse the remains. You should be able to see fine, glasslike particles in the container. Add a bit of vinegar. If bubbles form, the sponge is calcareous; if not, it is a demosponge.

Haliclona spp.
Indo-Pacific blue finger sponges

Maximum Size: Columns to 12 in. (30 cm) in height, 2 in. (5 cm) in diameter.

Range: Indonesian-Malay peninsula region; possibly elsewhere.

Minimum Aquarium Size: Moderate tanks, 50 gal. (190 L) or larger.

Lighting: Moderate to bright.

Foods & Feeding: Filter out and eat small particulate matter, mostly bacterial aggregates, found in the water.

Aquarium Suitability/Reef Aquarium Compatibility: Toxic; may overgrow or poison other animals. Not good aquarium animals.

Captive Care: Need bulk water movement, not the point-source water movement characteristic of powerheads. Grow from a small encrusting mass to a series of fingerlike projections with several large holes on each branch. They tolerate bright light quite well and can hold their own against competing algae. Often difficult to keep in captivity, as they need lots of food and exceptionally swift water flow over the entire body. Colonies should be placed in an area with strong currents and bright light and need to be fastened in place well until they securely overgrow the basal area.

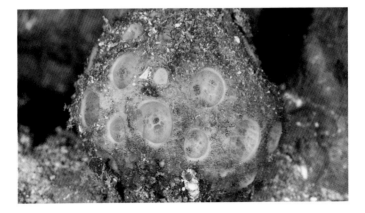

Cinachyra spp.
Orange ball sponges

Maximum Size: Spheres to about 6 in. (15 cm) in diameter.

Range: Several species are found with this common name; the genus is found in both the Caribbean and Indo-Pacific.

Minimum Aquarium Size: Moderate tanks, 50 gal. (190 L) or larger.

Lighting: Do well in both brightly lit or dimly lit areas of reef tanks.

Foods & Feeding: Filter out and eat small particulate matter, mostly bacterial aggregates found in the water. Do best in tanks with a sand bed and well-developed bottom fauna.

Aquarium Suitability/Reef Aquarium Compatibility: May be toxic and may overgrow or poison other immobile animals. Otherwise, they may be fine animals for an aquarium.

Captive Care: They need some current, but will do well in low-current conditions in reef tanks. Colonies are roughly spherical with many excurrent openings scattered over the surface. Often the area between the openings is covered with debris sucked in with its incoming feeding currents. This debris forms a dirty brownish layer between the excurrent apertures. They are not overly bothered by algae growing on their surfaces.

APLYSINA SP.

Amphimedon spp., Aplysina spp., Ptilocaulis spp.
Tree sponges

Maximum Size: Arborescent colonies to 18 in. (46 cm) or more in height; branches to about 1 in. (2.5 cm) in diameter.

Range: Similar species are found in the Caribbean and Indo-Pacific.

Minimum Aquarium Size: Large tanks, 100 gal. (380 L) or larger.

Lighting: Prefer dim lighting. These are deeper-water animals that do not need bright light, which may damage them.

Foods & Feeding: As with most sponges, they filter out and eat small particulate matter, mostly bacterial aggregates found in the water. Do best in a tank with a sand bed and well-developed bottom fauna.

Aquarium Suitability/Reef Aquarium Compatibility: Not good aquarium animals. Do not tolerate the point-source water movement characteristic of powerheads and will literally "melt away."

Captive Care: May be toxic, and may overgrow or poison other immobile animals. Typically found growing on reef walls or in areas of high current. They require a large aquarium and swift currents with bulk laminar flow to do well. Avoid oscillating flow and surge generators. They do not last very well in reef aquariums, primarily due to a lack of appropriate currents and foods. Additionally, they seem to lack the ability to prevent algal fouling.

Callyspongia spp.
Frilly sponges

Maximum Size: Vase-shaped or columnar, up to 18 in. (46 cm) tall.

Range: Similar species are found in the Caribbean and Indo-Pacific.

Minimum Aquarium Size: Large tanks, 100 gal. (380 L) or larger.

Lighting: From deeper water (30+ ft. [9+ m]) and prefer dim light; may be harmed by bright light.

Foods & Feeding: Filter out and eat small particulate matter, mostly bacterial aggregates found in the water. Do best in tanks with sand bed and well-developed bottom fauna.

Aquarium Suitability/Reef Aquarium Compatibility: May be toxic, and may overgrow or poison other immobile animals. Not good aquarium animals.

Captive Care: Prefer areas of high water flow, with intermittent and brief calm periods. Avoid air bubbles. They do not tolerate the point-source water movement characteristic of powerheads. Frills on the surface look soft, but are rather stiff. There are many undescribed species, so identification past genus level is problematic. Vary from white and gray to oranges, greens, blues, and vibrant violet. In nature, some species are covered with symbiotic zoanthids and brittle stars.

PADDLE SPONGE, POSSIBLY *CLATHRIA* SP.

Clathria spp.
Orange tree sponges, orange paddle sponges

Maximum Size: Arborescent, fingerlike, or paddlelike to about 3.3 ft. (1 m) or more in height.

Range: Similar species are found in the Caribbean and Indo-Pacific.

Minimum Aquarium Size: Large tanks, 100 gal. (380 L) or larger. Deep tanks are a necessity.

Lighting: Prefer dim light; may be harmed by bright light.

Foods & Feeding: Filter out and eat small particulate matter, mostly bacterial aggregates found in the water. They will feed on nano-plankton comprised of small phytoplankton.

Aquarium Suitability/Reef Aquarium Compatibility: Toxic; may overgrow or poison other animals. Not good aquarium animals.

Captive Care: In the wild, these sponges are found projecting laterally from vertical cliff faces and do best in similar conditions in captivity. Water flow should be laminar along a "pseudo cliff." Avoid oscillating flow and surge. Require high currents and plenty of microscopic food. Will not tolerate the point-source water movement characteristic of powerheads. These sponges have flexible branches that bend in currents. Many are preyed upon by various cryptically colored nudibranchs, which should be removed.

Feathery hydroids resemble delicate terrestrial ferns but are capable of delivering the stinging welts of other cnidarians, such as sea anemones and corals.

Introduction to Hydroids

Hydroids belong to the Phylum Cnidaria, along with sea anemones, corals, soft corals, and jellyfishes. These are all simple animals whose body is in the form of a polyp: basically a cylinder with a mouth at one end surrounded by tentacles. The outside skin, or epidermis, is a single layer of tissue. The gut consists of a simple bag lined with a single layer of digestive and absorptive tissue. Between these two layers is a layer of proteins and other material, called the mesoglea or "middle jelly."

Hydroids are members of the Class Hydrozoa, and differ from the other cnidarians by the simplicity of the gut, which consists of a simple sac without interior folds or septa, and by the relative thinness of their body wall, due to the lack of a thick mesoglea. In this group of animals, the mesoglea serves primarily as a cement, gluing the two tissues together, and is very thin.

Hydroids typically show an alternation of sexually and asexually reproducing stages. The sexually reproducing stages are generally pelagic and a type of jellyfish. The asexually reproducing stages

Feathery hydroids occasionally hitchhike into reef aquariums on live rock. These attractive animals must receive planktonic feeding to survive.

generally live on the bottom and are typically in the form of large colonies consisting of numerous interconnected polyps. Hydroid colonies have specific and typical branching patterns, polyp positions, and shapes. These are the characteristics that experts mostly use to discriminate between types. The colonies also form asexual buds, and the positions and shapes of those buds are also used for identification purposes.

Some hydroids are capable of delivering potent stings to humans and demand both respect and special handling—or avoidance.

Myriothela (?) spp.
Finger hydroid (digitate hydroid)

Maximum Size: Up to 0.5 in. (1.3 cm).
Range: Tropical seas.
Minimum Aquarium Size: Immaterial.
Lighting: Immaterial.
Foods & Feeding: Feeds on suspended particulate material.
Aquarium Suitability/Reef Aquarium Compatibility: Serious pest. Can kill corals.
Captive Care: These small hydroids can contract down to a nondescript nubbin, but will expand into a fingerlike projection. Small tentacles may be visible on their surfaces. They prefer crevices or grooves in rocks, and extend out from them. When fully expanded, they sting and may kill adjacent animals. They reproduce well asexually and may soon come to spread throughout the aquarium. Once their population has become widespread in a tank, they are difficult to eradicate. Peppermint shrimp (*Lysmata wurdemanni*) do not seem to eat them, nor do copperband butterflyfishes (*Chelmon rostratus*). Manual removal is probably the best option.

Sertularella speciosa
Caribbean branching hydroid

Maximum Size: Colonies to 8 in. (20 cm) in height; polyps about 3 mm in diameter.
Range: Caribbean.
Minimum Aquarium Size: Nano tanks, 1 gal. (3.8 L) or less.
Lighting: Immaterial.
Foods & Feeding: Polyps eat small plankton and particulate foods.
Aquarium Suitability/Reef Aquarium Compatibility: Aggressive and stinging. May harm neighboring animals.
Captive Care: This hydroid is a common hitchhiker on aquacultured live rock. It grows well in moderate currents in well-established, well-fed tanks. Handle with care! It is toxic and capable of inflicting a mild sting, although this may not be enough to deter many competitors and it may need help to keep from being overgrown. Stalk material is brown, polyps are white; alternately branched on opposite sides of the main stalk. Relatively large polyps alternate on tops and bottoms of the stalks. Several similar branching hydroids look like this species. Close examination of branching patterns may distinguish them, but unless colonies are budding off jellyfish, definitive identification is impossible.

Distichopora (?) (red) spp.
Red lace corals

Maximum Size: About 6 in. (15 cm).
Range: Indo-Pacific.
Minimum Aquarium Size: Large tanks, 100 gal. (380 L) or more.
Lighting: Dim lighting is necessary to prevent algal overgrowth.
Foods & Feeding: Actual diets in nature are not known. May need phytoplankton, in addition to bacterial particulates, small particulate organic matter, and microzooplankton for good health.
Aquarium Suitability/Reef Aquarium Compatibility: Nearly impossible to keep alive for extended periods. Should not be purchased.
Captive Care: Need high currents oriented perpendicular to the main colony orientation. Turbulent flow or surge is not recommended. Experienced aquarists with large systems with productive sand beds may be able to keep them alive; not recommended for the average hobbyist. Similar species can be distinguished by color, cross-sectional shape of branches, and polyp arrangement. Scientific names are uncertain, as the group is poorly characterized and in need of much work. The "red" form is characterized by massive main stems and short, white-tipped lateral branches. Main stems are ellipsoid in cross-section.

Distichopora (?) (violet) spp.
Violet lace corals

Maximum Size: To about 8 in. (20 cm).

Range: Indo-Pacific, in caves or very shady areas.

Minimum Aquarium Size: Large tanks, 100 gal. (380 L) or more.

Lighting: Dim lighting is necessary to prevent algal overgrowth; unable to survive for long under bright lighting.

Foods & Feeding: Actual diets in nature are not known. May need phytoplankton, in addition to bacterial particulates, small particulate organic matter, and microzooplankton for good health.

Aquarium Suitability/Reef Aquarium Compatibility: Nearly impossible to keep alive in captive systems. Not suggested for average hobbyists.

Captive Care: Experienced aquarists with large systems that have productive sand beds may be able to keep them alive. They need high currents oriented perpendicular to the main colony orientation. Turbulent flow or surge is not recommended. They are slow-growing. This is one of several species recently imported for captivity. Scientific names are uncertain. The "violet" species form is characterized by a cylindrical main stem and short, "lumplike" lateral branches that are often white-tipped.

Distichopora (?) (yellow) spp.
Burning ember lace corals

Maximum Size: To about 12 in. (30 cm).

Range: Indo-Pacific, in caves or very shady areas.

Minimum Aquarium Size: Large tanks, 100 gal. (380 L) or more.

Lighting: Dim lighting is necessary to prevent algal overgrowth; unable to survive for long under bright lighting.

Foods & Feeding: Actual diets in nature not known. May need phytoplankton, in addition to bacterial particulates, small particulate organic matter, and microzooplankton for good health.

Aquarium Suitability/Reef Aquarium Compatibility: Almost impossible to keep alive for any extended period of time. Not suggested for average hobbyists.

Captive Care: These slow-growing, attractive corals need high currents oriented perpendicular to the main colony orientation. Turbulent flow or surge is not recommended. Experienced aquarists with large systems and productive sand beds may be able to keep them alive. This is one of several species recently imported for captivity. Scientific names are uncertain. The "yellow" species or form is characterized by a rounded, highly branched main stem and short, rounded, white-tipped lateral branches.

Stylaster (pink) spp.
Pink lace corals

Maximum Size: To about 6 in. (15 cm).

Range: Indo-Pacific, on vertical surfaces and cliffs in shady areas.

Minimum Aquarium Size: Large tanks, 100 gal. (380 L) or more.

Lighting: Dim lighting is necessary to prevent algal overgrowth; unable to survive for long under bright lighting.

Foods & Feeding: Actual diets in nature are not known. May need phytoplankton, in addition to bacterial particulates, small particulate organic matter, and microzooplankton for good health.

Aquarium Suitability/Reef Aquarium Compatibility: Unlikely to survive for any extended period of time. Should not be purchased.

Captive Care: This stylasterine is related to *Distichopora* and is equally difficult to maintain. Needs high currents oriented perpendicular to the main colony orientation. Turbulent flow or surge is not recommended. Not suggested for average hobbyists. Experienced aquarists with large systems that have productive sand beds may be able to keep them alive. The group is poorly characterized; scientific names are uncertain. This species or form is characterized by robust, brilliant pink main stems and very finely multiple-branched white lateral branches.

Stylaster (white) spp.
White lace corals

Maximum Size: To about 12 in. (30 cm).

Range: Indo-Pacific, in caves or very shady areas.

Minimum Aquarium Size: Large tanks, 100 gal. (380 L) or more.

Lighting: Dim lighting is necessary to prevent algal overgrowth; unable to survive for long under bright lighting.

Foods & Feeding: Actual diets in nature are not known. May need phytoplankton, in addition to bacterial particulates, small particulate organic matter, and microzooplankton for good health.

Aquarium Suitability/Reef Aquarium Compatibility: Not likely to survive in captivity. Should not be purchased.

Captive Care: These corals will simply starve in most aquariums. However, experienced hobbyists with large systems with productive refugiums or sand beds and minimal protein skimming may be able to keep them alive. Can tolerate some turbulence, but steady currents perpendicular to the main colony orientation are better. Surge not recommended. Scientific names are uncertain. This species or form is characterized by rounded, pale pink to pale orange, moderately branched main stems and long, repeatedly branched white lateral branches.

Millepora (branching) spp.
Branching fire corals

Maximum Size: To about 12 in. (30 cm).
Range: Circumtropical.
Minimum Aquarium Size: Nano tanks, 1 gal. (3.8 L) or larger.
Lighting: Zooxanthellate; prefer bright illumination.
Foods & Feeding: Bacterial particulates, small particulate organic matter, and microzooplankton.
Aquarium Suitability/Reef Aquarium Compatibility: Hardy, but aggressive and may overgrow other sessile animals. Potent sting! Do not touch.
Captive Care: Fire corals grow rapidly and are easily kept. Hairlike polyps protrude from small, star-shaped holes in the calcareous matrix. Stings are strong! Most people will be bothered; sensitive individuals may experience severe "burns" or anaphylactic shock. Handle with care. Two morphs are imported for captivity: branching and encrusting (see next page). These are not species, but "shapes" shared among several species. The branching form is characterized by a growth pattern of two more-or-less equal branches each time splitting occurs. The branching is usually planar—in one plane. These are typically light tan to yellowish brown.

ENCRUSTING FIRE CORAL GROWING OVER A GORGONIAN.

Millepora (encrusting) spp.
Encrusting fire corals

Maximum Size: To about 0.5 in. (1.3 cm).

Range: Circumtropical.

Minimum Aquarium Size: Nano tanks, 1 gal. (3.8 L) or more.

Lighting: Zooxanthellate; prefer bright illumination.

Foods & Feeding: Bacterial particulates, small particulate organic matter, and microzooplankton.

Aquarium Suitability/Reef Aquarium Compatibility: Aggressive and may overgrow other sessile animals. Potent sting! Do not touch.

Captive Care: The encrusting form of fire coral grows quite rapidly, spreading across any hard substrate and even smothering many sessile organisms. Hairlike polyps protrude from small, star-shaped holes in the calcareous matrix. The stings from this species are strong! Most people will be bothered by contact; sensitive individuals may experience severe "burns" or anaphylactic shock. Use appropriate caution when handling them. Whether or not this is one separate species, several species, or just an ecologically determined growth form is not known. Many closely related stylasterines change shape, depending on currents and colony orientation. *Millepora* spp. are typically brown to light tan to yellowish brown.

Cassiopeia frondosa
Upside-down jelly

Maximum Size: Diameter to about 10 in. (25 cm).
Range: Lives upside down on sandy bottoms in the shallow waters of the Caribbean.
Minimum Aquarium Size: Large tanks, 100 gal. (380 L) or more.
Lighting: Bright illumination is necessary.
Foods & Feeding: Zooxanthellate; can subsist for long periods without feeding if dissolved nutrient level is high. Feeds on small planktonic animals, such as *Artemia* or *Mysis*, or feeder fishes like mollies.
Aquarium Suitability/Reef Aquarium Compatibility: Not a good community member; can sting and kill other animals. It has nematocysts and may be toxic to humans.
Captive Care: This is a bizarre, unusual, and very interesting animal that will do best in its own tank. It needs an aquarium with a good sand bed and little current. Outflow apertures and overflow boxes should be well screened. Scyphozoans, such as this, have an alternation of generations, with a hydroidlike polyp as one stage and a swimming medusa the other. If polyps become established, they reproduce asexually and become a nuisance.

Cassiopeia xamachana
Mangrove upside-down jelly

Maximum Size: Diameter to about 12 in. (30 cm).
Range: Lives on sandy bottoms in shallow waters of the Caribbean.
Minimum Aquarium Size: Large tanks, 100 gal. (380 L) or more.
Lighting: Bright illumination is necessary.
Foods & Feeding: Zooxanthellate; can subsist for long periods without feeding if dissolved nutrient level is high. Feeds on small planktonic animals, like *Artemia* or *Mysis*, or feeder fishes such as mollies.
Aquarium Suitability/Reef Aquarium Compatibility: Not suitable for the standard reef tank. Can sting and kill other animals. Has nematocysts and may be toxic to humans.
Captive Care: This curious, fascinating creature requires water with little motion and will do best in a lagoon-type biotope or species tank. Outflow apertures and overflow boxes must be well screened. A well-established, productive sand bed is important as a source of live food. In this species, the oral tentacles have large lateral appendages. These jellies have an alternation of generations, with a hydroidlike polyp as one stage, a swimming medusa the other. If polyps become established, they reproduce asexually and become a nuisance.

Subergorgia spp.
Pacific sea fans

Maximum Size: Height to 10 ft. (3 m); aquarium specimens seldom exceed 12 in. (30 cm) in height.

Range: Caribbean.

Minimum Aquarium Size: Large tanks, 100 gal. (380 L) or larger

Lighting: Need dim illumination. Bright illumination may lead to algal overgrowth.

Foods & Feeding: Nonzooxanthellate. Must be fed. Do best on small particulate foods such as enriched *Artemia* nauplii, dust-size pelleted foods, rotifers, or other foods that disperse to form fine particulate material in the water.

Aquarium Suitability/Reef Aquarium Compatibility: Poor survival in captivity, probably due to insufficient or unsuitable foods and inappropriate lighting causing algal overgrowth.

Captive Care: Deeper-water gorgonians; beige to pinkish orange, and yellow; may appear reddish due to a filmy red covering, perhaps of cyanobacteria. Mesh openings are elongate, typically about 0.5 to 1 in. wide, 2 to 3 in. long. Polyps red, orange, sometimes yellow. Must be securely fastened in place; require strong water currents of laminar flow. Do not place in areas of turbulent flow.

Briareum asbestinum
Corky sea fingers

Maximum Size: Height to 24 in. (61 cm). Most colonies are smaller.
Range: Caribbean.
Minimum Aquarium Size: Medium tanks, 50 gal. (190 L) or more.
Lighting: Prefers bright illumination.
Foods & Feeding: Zooxanthellate. Does best when fed live plankton, such as enriched *Artemia* nauplii and other planktonic animals. Nonliving foods may be accepted if care is taken to ensure feeding.
Aquarium Suitability/Reef Aquarium Compatibility: Grows well if well fed. May overgrow other sessile animals.
Captive Care: When well fed and cared for, this species is an aggressive competitor for space and may overgrow other soft corals, stony corals, and gorgonians. It needs moderate to high currents to do well. This encrusting form extends up into thick, fingerlike extensions. It doesn't form fanlike colonies. Colony color ranges from yellow to brown or purple. The large polyps are brownish green to light tan, colors indicative of their zooxanthellae. When fully extended, the polyps appear to have a "furry" covering; when they sway in the current, this can be very attractive.

Diodogorgia nodulifera
Orange or yellow gorgonian (colorful sea rod)

Maximum Size: Height to 16 in. (41 cm).

Range: Caribbean.

Minimum Aquarium Size: Medium tanks, 50 gal. (190 L) or more.

Lighting: Needs dim lighting. When kept in brightly illuminated tanks, it tends to become covered with cyanobacteria or algae, which will eventually kill it.

Foods & Feeding: Lacks zooxanthellae and needs to be fed regularly; daily is best. Does well on small planktonic animals, but will also accept thawed frozen foods as long as they break up into small particles and disperse throughout the tank water.

Aquarium Suitability/Reef Aquarium Compatibility: Survival is poor in captivity, probably due to the lack of sufficient or appropriate foods or overgrowth by aggressive algae.

Captive Care: Slow-growing, this colorful gorgonian needs good current flow. It must be securely anchored; it doesn't tolerate handling and should be disturbed as little as possible. It may be brilliant red, yellow, or orange; large polyps are dazzling bright white. When withdrawn, the polyp is noticeable by the swollen and protruding calyx, or polyp cover.

Erythropodium spp.
Caribbean encrusting gorgonians

Maximum Size: Encrusting, may be up to 0.5 in. (13 mm) thick. Colonies may cover extensive areas.

Range: Caribbean.

Minimum Aquarium Size: Small tanks, 10 gal. (38 L) or more.

Lighting: Need bright illumination.

Foods & Feeding: These species are zooxanthellate, but also benefit from feedings of *Artemia* nauplii, rotifers, or dissolved frozen foods that disperse to form fine particulate material in the water.

Aquarium Suitability/Reef Aquarium Compatibility: Good aquarium animals. Moderately aggressive toward other sessile animals.

Captive Care: These easy-to-maintain gorgonians grow well and form a tan mat from which tan polyps extend. The polyps have fine, long tentacles; when extended from the colony, these tentacles look like a fur covering. When retracted, the colonies are basically smooth, with small apertures for the polyps to retract into. These animals are found in shallow water reef flats and do best in brightly lit situations. These species will overgrow other sessile organisms, but seem less aggressive than the similar Corky Sea Fingers (page 45).

Eunicea spp.
Knobby sea rods

Maximum Size: Colonies may exceed 39 in. (1 m) in height. Aquarium individuals are much smaller.

Range: Caribbean.

Minimum Aquarium Size: Large tanks, 100 gal. (380 L) or more.

Lighting: Need bright illumination.

Foods & Feeding: As with all zooxanthellate animals, they benefit from feeding, especially foods such as enriched *Artemia* nauplii, rotifers, or dissolved frozen foods that disperse to form fine particulate material in the water.

Aquarium Suitability/Reef Aquarium Compatibility: Good aquarium growth if well fed. Not aggressive.

Captive Care: These reasonably hardy animals benefit from good water movement, but tolerate low-motion areas. Several species have the common name "knobby sea rods" and are indistinguishable without microscopic examination. When polyps are retracted, there are large protruding bumps where each is found. The polyps have short tentacles and are able to stand without much deformation even in high current flows. Colony color ranges from tan to pastel purple.

Gorgonia ventalina
Common Caribbean sea fan

Maximum Size: Colonies may exceed 24 in. (61 cm) in height and width. Aquarium individuals are usually much smaller.
Range: Caribbean.
Minimum Aquarium Size: Large tanks, 100 gal. (380 L) or more.
Lighting: Needs bright illumination.
Foods & Feeding: Zooxanthellate. Benefits from feeding, especially foods like enriched *Artemia* nauplii, rotifers, or dissolved frozen foods that disperse to form fine particulate material in the water.
Aquarium Suitability/Reef Aquarium Compatibility: Poor survival in captivity.
Captive Care: Prefers areas of moderate current and must be oriented perpendicular to the flow. Needs bulk current flow, not point-source flow generated by powerheads. Must be securely fastened. If not oriented correctly, portions may die and become covered with algae. Fans composed of a meshwork of interconnected branches with relatively small holes. Polyps are small and when retracted, the branches are flattened. This sea fan is a preferred prey of the Flamingo Tongue Snail (*Cyphoma gibbosum*). Snails must be removed and humanely killed (frozen), as they will eat the living tissue of a sea fan in a short time.

Leptogorgia miniata
Carmine sea spray

Maximum Size: Colonies seldom exceed 6 in. (15 cm) in height.
Range: Caribbean.
Minimum Aquarium Size: Moderate tanks, 50 gal. (190 L) or larger
Lighting: Needs dim illumination. Becomes overgrown with algae in brightly lit situations.
Foods & Feeding: Nonzooxanthellate. Must be fed. Does best on small particulate foods such as enriched *Artemia* nauplii; dust-size pelleted food, rotifers, or other foods that disperse to form fine particulate material in the water.
Aquarium Suitability/Reef Aquarium Compatibility: Poor survival in captivity, probably due to insufficient or unsuitable foods and inappropriate lighting causing algal overgrowth.
Captive Care: This is a deeper-water gorgonian, colored in shades of red. Polyps are white, often translucent. Colonies are bushy, nonplanar, with branches in all directions. Needs to be securely fastened in place and requires strong water currents. Does well in areas of turbulent flow or flow from differing directions. Likely lacks algicides and has no defense against algal fouling.

Muricea spp.
Spiny sea fans

Maximum Size: Colonies reach about 12 in. (30 cm) in height, but may be up to 24 in. (61 cm) wide.

Range: Caribbean.

Minimum Aquarium Size: Large tanks, 100 gal. (380 L) or more.

Lighting: Need bright illumination.

Foods & Feeding: Zooxanthellate, but must be fed foods such as enriched *Artemia* nauplii, rotifers, or dissolved frozen foods that disperse to form fine particulate material in the water.

Aquarium Suitability/Reef Aquarium Compatibility: Do well if well fed; otherwise, survival in reef tanks is poor. Will overgrow or encrust other animals.

Captive Care: Form low-growing colonies that are much wider than tall. Thick branches, light brown to tan, are covered with sharp, protruding areas that cover the retracted polyps. Branches do not intersect or fuse; shaped like a squat candelabrum. Prefer moderate currents; must be securely fastened in place, perpendicular to the main current flow. Will overgrow or encrust other animals. These fans are a preferred prey of *Cyphoma gibbosum* snails, which must be removed, as they will eat the living tissue in a relatively short time.

Muricea pendula
Pinnate sea fan

Maximum Size: Colonies reach about 24 in. (61 cm) in height.
Range: Caribbean.
Minimum Aquarium Size: Large tanks, 100 gal. (380 L) or more.
Lighting: Needs dim lighting.
Foods & Feeding: Nonzooxanthellate. Must be fed foods such as enriched *Artemia* nauplii, rotifers, or dissolved frozen foods that disperse to form fine particulate material in the water.
Aquarium Suitability/Reef Aquarium Compatibility: Not a reef tank animal, although it is sold as such. Survival in reef tanks is poor.
Captive Care: This attractive small sea fan is found in deeper-water environments. It needs a dedicated, dimly lit tank with moderate currents. This is not a species for a true reef tank. It is not adapted to withstand bright lighting, nor can it acclimate to it and will quickly become fouled with algae if kept in such conditions. The basic colony color varies from reddish brown through reds to orange or yellow. The polyp bodies are reddish, orange, or yellow, and the tentacles are clear and translucent, often with a white cast.

Plexaura flexuosa
Bent sea rod

Maximum Size: Colonies reach about 39 in. (1 m) in height.

Range: Caribbean, in shallow waters to depths of 30 m.

Minimum Aquarium Size: Large tanks, 100 gal. (380 L) or more.

Lighting: Needs bright illumination.

Foods & Feeding: Zooxanthellate, but must be fed foods such as enriched *Artemia* nauplii, rotifers, or dissolved frozen foods that disperse to form fine particulate material in the water.

Aquarium Suitability/Reef Aquarium Compatibility: Survival is poor in reef tanks, due to the lack of sufficient foods. Not aggressive.

Captive Care: Needs a large aquarium with plenty of breadth as well as width. Tolerates low currents well and looks like a sea bush with branches in all directions. Has the basic candelabrum pattern, but with secondary branching some distance out on the main branches. The branching pattern is usually dichotomous, giving rise to two equal branches. The color is pastel beige to purple. The polyps are tan to light yellow, cover the branches, and are not arranged in discrete rows. This growth form is in decided contrast to most sea fans, where the branching pattern is quite planar.

Pseudopterogorgia spp.
Sea plumes

Maximum Size: Colonies reach about 10 ft. (3 m) in height and 16.5 ft. (5 m) wide.
Range: Caribbean.
Minimum Aquarium Size: Large tanks, 100 gal. (380 L) or more.
Lighting: Need bright illumination.
Foods & Feeding: Zooxanthellate, but must be fed foods such as enriched *Artemia* nauplii, rotifers, or dissolved frozen foods that disperse to form fine particulate material in the water.
Aquarium Suitability/Reef Aquarium Compatibility: Sold as "cuttings," these are not really suitable for reef aquariums. They seldom reattach to the surface even if glued well. Not particularly aggressive.
Captive Care: Because of their size at maturity, these are not really good aquarium animals for the majority of hobbyists, although they are occasionally collected and sold. They prefer slow to moderate currents. Again, depending on the species and ecological situation, they may become quite large. Long, secondary branches off each side of the main branches give the appearance of a "droopy" feather. Colony colors range from yellow through tans to pastel purples, with zooxanthellate tan polyps.

Swiftia exserta
Red polyp octocoral

Maximum Size: Colonies reach about 18 in. (46 cm) in height.
Range: Caribbean, at depths of 330 ft. (100 m).
Minimum Aquarium Size: Large tanks, 100 gal. (380 L) or more.
Lighting: Needs dim lighting.
Foods & Feeding: Nonzooxanthellate. Must be fed foods such as enriched *Artemia* nauplii, rotifers, or some dissolved frozen foods that disperse to form fine particulate material in the water.
Aquarium Suitability/Reef Aquarium Compatibility: Should not be purchased for typical reef tanks. Survival in captivity is poor due to algal overgrowth and the lack of appropriate foods.
Captive Care: This deep cherry-red-polyped octocoral lacks zooxanthellae and is thus a creature of low light. It will usually perish in the aquarium, generally from the side effects of bright lighting, as it tends to become fouled with algae. An experienced aquarist might succeed by creating the right conditions, feeding religiously and keeping water quality high. The stalks range in color from orange to deep red. In higher-current areas, this species forms bushes rather than fans, while in sheltered areas it grows in a more planar manner.

Virgularia sp.: sea pens require a good supply of suspended particulate food in the aquarium setting as well as a deep sand bed in which to anchor.

Introduction to Sea Pens

Sea pens are complex, fascinating animals that typically live in sandy or muddy sand environments. Certain species make spectacular display animals, as they are brilliantly bioluminescent, and often glow brightly with this spontaneous display.

Removed from the sediment, a sea pen tends to look rather like a withered, off-color carrot. There is an anchoring bulb that corresponds to the body of the carrot, and a stalk extending upward. The anchoring bulb and stalk are considered to be one polyp, derived from the first polyp that formed after larval metamorphosis. There is a long, thin sliver of calcareous skeleton found in the center of the stalk and extending into the bulb.

Three different kinds of polyps are found on all sea pens. For this reason, biologists refer to a single sea pen specimen as a colony. The stalk contains two more types of polyps. Representatives of the first type are feeding polyps, which look rather like the feeding polyps of all other soft corals, with eight pinnately branched tentacles and a central mouth. The second type of polyp is a siphonozoid, which is basically just a mouth with no surrounding tentacles. The gullet of this mouth is furnished with millions of beating microscopic filaments, called cilia, and these pump water into the colony.

Sea pens live anchored in the sediment by the bulb, and extend their feeding polyps to catch food. If this were all they did, they would be easy to keep, but it isn't and they aren't. All sea pens appear to have an intrinsic rhythm of deflation, whereupon they bury themselves in the sediment. Some time later, they climb back up and inflate to feed. They may do this several times a day or only infrequently—but they all do it. This behavior pattern means that sea pens need a minimum of 8 in. (20 cm) of sediment in which to bury, and actually 12 to 24 in. (30 to 61 cm) would be better. Not many hobbyists have aquariums with sand beds this deep, and it is best that these animals not be routinely imported or purchased.

If you have purchased one, however, you might try to arrange the sand it needs—very fine sand or muddy sand—in a deep flowerpot or a large section of PVC pipe. In a large, deep aquarium, such a pot or pipe might be able to be set in the rockwork and not be obtrusive. The sea pen can then be placed on the sand, and if the sand bed is appropriate the pen will bury itself.

Some time later it will emerge from the sand, inflate, and begin to feed. If they do bury, and then emerge and start to feed, the battle has been won and the sea pen should thrive, if it has enough food. Most are from deeper-water environments and probably will do best in dimly lit tanks.

Cavernularia spp.
Sea pens

Maximum Size: Colonies to about 18 in. (46 cm) in height.

Range: Circumtropical.

Minimum Aquarium Size: Large tanks, 100 gal. (380 L) or more, with a very deep (8 to 12 in. [20 to 30 cm]) sand bed in which to burrow.

Lighting: Prefer dim illumination.

Foods & Feeding: Nonzooxanthellate. Must be fed foods such as *Artemia* nauplii, rotifers, or dissolved frozen foods that disperse to form fine particulate material in the water.

Aquarium Suitability/Reef Aquarium Compatibility: Unsuitable for most reef tanks.

Captive Care: Sea pens must have a very deep sand bed to survive and thrive. They live anchored in the sediment by the bulb and extend their feeding polyps to catch food. Several times a day they deflate, bury themselves in the sediment, and later climb back up and inflate to feed. This behavior indicates they will thrive as long as there is enough food. Sea pens in this genus have a rather thick central stalk with a profusion of feeding polyps arising directly from the stalk. Siphonozoids are also scattered over the stalk surface. Sea pens in this genus tend to be brown or tan.

Virgularia spp.
Sea pens

Maximum Size: Colonies to about 18 in. (46 cm) in height.

Range: All seas.

Minimum Aquarium Size: Large tanks, 100 gal. (380 L) or more, with a very deep (8 to 12 in. [20 to 30 cm]) sand bed in which to burrow.

Lighting: Prefer dim illumination.

Foods & Feeding: Nonzooxanthellate. Must be fed foods such as *Artemia* nauplii, rotifers, or dissolved frozen foods that disperse to form fine particulate material in the water.

Aquarium Suitability/Reef Aquarium Compatibility: Unsuitable for most reef tanks. Need a very deep sand bed.

Captive Care: These large sea pens need a muddy sediment layer twice as deep as the length of the internal skeleton. They prefer relatively high currents and extend far out of the sediment to feed. They turn in their burrows to orient into the currents so the feeding polyps are at the trailing edge of the leaves. Food is captured as it eddies around the leaves. Colonies in this genus are white, tan, or delicate pale orange.

Pteroeides spp.
Sea pens

Maximum Size: Colonies reach about 18 in. (46 cm) in height.
Range: Circumtropical.
Minimum Aquarium Size: Large tanks, 100 gal. (380 L) or more, with a very deep (16 to 24 in. [41 to 61 cm]) sand bed in which to burrow.
Lighting: Prefer dim illumination.
Foods & Feeding: Nonzooxanthellate. Must be fed foods such as *Artemia* nauplii, rotifers, or dissolved frozen foods that disperse to form fine particulate material in the water.
Aquarium Suitability/Reef Aquarium Compatibility: Unsuitable for most reef tanks. Need a very deep sand bed.
Captive Care: Several species in this genus are probably the most commonly imported sea pens. Care is similar to *Virgularia*, but the sediment needn't be as muddy. Some sea pens generate hydrodynamic lift, similar to the lift generated by a box kite, when water flows over their leaves. When "unhappy," the pen will inflate, crawl out of the sediment and drift away in the current, so you may need to find another type of sediment. They have a more inflated central stalk and bigger leaves than *Virgularia*. They tend to be gold or yellow and often have brightly colored purple or red markings on either the central stalk or leaves.

Heliopora coerulea
Blue coral (blue-ridge coral)

Maximum Size: Colonies may form reefs several feet high.
Range: Indo-Pacific; shallow- and deeper-water areas; in deeper water the zooxanthellae tend to be reduced or absent.
Minimum Aquarium Size: Moderate tanks, 50 gal. (190 L) or more.
Lighting: Prefer bright illumination.
Foods & Feeding: Zooxanthellate, but must be fed with foods such as *Artemia* nauplii, rotifers, or dissolved frozen foods that disperse to form fine particulate material; benefit from a good sand bed.
Aquarium Suitability/Reef Aquarium Compatibility: Good aquarium animal. Not particularly aggressive. Slow-growing.
Captive Care: This animal gets its name from the color of its skeleton. If the coral is alive and healthy, the blue color is invisible, as it is covered with brown or tan living tissue. Small polyps are found scattered over the surface of the colony and will periodically extend when the animal is feeding. Colonies form flat plates with deep intervening valleys or thickened, flattened fingerlike projections. Like all other corals, this species benefits from high levels of dissolved calcium carbonate in the water; it can build skeleton and grow noticeably over the course of a year.

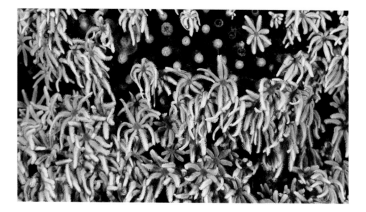

Tubipora musica
Pipe organ coral

Maximum Size: Colonies may reach 12 in. (30 cm) or more in height, and twice that in width.

Range: Indo-Pacific.

Minimum Aquarium Size: Moderate tanks, 50 gal. (190 L) or more.

Lighting: Prefers bright illumination.

Foods & Feeding: Zooxanthellate, but must be fed with foods such as *Artemia* nauplii, rotifers, or dissolved frozen foods that disperse to form fine particulate material in the water.

Aquarium Suitability/Reef Aquarium Compatibility: Delicate reef aquarium animal that requires a deep sand bed or refugium to produce bacterial particulates in the water.

Captive Care: This coral was once thought difficult to maintain, but with the development of systems with good sand bed fauna, it has been kept successfully. Will do well with moderate to strong currents. It is a "soft" coral with a deep red stony skeleton composed of vertical tubes passing through horizontal plates of calcium carbonate. White, tan, or green polyps are found in the ends of the skeletal tubes. While the eight tentacles of each polyp are evident, their pinnate nature is not as clear as it is on some other "soft" corals.

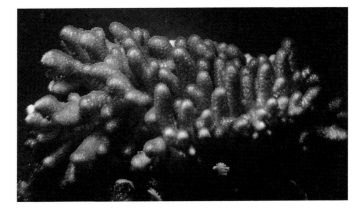

Alcyonium spp.
Temperate soft corals (dead man's fingers)

Maximum Size: Colonies may reach 6 in. (15 cm) in height.

Range: Temperate or subtropical. Cosmopolitan.

Minimum Aquarium Size: Small tanks, 10 gal. (38 L) or more.

Lighting: No preference.

Foods & Feeding: These corals lack zooxanthellae and need to be fed on foods like *Artemia* nauplii, rotifers, or dissolved frozen foods that will disperse to form fine particulate material in the water.

Aquarium Suitability/Reef Aquarium Compatibility: Not good aquarium animals, as food is difficult to provide and reef temperatures generally cause early death.

Captive Care: These corals require temperatures of no more than 59°F (15°C). Under good conditions, *Alcyonium* spp. grow rapidly and will overgrow and smother many other sessile invertebrates. However, at reef temperatures of 82 to 84°F (28 to 29°C), they generally live only a few weeks. Only occasionally offered for sale, these colonies are rather drab; they form gray, tan, or pale yellow blobs with fingerlike projections that reach heights of 4 to 6 in. (10 to 15 cm). Translucent polyps, usually the same color as the entire colony, arise from holes spreading across the colony surface.

Alcyonium spp.
Finger corals (colt corals)

Maximum Size: Colonies may reach 6 in. (15 cm) in height.
Range: Indo-Pacific.
Minimum Aquarium Size: Moderate tanks, 50 gal. (190 L) or more.
Lighting: Require bright illumination.
Foods & Feeding: Zooxanthellate, but need to be fed. Feeding reports on zooplankton are rare; may require phytoplankton for best growth.
Aquarium Suitability/Reef Aquarium Compatibility: Good aquarium animals. They grow well under normal reef conditions. May overgrow other sessile animals.
Captive Care: These hardy soft corals grow well in reef aquarium conditions with bright light and good water movement. One of several genera confusingly sold under the common name of "colt coral," several species of *Alcyonium* make their way into the aquarium trade. See Eric Borneman's *Aquarium Corals* (Microcosm/ T.F.H., 2001) for a discussion of the problems with the name "colt coral." The colonies form gray, tan, or yellow masses with fingerlike projections. Translucent polyps arise from holes spread across the surface of the colony. These polyps are generally the same color as the entire colony.

Anthelia spp.
Waving hand corals

Maximum Size: Colonies may reach 12 in. (30 cm) in height.
Range: Indo-Pacific.
Minimum Aquarium Size: Small tanks, 10 gal. (38 L) or more.
Lighting: Require bright illumination.
Foods & Feeding: Zooxanthellate, but will need to be fed on foods such as *Artemia* nauplii, rotifers, or dissolved frozen foods that will disperse to form fine particulate material in the water.
Aquarium Suitability/Reef Aquarium Compatibility: They do moderately well in reef aquariums. Not particularly aggressive, but they may overgrow sessile animals.
Captive Care: Prefer moderately strong currents. Their diet in nature is unclear, but it is likely they need small microplankton to thrive. *Anthelia* species have relatively large and robust polyps arising from a common basal colony. The polyps in some species may be as small as 5 mm in diameter, but most are larger. As with all octocorals, the polyps have pinnate tentacles; this branching pattern is particularly visible in *Anthelia* species and serves as a distinguishing characteristic. In particular, the lateral branches from the tentacles are fewer, larger, and somewhat shorter than in other soft corals.

Cladiella spp.
Finger leather corals (cauliflower corals, colt corals)

Maximum Size: Colonies may reach 16 in. (41 cm) in height.
Range: Large number of species found in the Indo-Pacific.
Minimum Aquarium Size: Small tanks, 10 gal. (38 L) or more.
Lighting: Require bright illumination.
Foods & Feeding: Zooxanthellate, but benefit from phytoplankton additions and do best in tanks with well-developed sand bed infauna that produce small invertebrate larvae.
Aquarium Suitability/Reef Aquarium Compatibility: Good aquarium animals. They may overgrow some sessile animals.
Captive Care: These soft corals grow rapidly and need to be trimmed. They respond well to judicious pruning as they get larger, and the aquarist can easily propagate the cuttings into new colonies. Some species do not do well in a tank with lots of hermit crabs, which crawl over their surfaces, causing deleterious interruptions in feeding and other activities. Identification is very challenging. In general, polyps are usually about 3 to 5 mm in diameter, generally dark colored—brown to green—in a whitish matrix. Colonies have short, thick stalks and the surface is often lobulate, hence the common name "cauliflower coral."

Dendronephthya spp.
Carnation corals (cauliflower corals, tree corals)

Maximum Size: Colonies may reach 6 ft. (1.8 m) in height and 3.3 ft. (1 m) in diameter.

Range: Indo-Pacific, often on vertical rock surfaces in shaded areas.

Minimum Aquarium Size: Large tanks, 100 gal. (380 L) or more.

Lighting: Bright illumination may be harmful.

Foods & Feeding: Need to be fed heavily, as they lack zooxanthellae. Benefit from phytoplankton additions; do best in tanks with well-developed sand bed infauna that produces small invertebrate larvae.

Aquarium Suitability/Reef Aquarium Compatibility: Essentially impossible to maintain. Should not be purchased.

Captive Care: These are among the most colorful and beautiful soft corals, but are also some of the most difficult to keep. Mimic natural conditions as closely as possible. They seem to need strong, alternating currents and probably require bulk flows rather than vortices produced by powerheads and pumps. There are several similar-looking species. The small polyps are often brilliant reds, yellows, or purples and are found on the ends of large, inflatable white branches and stalks. Spicules are embedded in the walls of the branches and extend out to support the polyps, giving them a spiny look.

Lemnalia spp., *Litophyton* spp., *Nephthea* spp.
Tree corals

Maximum Size: Colonies may reach 16.6 ft. (5 m) in height and width; most are smaller.
Range: Indo-Pacific.
Minimum Aquarium Size: Moderate tanks, 50 gal. (190 L) or more.
Lighting: Require bright illumination.
Foods & Feeding: Zooxanthellate, but need to be fed heavily. Given enriched newly hatched *Artemia* or other small particulate foods, they will grow rapidly.
Aquarium Suitability/Reef Aquarium Compatibility: Good aquarium animals. Often very rapid-growing.
Captive Care: Tree corals prefer slow to moderate currents. They do not do well in close proximity to stony corals or sea anemones, and will be aggressive. However, they tend to lose these battles and will regress or die if not moved. These three genera are almost indistinguishable. The basic color is tan, light green, or greenish white; polyps tend to be darker brown or green; some may be the same color as the colony's background coloration. The "devil's plague" anemones (*Aiptasia* spp.) will kill these corals within a short time.

Lobophytum spp.
Leather corals

Maximum Size: Colonies of some species may reach 3.3 ft. (1 m) in height and width; aquarium colonies are smaller.

Range: Indo-Pacific, 20 to 60 ft. (6 to 18 m) deep.

Minimum Aquarium Size: Moderate tanks, 50 gal. (190 L) or more.

Lighting: Prefer bright lighting, but can tolerate dimly lit tanks if they are provided with supplemental foods.

Foods & Feeding: Zooxanthellate, but do well on phyto- and micro-zooplankton. Enriched *Artemia* may be too large for smaller species, but are fine for larger.

Aquarium Suitability/Compatibility: Easy to maintain; dangerous to some other animals.

Captive Care: Prefer moderate to strong currents. React poorly with sea anemones or mushroom polyps, secreting potent chemicals that can cause these animals to move away or die. Half a dozen of the 45 or so *Lobophytum* spp. are found in the reef hobby. Many are similar and are difficult to distinguish. All are leathery and possess a discoidal or irregular base with prominent ridges or fingerlike projections extending upward. Polyps are often white, relatively large; may extend 5 to 10 mm out from the surface. Color is gray to brown to green.

Pachyclavularia spp.
Green star polyps

Maximum Size: Colonies of some species may reach up to 12 in. (30 cm) in diameter, but individual polyps are seldom more than about 0.5 in. (13 mm) high, and about the same diameter.
Range: Indo-Pacific.
Minimum Aquarium Size: Moderate tanks, 50 gal. (190 L) or more.
Lighting: Prefer bright lighting, but can tolerate dimly lit tanks if they are provided with supplemental foods.
Foods & Feeding: Zooxanthellate. Get most of their nutrition from their symbiotic algae, but will also benefit from occasional feedings.
Aquarium Suitability/Compatibility: Easy to keep; good for reef tanks.
Captive Care: These are some of the most popular animals kept in aquariums. They prefer moderate to high currents and will not thrive in areas with low current. They are occasionally preyed upon by *Lysmata* or *Saron* shrimps. They do not do well with several species of green algae, particularly *Batophora* spp., which will overgrow them. The polyps arise from a matlike, low-growing base that is purple, tan, or brown and can extend upward for a distance equal to their diameter. Polyps typically have a white center, but the tentacles can be almost any shade of brown or green.

Sarcophyton spp.
Mushroom corals (toadstool or leather corals)

Maximum Size: Colonies of some species may reach over 3.3 ft. (1 m) in height and twice that in width.

Range: Indo-Pacific.

Minimum Aquarium Size: Moderate tanks, 50 gal. (190 L) or more.

Lighting: Prefer bright lighting, but can tolerate dimly lit tanks if they are provided with supplemental foods.

Foods & Feeding: Zooxanthellate. Do not appear to feed in the aquarium, but do better in tanks that get relatively heavy regular feedings.

Aquarium Suitability/Compatibility: Easy to keep, but may poison other tank inhabitants.

Captive Care: These hardy, leatherlike corals, resembling either mushrooms or flared vases, can develop into magnificent aquarium specimens. Effective competitors for space, they secrete numerous chemicals that inhibit many other animals. Occasionally preyed upon by the *Rapa rapa* snail that eats them from the inside out, they are very resilient if the snail is removed and damaged areas cut off with a knife. Colonies go through cycles of polyp extension and retraction, and at times the top of the colony can be quite smooth. Cuttings are easily propagated. Color ranges from yellow to tan to purple or light green.

Sarcophyton sp. (mushroom coral) displays a delicate green, smooth appearance with its polyps totally withdrawn, a regular occurrence.

Sarcophyton sp. (mushroom coral) with its polyps expanded in the wild. (Note the tunicate *Polycarpa aurata* at the left.)

Sarcophyton sp. (mushroom coral): when kept in a crowded aquarium, its potent natural chemical defenses will often negatively impact close neighbors.

Sarcophyton sp. (mushroom coral) may outgrow its aquarium in time.

Scleronephthya spp.
Tree corals

Maximum Size: Colonies of some species may reach over 24 in. (61 cm) in height.
Range: Indo-Pacific, in current-swept areas.
Minimum Aquarium Size: Moderate tanks, 50 gal. (190 L) or more.
Lighting: Prefer dim lighting; may be negatively affected by algae.
Foods & Feeding: Nonzooxanthellate. Must be fed microplankton. Enriched *Artemia* nauplii and rotifers may be accepted. One species is known to feed on phytoplankton; others probably do as well.
Aquarium Suitability/Compatibility: Essentially impossible to keep.
Captive Care: Unfortunately, the food and current requirements for these often spectacular corals are not known with certainty. They probably benefit from a broad and wide water flow, with most of the water in the tank moving at the same rate; avoid powerheads. They are shorter and more compact than *Dendronephthya*, but otherwise similar. Also, the polyps are clustered instead of being diffusely scattered over the ends of the stalks. Spicules are more numerous in the stalk, making the animal more robust than *Dendronephthya*, but the polyps lack supporting spicules and are not spiny. There are numerous species and color forms—all difficult to identify.

Sinularia spp., *Sinularia dura*, and others
Cabbage leather corals

Maximum Size: Some colonies may exceed 24 in. (61 cm) in height and width, but most are smaller.

Range: Indo-Pacific.

Minimum Aquarium Size: Moderate tanks, 50 gal. (190 L) or more.

Lighting: Prefer bright lighting, but can tolerate dimly lit tanks if they are provided with supplemental foods.

Foods & Feeding: Zooxanthellate, but may benefit from feedings of microplankton.

Aquarium Suitability/Compatibility: Easy to keep, but may poison other nearby animals.

Captive Care: The colonies are robust and stalked, but branches appear drooping and sagging like old cabbage leaves. This genus can tolerate high currents and requires direct current flow to keep the surface of the colonies free of excess mucus and debris. Basic colors are brown, tan and gray; occasionally more colorful. Retractile polyps are concentrated near the edges of the leaves. Mature colonies will fragment and drop branches to produce clones. May be easily propagated by cuttings. Highly competitive; secrete noxious chemicals that kill competitors such as other corals.

Sinularia flexibilis, Sinularia procera, Sinularia sandensis
Flexible leather corals, finger leather corals (slime corals)

Maximum Size: May exceed 3.3 ft. (1 m).
Range: Indo-Pacific.
Minimum Aquarium Size: Moderate tanks, 50 gal. (190 L) or larger.
Lighting: Prefer bright illumination.
Foods & Feeding: Zooxanthellate, but these species need microplankton feedings for good growth.
Aquarium Suitability/Reef Aquarium Compatibility: Easy to keep. Very competitive and will poison many other sessile animals with noxious secretions.
Captive Care: These three species are not distinguishable without microscopic examination of their spicules. They need high currents; surge tanks or turbulent flow is best. White, gray, or various shades of brown. They produce excessive amounts of mucus and need a tank with good skimming and nutrient export. These species are one of several "species groups" within the genus *Sinularia*. Many of these species are exceptionally difficult for experts to distinguish. All are "specialists" in chemical warfare. They are generally easy to grow, and will inhibit or kill most other corals.

Siphonogorgia spp.
China corals

Maximum Size: Some colonies may reach over 24 in. (61 cm) in height and width, but most are smaller.

Range: Mostly Indo-Pacific, but one species is in the Caribbean.

Minimum Aquarium Size: Large tanks, 100 gal. (380 L) or more.

Lighting: Do best under, and may need, low-light intensity to prevent fouling by diatoms and other adherent organisms.

Foods & Feeding: Nonzooxanthellate. Probably need a diet of phytoplankton and microzooplankton.

Aquarium Suitability/Compatibility: Difficult to keep.

Captive Care: Similar to the gorgonians, corals in this genus defy easy keeping in the aquarium. They are found in high-current areas with the fans oriented perpendicularly to the predominant currents to catch passing plankton. When current is reduced, the animals may collapse a bit. The body is inflatable, branches slender and "semi-rigid" due to the high concentration of spicules. In some species, polyps are found on the sides of the main branches, as well as elsewhere; most species have polyps only on the small branches, occurring as terminal clusters. Polyps may withdraw into the branches totally. Body color is red or orange; polyps may be white or yellow.

Studeriotes longiramosa
Christmas tree coral

Maximum Size: Some colonies may reach over 24 in. (61 cm) in height, but most are smaller.
Range: Indo-Pacific.
Minimum Aquarium Size: Moderate tanks, 50 gal. (190 L) or more.
Lighting: Does best under, and may need, low-light intensity to prevent fouling by diatoms and other adherent organisms.
Foods & Feeding: Zooxanthellate. Eats small particulates and microzooplankton, such as enriched *Artemia*; may require phytoplankton.
Aquarium Suitability/Compatibility: Hard to keep; requires expert care.
Captive Care: This bizarre-looking species folds inward on itself during the night and extends out during the day. When folded, the branches are pulled down and inward, and the body closes tightly over them with strong, sphincterlike muscles. Lives in loose sediments, anchored in place by rootlike processes. Brown or tan, lacks zooxanthellae and must be fed. The relatively small polyps are distributed along the branches and the animal can only feed during periods of expansion (i.e., daylight). Colonies do best in moderate currents, which bring them food. Food and current requirements are difficult for most hobbyists to provide.

Xenia spp.
Waving hand corals (pulse corals, pulsing *Xenia*)

Maximum Size: Colonies can reach heights of about 4 in. (10 cm); most are smaller. Polyps reach diameters of about 0.5 in. (13 mm).
Range: Indo-Pacific.
Minimum Aquarium Size: Nano tanks, 1 gal. (3.8 L) or more.
Lighting: Do best under moderate to bright lighting.
Foods & Feeding: Get most of their nutrition from their zooxanthellae but do well with microphytoplankton supplements.
Aquarium Suitability/Compatibility: Easy to grow and keep.
Captive Care: *Xenia* species are specialized for different microhabitats, but normal reef conditions with temperatures in the 81 to 84°F (27 to 29°C) range, with salinities of 35 to 36 ppt will be a good starting point. They like moderate, continuous current. They do not tolerate rapid changes in pH and appear particularly sensitive to a high pH, so care should be taken during the addition of kalkwasser to prevent the pH from rising too quickly. *Xenia* are characterized by having large polyps arising off a central stalk or core. The distinctive pulsing actions of the polyps will mesmerize viewers, but this behavior is not yet fully understood and not all colonies can be counted upon to pulse.

Cespitularia sp. (blue *Xenia*) is a close relative of the genus *Xenia,* with more prominent stalks. Colonies may or may not have pulsing habits.

Xenia sp. (waving hand coral) is almost weedlike in ideal conditions, spreading rapidly across hard, rocky substrates and even up aquarium walls.

Xenia sp. (waving hand coral) is now widely available as captive-propagated colonies, which tend to be easier to keep and, it is claimed, more likely to pulse.

Xenia sp. (waving hand coral) is a good beginner's coral, requiring good light and water conditions, but often thriving without extraordinary care or husbandry.

Heteractis crispa anemone with *Amphiprion chrysopterus* clownfish: overharvesting of large, wild sea anemones is of great concern to many marine biologists.

Introduction to Sea Anemones

Probably the most enduring closeup image of a coral reef is that of a clownfish (anemonefish) nestled down in its host anemone. Indeed, this relationship is quite symbolic of the entire symbiotic nature of many reef animals. More to the point, for the general public, clownfishes are simply cute and attractive. Because of this, almost every beginning aquarist thinks he or she wants an anemone and clownfish duo in his or her aquarium.

With respect to the anemones, this is an exceptionally unfortunate desire for several reasons. First, they are difficult for most aquarists to keep healthy. Second, most anemones sold in aquarium shops are wild-caught, although captive propagation is now beginning. Third, any anemone removed from a coral reef area also removes any possibility of clownfishes from that area, because in the wild these fishes require the anemone's presence for their survival. Finally, it has been documented that sea anemones reproduce and spread slowly in nature, and small individuals are almost never seen. Some researchers have indicated that adult anemones may be several

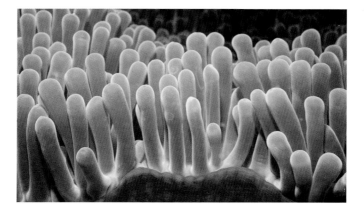

Heteractis magnifica tentacles: bearing microscopic stinging nematocysts, they can deliver irritating or even serious skin reactions if handled without gloves.

centuries old. So if a hobbyist tries to keep a host anemone and fails, not only have they killed that one animal, they have also killed any clownfishes in the wild that might have been found on it. Additionally, they will have removed a potential breeding animal from a population that may need all the breeders it can get.

Removal of even one of these animals from the wild might seem bad enough, but collectors are removing literally all the anemones from some reef areas. Given normal proliferation rates, this means anemones are unlikely to be found in these regions again for centuries, if ever. And all the associated symbionts, such as the clownfishes, anemone shrimps, and anemone crabs, are similarly impacted.

I would urge any aquarist to be very hesitant to try keeping host anemones unless they are captive-bred. On the other hand, clown-fishes *can* be maintained and bred in captivity without an anemone. This is a guilt-free solution: one can keep the clownfish without the anguish of worrying about the anemone.

But for individuals who have acquired anemones, from whatever source, I suggest the following generalized care:

Host anemones are from several different evolutionary lineages

Stichodactyla haddoni (Haddon's carpet anemone): the conscientious reefkeeper will always look for captive-bred or sustainably harvested specimens.

but all require full strength salinity of 35 to 37 ppt, and temperatures of 81 to 84°F (27 to 29°C).

Despite the fact that they have zooxanthellae, all host anemones need to be fed and will do best with one, or a pair of, clownfish. However, the size of the clownfish needs to be tailored to the size of the anemone. Putting a pair of large maroon clowns (*Premnas biaculeatus*) with a small bulb-tipped anemone (*Entacmaea quadricolor*) will likely kill the anemone, as the clowns will buffet it to death.

Keep in mind that a moving or unattached anemone is an unhappy anemone, and is probably not long for this world unless conditions are changed. Conditions that may need correction might include: food quantity, food type, current, substrate, or light intensity (too much or too little). Be sure all powerheads and water pump intakes are carefully screened to prevent accidental injury to a roaming anemone. Tanks with large, heavily fed anemones must have excellent water flow and aggressive protein skimming.

See the species listings that follow and the bibliographic references at the back of this book for further instructions about anemone care.

Cryptodendrum adhaesivum
Adhesive anemone (pizza anemone)

Maximum Size: Disc about 12 in. (30 cm) in diameter.
Range: Indo-Pacific.
Minimum Aquarium Size: Large tanks, 100 gal. (380 L) or more.
Lighting: Does best when kept under bright lighting.
Foods & Feeding: Needs to be fed frequently with meaty foods. Diced large or whole small fishes will be good food choices.
Aquarium Suitability/Reef Compatibility: Compatible with most animals. Ecologically important; do not buy wild-caught specimens. Warning: surface is exceptionally sticky and will sting humans.
Captive Care: This beautiful anemone is seldom seen in stores and is hard to keep. Needs to be anchored in rocks with the disc extending out over the rocks. Let it choose its own anchorage and arrange other livestock well away from it. Likes moderate, but not vigorous, steady current flow over its surface. Good protein skimming is a must. Possesses two types of tentacles, often of different colors. One type covers most of the disc and is short, but branched several times. The second type, colored pink, gray, green, brown, yellow or blue, lines the edge of the disc and is tightly packed. *Amphiprion clarkii* is the only clownfish in nature that will use this host.

Entacmaea quadricolor
Bubble-tip anemone (bulb-tip anemone)

Maximum Size: Disc about 12 in. (30 cm) in diameter.
Range: Indo-Pacific.
Minimum Aquarium Size: Moderate tanks, 50 gal. (190 L) or more.
Lighting: Does best when kept under bright lighting.
Foods & Feeding: Zooxanthellate; needs regular feeding with meaty foods such as whole or diced shrimp and marine fish.
Aquarium Suitability/Reef Compatibility: Does well in many aquariums. Captive-propagated specimens are commonly available and are hardier and easier to keep than wild-caught animals. Will occasionally eat aquarium fishes.
Captive Care: The hardiest and easiest to keep of the host anemones and compatible with most clownfish species. Needs moderate to strong currents. Attachment disc must be buried in a deep crevice. This anemone tends to be brown or greenish-brown, with bright green tentacles that often form a bulb at the tip. When large, these anemones often split into several (2 to 5) smaller individuals that may or may not remain together. If they don't remain together, a resident pair of clownfish may inadvertently kill the anemones, as each smaller anemone may be too small to withstand the clowns' buffeting.

One of the sea anemones almost universally accepted by different clownfish species, *Entacmaea quadricolor* is also the best choice for most aquarists.

Captive-propagated bubble-tip anemones are becoming widely available, as healthy specimens frequently undergo fission, or splitting, to produce two clones.

Entacmaea quadricolor
Rose anemone

Maximum Size: Disc about 12 in. (30 cm) in diameter.
Range: Indo-Pacific.
Minimum Aquarium Size: Moderate tanks, 50 gal. (190 L) or more.
Lighting: Does best when kept under bright lighting.
Foods & Feeding: Zooxanthellate, but feed frequently with diced large, or whole, small fishes.
Aquarium Suitability/Reef Aquarium Compatibility: Relatively hardy captive-propagated specimens are available and are hardier and easier to keep than wild-caught animals. Will occasionally eat aquarium fishes.
Captive Care: This popular anemone is a color variety of the Bubble-Tip Anemone (see pages 86-87) and requires similar care. It does well in moderate to strong currents and will expand fully under these conditions. The tentacle tips form bulbs, as in the more common form, but more frequently. The tips may be colored in a contrasting color, such as white or blue. Most clownfishes will use this anemone as a host.

Heteractis aurora
Beaded anemone

Maximum Size: Disc about 10 in. (25 cm) in diameter.
Range: Indo-Pacific.
Minimum Aquarium Size: Moderate tanks, 50 gal. (190 L) or more.
Lighting: Moderate lighting.
Foods & Feeding: Zooxanthellate, but feed every other day with diced large, or whole, small fishes.
Aquarium Suitability/Reef Aquarium Compatibility: Difficult to keep. Will occasionally eat aquarium fishes.
Captive Care: Probably the most distinctive host sea anemone. Relatively short tentacles have regular swellings along their length, giving them a "beaded" appearance. Pale gray, brown, or greenish in color with white markings. It lives in the sand, where it extends vertically in the sediment with the oral disc lying flat on the surface and the pedal disc fastened to some object below the sediment surface. May retract fully under the surface, reinflating later. Needs a sand bed 4 to 6 in. (10 to 15 cm) in depth. Place the anemone where rock is partially buried in the sand. The anemone will attach to the rock and move down into the sand. Good protein skimming is a must. Clark's clownfish and several related species are found with this anemone in nature.

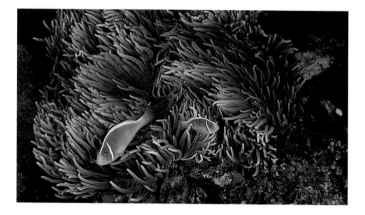

Heteractis crispa
Leathery sea anemone (sebae anemone)

Maximum Size: Disc about 12 in. (30 cm) in diameter.
Range: Indo-Pacific.
Minimum Aquarium Size: Moderate tanks, 50 gal. (190 L) or more.
Lighting: Does best when kept under bright lighting.
Foods & Feeding: Feed every other day with diced large, or whole, fishes, shrimps or squids. Bleached or white animals need to be fed more until they become gray or brown, at which time feedings can be reduced, but still need to be continued for the health of the animal.
Aquarium Suitability/Reef Aquarium Compatibility: Difficult to keep. Will occasionally eat aquarium fishes.
Captive Care: This anemone is frequently available but has a low survival rate. Pale greenish tan, with long tentacles tipped in blue or pink. Needs a clownfish for full tentacle extension. Place where rock horizontally overlies a sand bed to create a narrow crevice. Needs moderate current. The column in healthy animals has a pronounced leathery texture and bears many adhesive bumps. Normally zooxanthellate, but often animals seen in the trade are bleached white. Unless it reacquires zooxanthellae, it is doomed to a slow death. About a dozen species of clownfishes can use this anemone as a host in nature.

Heteractis magnifica
Magnificent sea anemone (Ritteri anemone)

Maximum Size: Disc over 39 in. (1 m) in diameter.

Range: Indo-Pacific, in moderate to shallow water.

Minimum Aquarium Size: Very large tanks, 500 gal. (1,900 L) or more.

Lighting: Does best kept under bright lighting.

Foods & Feeding: Needs to be fed well and often. A large specimen will eat the equivalent of a good-sized herring every couple of days.

Aquarium Suitability/Reef Compatibility: Almost impossible to keep alive more than a few months. Do not buy wild-caught specimens. Will fatally sting many other reef anemones and corals.

Captive Care: This is a spectacular animal best left on the reef. It requires good water quality and moderate water movement, along with a solitary perch where it cannot contact any other anemone or nearby coral. Its nematocysts can kill almost all other animals in an aquarium. Color ranges from deep rose to brilliant orange. Observations from natural populations indicate that some may reproduce asexually, but this has rarely been seen in captivity, probably because it is seldom kept under appropriate conditions. This species is naturally home to about eight or ten clownfish species.

Heteractis malu

Delicate anemone (Hawaiian, sebae, or white sand anemone)

Maximum Size: Disc about 8 in. (20 cm) in diameter.
Range: Indo-Pacific.
Minimum Aquarium Size: Large tanks, 100 gal. (380 L) or more.
Lighting: Does best when kept under bright lighting.
Foods & Feeding: Has zooxanthellae, but needs to be fed every other day or so with meaty foods.
Aquarium Suitability/Reef Compatibility: Needs a deep sand bed in which to bury its column. It has potent nematocysts that can raise welts on humans.
Captive Care: This is another sediment-dwelling anemone normally found with its column buried in the sediment and the green or tan oral disc on the sediment surface. May or may not have lines radiating outward from the mouth. The tentacles tend to be rather short and tubular, often magenta, pink, green, or lavender in color. The outer ones in any row may be inflated about the middle, so the animal has the appearance of having two different types of tentacles. *Amphiprion clarkii* is the only clownfish reported to be found with this species in nature.

Macrodactyla doreensis
Corkscrew anemone (long-tentacled anemone)

Maximum Size: Disc about 19 in. (48 cm) in diameter.
Range: Indo-Pacific.
Minimum Aquarium Size: Large tanks, 100 gal. (380 L) or more.
Lighting: Does best when kept under bright lighting.
Foods & Feeding: Has zooxanthellae, but needs to be fed every other day or so with meaty foods.
Aquarium Suitability/Reef Compatibility: Ecologically important. Survival in aquariums is poor; avoid wild-caught specimens.
Captive Care: Normally found in sediments with its oral disc flat on the surface, and proper aquarium conditions would call for a bed of fine sediments like silt or mud. Needs relatively little current. Major identifying characteristic is the presence of long and slightly tapering tentacles that may be as long as 8 in. (20 cm) in a large individual. The column, which is buried in the sediment, is brown to orange and is lined with prominent white spots. The oral disc is typically brown to green. The tentacles are often the same color as the disc, although they may be a translucent gray. In nature, only four species of clownfishes are reported with this anemone: *Amphiprion clarkii, A. chrysogaster, A. perideraion,* and *A. polymnus.*

Stichodactyla gigantea
Giant carpet anemone (gigantic sea anemone)

Maximum Size: Disc about 19.5 in. (50 cm) in diameter.
Range: Indo-Pacific.
Minimum Aquarium Size: Large tanks, 100 gal. (380 L) or more.
Lighting: Does best when kept under bright lighting.
Foods & Feeding: Has zooxanthellae, but needs to be fed frequently, every other day or so, with diced large, or whole, small fishes.
Aquarium Suitability/Reef Compatibility: Ecologically important; collection should be discouraged. Sting is potent and will kill nearby sessile invertebrates.
Captive Care: In nature, this species often lives in sand pockets in shallow coral rock with the adhesive pedal disc fastened to some subsurface rock. Found in very shallow sand habitats, occasionally reported to be exposed at low tide in some localities. In captivity, it will likely do best living in a shallow sand bed surrounded by rocks. The color is quite variable: the tentacles may be purple, pink, blue, or green. The tentacles are small, about 8 mm long, and move constantly. Six clownfish species are reported to associated with this species in nature: *Amphiprion akindynos, A. bicinctus, A. clarkii, A. ocellaris, A. percula, A. perideraion,* and *A. rubrocinctus.*

Stichodactyla haddoni
Haddon's carpet anemone (sand carpet anemone)

Maximum Size: Disc about 39 in. (1 m) in diameter.
Range: Indo-Pacific.
Minimum Aquarium Size: Large tanks, 100 gal. (380 L) or more.
Lighting: Prefers bright lighting.
Foods & Feeding: Has zooxanthellae, but to be healthy it needs to be fed a diet of meaty foods. An individual with a 24 in. (61 cm) oral disc needs about a teaspoon of fish, such as lance fish or silversides, per day.
Aquarium Suitability/Reef Compatibility: Ecologically important. Unsustainable wild collection should be discouraged. Will eat aquarium fishes.
Captive Care: This animal can become massive. A specimen with a 24 in. (61 cm) diameter disc may have a column exceeding 6 in. (15 cm) in diameter. Lives under the sand; sand bed should be at least 6 to 8 in. (15 to 20 cm) deep. Will extend upward so the basic shape is that of a large trumpet or mushroom. Prefers low to moderate currents. Bulbous tentacles, expanded from a narrow base, may be very sticky. Some tentacles may move, others are motionless. Clownfishes reported to associate with it are: *Amphiprion akindynos, A. chrysogaster, A. chrysopterus, A. clarkii, A. polymnus, A. sebae,* and *A. omanensis.*

Stichodactyla mertensii
Merten's carpet anemone

Maximum Size: Disc over 39 in. (1 m) in diameter.
Range: Indo-Pacific.
Minimum Aquarium Size: Large tanks, 100 gal. (380 L) or more.
Lighting: Prefers bright lighting.
Foods & Feeding: Has zooxanthellae but needs to feed to be healthy. An individual with a 24 in. (61 cm) oral disc needs about a teaspoon of fish, such as lance fish or silversides, per day. If fed inappropriately, it will slowly shrink and move around the aquarium.
Aquarium Suitability/Reef Compatibility: Ecologically important, so collection should be discouraged.
Captive Care: One of the largest sea anemones, this impressive animal lives in rocks with the adhesive pedal disc extended down into a crevice, and the column in contact with rocks on all sides. It is reluctant to withdraw into the crevice and retracts only after repeated stimulation. This anemone prefers relatively strong currents and will do well in a tank with a wavemaker. The disc is only moderately folded and the tentacles are green, sometimes a brilliant yellow green. The tentacles are not adhesive to human skin. About 13 species of clownfishes are found with this species in nature.

Stichodactyla helianthus
Caribbean carpet anemone

Maximum Size: Disc to about 12 in. (30 cm) in diameter.
Range: Caribbean.
Minimum Aquarium Size: Large tanks, 100 gal. (380 L) or more.
Lighting: Needs bright lighting.
Foods & Feeding: Has zooxanthellae, but needs to be fed to be healthy.
Aquarium Suitability/Reef Compatibility: Ecologically important and common but seldom collected for sale. Has a potent sting.
Captive Care: Lives in shallow sandy areas in protected environments. To provide the proper conditions, place where rock horizontally overlies a sand bed to create a narrow crevice; keep the sand depth at 4 in. (10 cm) or less. Moderate water currents are acceptable, but more excessive water flow may prompt the animal to withdraw frequently under the sand. *Stichodactyla helianthus* is superficially similar to *Stichodactyla haddoni* (page 95) but folds its oral disc relatively little. The green or green-gray tentacles are small, less than 0.25 in. (6 mm) long, and very "sticky" with a sting that can harm other aquarium life. Several fishes and over 40 species of invertebrates, including shrimps and crabs, have been reported to associate with this Caribbean anemone.

Actinodendron spp.
Hellfire anemones (knobby-tentacled anemones, beaded-tentacled anemones, tree anemones)

Maximum Size: Disc to about 12 in. (30 cm) in diameter.
Range: Indo-Pacific.
Minimum Aquarium Size: Moderate tanks, 50 gal. (190 L) or more.
Lighting: Prefer moderate lighting.
Foods & Feeding: Have zooxanthellae, but need to feed to be healthy. Probably feed on small fishes or crustaceans and will do well in an aquarium on a mixture of both.
Aquarium Suitability/Reef Compatibility: Reasonably hardy, but reported to kill fishes. Handle with gloves and extreme care; stings are notoriously painful.
Captive Care: Do best in moderately strong currents and need a relatively deep sand bed to allow for burrowing activities. Some bury during the day and emerge to feed at night while others have the reverse behavior pattern. *Actinodendron plumosum*, a night emerging species, has tentacles that extend upward from the sediment, while other species keep their tentacles close to the substrate. No clownfishes naturally associate with them. Some *Periclimenes* shrimps do well with these hosts.

Calliactis spp.
Hermit crab anemones

Maximum Size: Disc about 0.4 in. (10 mm) in diameter, column to about 2 in. (5 cm) high.

Range: Indo-Pacific.

Minimum Aquarium Size: Small tanks, 10 gal. (3.8 L) or more.

Lighting: Immaterial.

Foods & Feeding: Feed on particulate material in the water column and can be fed any foods that fishes will eat.

Aquarium Suitability/Reef Compatibility: Once the particular conditions of their carrier crabs are met, they are reasonably hardy and good aquarium inhabitants.

Captive Care: A number of anemone species are found living attached to hermit crabs, and they make an interesting display of symbiosis in a smaller species tank. The oral discs of *Calliactis* species are proportionally rather wide. The column is narrower and often about 1.2 to 1.5 in. (3 to 3.8 cm) high and is usually longitudinally striped with dark lines and may be mottled. This association is a true mutualism. The crab gets protection by having the anemones on its shell, and the anemones benefit by getting food from the crab's sloppy eating habits.

Bartholomea annulata
Curleycue anemone

Maximum Size: To about 8 in. (20 cm) across the tentacles.
Range: Caribbean.
Minimum Aquarium Size: Moderate tanks, 50 gal. (190 L) or more.
Lighting: Immaterial.
Foods & Feeding: Nonzooxanthellate. Will feed on particulate material in the water column and can be fed any meaty foods fishes will eat. Live or frozen foods are better than flake.
Aquarium Suitability/Reef Compatibility: Once its particular conditions are met, it is reasonably hardy and a good aquarium inhabitant.
Captive Care: This anemone lives in rocks or gravel with the body protected in a hole, crevice, or cave, and only the tentacles extending into view. The body is often buried quite deeply into the substrate and when the tentacles are visible, the animal is significantly extended. If disturbed, it can withdraw very rapidly. This species will benefit from moderately strong currents, but overly vigorous currents will prevent any extension at all. The clear, transparent tentacles have characteristic white corkscrew markings running along them.

Condylactis gigantea
Caribbean giant anemone (Haitian anemone, condy)

Maximum Size: To about 12 in. (30 cm) high and across the tentacles.
Range: Caribbean.
Minimum Aquarium Size: Moderate tanks, 50 gal. (190 L) or more.
Lighting: Does best under bright light.
Foods & Feeding: Zooxanthellate. Also feeds on particulate material in the water column and can be fed any meaty foods that fishes will eat.
Aquarium Suitability/Reef Compatibility: Reasonably hardy and a good aquarium inhabitant, but may sting nearby sessile invertebrates.
Captive Care: *Condylactis* individuals are some of the most beautiful animals imported for the aquarium hobby. As with many anemones, the Caribbean giant anemone prefers to have its body protected in a crevice or cavity, while the tentacles extend out to collect food. In captivity, it prefers moderate currents. The basic column color is white, often lightly colored with hints of brown, tan, green, or yellow. The tentacles are the same color as the column, except for their bulbous tips, which can be pink, red, purple, green, or yellow. Some clown-fishes, including *Amphiprion frenatus*, may associate with this anemone in captivity. Many invertebrates and a few fishes associate with this species in nature.

Aiptasia spp.
Glass anemones (glassrose anemones, devil's plague)

Maximum Size: To about 4 in. (10 cm) high and across the tentacles.
Range: Widespread in warm seas.
Minimum Aquarium Size: Will live in any tank.
Lighting: Immaterial.
Foods & Feeding: Zooxanthellate, but well able to survive in the dark eating fish food or absorbing dissolved nutrients.
Aquarium Suitability/Reef Compatibility: These are dangerous pests. Their nematocysts are particularly virulent; they will attack and kill most corals and many other kinds of anemones, sea mats, or polyps.
Captive Care: These nuisance anemones typically arrive on live rock and can easily reach plague proportions. A large, well-fed specimen can asexually produce dozens of tiny juveniles in a day. Juveniles and adults are mobile, creep rapidly over the substrate, or detach and float to a new spot. The most effective biological control is a copperband butterflyfish (*Chelmon rostratus*). Peppermint shrimp (*Lysmata wurde-manni*) can be used in some tanks, but in well-fed tanks, the shrimp will scavenge on excess food and refuse to eat the anemones. At present, there is no way to completely remove the anemones and leave all other life in the tank.

Boloceroides mcmurrichi
Swimming anemone

Maximum Size: Up to 4 in. (10 cm) high and across the tentacles.
Range: Indo-Pacific.
Minimum Aquarium Size: Will live in any tank.
Lighting: Zooxanthellate, but lighting appears immaterial.
Foods & Feeding: Zooxanthellate, but able to survive in the dark eating fish food or absorbing dissolved nutrients.
Aquarium Suitability/Reef Aquarium Compatibility: Pest. Similar to *Aiptasia*; if left uncontrolled, it can completely take over a tank.
Captive Care: Body is tan or brown and the column is short; the tentacles are robust and may be banded. The disc may have whitish radial or blotchy marking. Reproduce by producing asexual larvae or by pinching off small chunks of pedal disc tissue, which then differentiate into a small anemone. Are mobile, creeping rapidly over the substrate or detaching and floating to a new spot. If disturbed, will swim by the use of rhythmic contraction and flexion of the tentacles. Manual control by any of several methods (injection with toxic materials or smothering) is possible if they are removed when the populations are small. Copperband butterflyfish (*Chelmon rostratus*) are most effective, but may eat other tank residents.

Protopalythoa spp.
Green zoanthids

Maximum Size: Colonies may be up to 12 in. (30 cm) in length and breadth. Individual polyps to about 1 in. (2.5 cm) across and high.
Range: Indo-Pacific.
Minimum Aquarium Size: Nano tanks, 1 gal. (3.8 L) or more.
Lighting: Zooxanthellate. Need bright illumination.
Foods & Feeding: Target feeding unnecessary, but do best if occasionally fed with small crustacean food such as *Artemia*.
Aquarium Suitability/Reef Compatibility: Easy to care for, but not particularly hardy. Handle all zoanthids with extreme care to avoid contact with palytoxin, a powerful poison found in their mucus.
Captive Care: These zoanthids are found in nature living in shallow-water areas, often completely covered with sand. They will do well only in brightly lit tanks with moderate currents. The relatively large disc is fringed with a row of tentacles that alternate, projecting up and down. The color is a deep emerald green, often with reddish-brown highlights. *Palythoa* and *Protopalythoa* polyps produce a toxin that may be concentrated enough in the mucus to cause serious injury to the aquarist. Always wear gloves when handling these toxin-bearing animals.

Palythoa caribaeorum
White Caribbean zoanthid (brown Caribbean zoanthid)

Maximum Size: Colonies may be several yards (meters) in length and breadth. Individual polyps to about 1.2 in. (3 cm) across.
Range: Caribbean.
Minimum Aquarium Size: Nano tanks, 1 gal. (3.8 L) or more.
Lighting: Zooxanthellate. Needs bright illumination.
Foods & Feeding: Target feeding unnecessary, but does best if occasionally fed with small crustacean food such as *Artemia*.
Aquarium Suitability/Reef Compatibility: Relatively aggressive. Will grow toward and overgrow some animals. Handle all zoanthids with extreme care to avoid contact with palytoxin, a powerful poison found in their mucus.
Captive Care: Given bright reef aquarium illumination and reasonably good water motion, this zoanthid is hardy and easy to care for. Regardless of the common name, the coloration is white to a rich chestnut, with the brown coloration being more common in those that are offered for sale or kept under lower light intensities. They seem harmless to most mobile aquarium inhabitants, but probably have the capability of eating fish fry and maybe small crustaceans. Always wear gloves when handling these toxin-bearing animals.

Palythoa grandis
Giant zoanthid

Maximum Size: Colonies may be up to 12 in. (30 cm) in length and breadth. Individual polyps to about 1.5 in. (3.8 cm) across.
Range: Caribbean.
Minimum Aquarium Size: Nano tanks, 1 gal. (3.8 L) or more.
Lighting: Zooxanthellate. Needs bright illumination.
Foods & Feeding: Will do best if well fed. White forms lack zooxanthellae and need specific attention to ensure that they feed. Small crustaceans or diced fish are relatively good foods for this species.
Aquarium Suitability/Reef Compatibility: Good reef tank animal. Handle all zoanthids with extreme care to avoid contact with palytoxin, a powerful poison found in their mucus.
Captive Care: This is a hardy, not particularly aggressive, animal that does not form large mats and spreads slowly. It is harmless to most other aquarium inhabitants. The oral disc is erected on a long stalk and is held in a more flattened posture than many of the other larger zoanthids. Found in shades of green, brown, and white. *Palythoa* polyps produce a toxin that may be concentrated enough in the mucus to cause serious injury to the aquarist. Always wear gloves when handling these animals.

Parazoanthus swiftii
Caribbean golden zoanthid (yellow symbiotic zoanthid)

Maximum Size: Colonies about 0.75 in. (1.9 cm) high and about 0.5 in. (13 mm) across the tentacles.

Range: Caribbean.

Minimum Aquarium Size: Moderate tanks, 50 gal. (190 L) or more.

Lighting: Immaterial.

Foods & Feeding: Lacks zooxanthellae and needs to be target-fed frequently. Any small zooplankton, such as enriched baby brine shrimp, will do.

Aquarium Suitability/Reef Compatibility: Requires special feeding and is not particularly hardy. Well-being also depends on their sponge host's health.

Captive Care: These small, brilliant yellow polyps—and many similar species—live on sponges. Their sponge host should be placed in a high-current area. Light is not important, but they may be better able to resist cyanobacterial or microalgal fouling if they are in a dimmer area of the tank. As they are dependent upon the sponge's well-being, it is probably better not to add the sponge-zoanthid assemblage to a tank unless you already have sponges growing successfully in the system.

ZOANTHUS SOCIATUS: CLOSED POLYPS AT RIGHT

Zoanthus pulchellus, Zoanthus sociatus
Green sea mats

Maximum Size: Colonies about 0.25 in. (6 mm) high and less than 0.5 in. (13 mm) wide.
Range: Caribbean.
Minimum Aquarium Size: Nano tanks, 1 gal. (3.8 L) or more.
Lighting: Need bright lighting.
Foods & Feeding: Zooxanthellate; usually get most of their nutrition from zooxanthellate byproducts. Will eat small particulate foods.
Aquarium Suitability/Reef Compatibility: These are good reef aquarium animals that are generally harmless.
Captive Care: Easy to care for, these species form low-growing mats with the individual polyps tightly pressed together. Colors vary from brilliant green to dark brown. The two species can be distinguished on the basis of overall growth forms: *Zoanthus pulchellus* tends to grow in more-or-less circular mats, while *Z. sociatus* forms linear colonies of individuals in rows. They generally lose in competitive battles with *Palythoa* zoanthids, and several algal species will overgrow and smother them. These zoanthids are preyed upon by sundial snails, camelback shrimp (*Rhynchocinetes uritai*), and other shrimps from the genera *Saron* and *Lysmata*.

UNKNOWN GENUS OF CERIANTHID

Arachnanthus, Cerianthus, and *Pachycerianthus* spp.
Tube anemones

Maximum Size: Tentacle crown to 6 in. (15 cm) across.
Range: All seas.
Minimum Aquarium Size: Large tanks, 100 gal. (380 L) or more.
Lighting: Immaterial.
Foods & Feeding: Lack zooxanthellae and need to be fed well on small planktonic foods.
Aquarium Suitability/Reef Compatibility: Challenging to keep. Some species pack a powerful sting that can burn or kill fishes, giant clams, and other reef aquarium inhabitants.
Captive Care: These beautiful animals have a crown of tentacles with two whorls of distinctly different-sized banded tentacles and live in a mucuslike tube created from special types of nematocysts (stinging capsules). They need a lot of space around them, as their sting is potent and damaging to many other reef animals. The aquarist must provide a deep sand bed or sandy mud bed for their tubes and plenty of space around them. Some species can easily kill a large tridacnid clam or coral if their tentacles are allowed to sweep against them. Although the tentacles are large, they are also quite delicate and feeding large foods may damage them.

Discosoma sp.: among the best invertebrate choices for newcomers to reef aquarium husbandry, the corallimorphs are hardy and often very beautiful.

Introduction to Corallimorphs

Corallimorpharians (corallimorphs), also called mushroom polyps or mushroom anemones, may not resemble either mushrooms or anemones, but they are beautiful, alluring marine invertebrates. Some species may spread under good conditions. A few species are hardy and are good animals for beginners.

There are two basic types of mushroom polyps found in the aquarium hobby. One looks pretty much like a standard sea anemone in having relatively long tentacles, but is distinguished by the presence of knobby tips; these animals lack zooxanthellae. The other looks like a flat disk with rows of bumps, knobs, or frilly extensions arranged in lines radiating from a central mouth; these animals are zooxanthellate. This type also has fine tentacles fringing the edge of the disk. This latter type contains most of the species hobbyists refer to as "mushroom" polyps.

These polyps actually have an internal structure that is quite similar to corals. In fact, there has been a trend in the recent taxonomic literature to refer to them as "corals without skeletons." They

Discosoma sp.: these fleshy polyps do best in areas of moderate to lower lighting and gentle currents, with room to spread.

are characterized by a relatively narrow column with an expanded, flattened oral disc.

Most mushroom polyps are deep-water animals that require moderate light intensities and relatively low current velocities. They feed on microparticulate material from the water supplemented by the products of their zooxanthellae. Some species may tolerate less-than-ideal water conditions, but care must be taken to ensure that pH remains in the normal range.

As with all corals, these animals probably compete for space by secreting toxic materials as well as by stinging adjacent animals with their mesenterial filaments. They will attack and may kill nearby animals.

The taxonomy of this group is in a state of flux and is otherwise so poorly known that we cannot characterize most varieties even to genus. Additionally, they are exceptionally variable within even a single population with regard to color. Like most hobbyists, I probably have clones of some mushroom polyps that differ significantly in color from place to place in a single aquarium.

Amplexidiscus fenestrafer
Elephant ear

Maximum Size: To about 18 in. (46 cm) in diameter.
Range: Indo-Pacific.
Minimum Aquarium Size: Moderate tanks, 50 gal. (190 L) or more.
Lighting: Moderate to dim lighting preferred.
Foods & Feeding: Zooxanthellate, but needs to be fed. It is a fish predator, although it occasionally snacks on shrimps and crabs.
Aquarium Suitability/Reef Compatibility: Hardy and easy to keep.
Captive Care: This fascinating but deadly predator mimics anemones, attracting and eating clownfishes. When the prey lingers near or nestles in the elephant ear's disc, it triggers a feeding response: the anemone rapidly closes, forming a ballooning, purselike container that is closed tight, and the internal mouth is opened. The bag then contracts and the prey is ingested. It will catch and eat all manner of fishes, and should be kept in tanks with nonedible tankmates, such as other cnidarians. Does best in tanks with low to moderate current flow, oriented vertically on rock walls. It should be fed regularly with pieces of marine fish, crab, or shrimp. Colors vary from light beige to a vivid dark green.

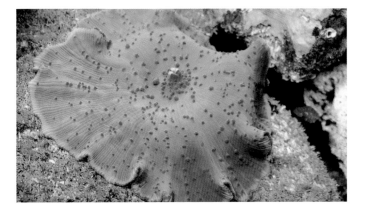

Discosoma (*Actinodiscus*) spp.
Mushroom polyps (various genera and species)

Maximum Size: To about 4 in. (10 cm) in diameter.
Range: Caribbean and Indo-Pacific.
Minimum Aquarium Size: Nano tanks, 1 gal. (3.8 L) or more.
Lighting: Moderate lighting; some prefer dim, others bright.
Foods & Feeding: Zooxanthellate, but need to be fed small particulate material and, occasionally, enriched newly hatched *Artemia*.
Aquarium Suitability/Reef Compatibility: Good aquarium animals. Often reproduce well. Occasionally overgrow other animals.
Captive Care: The correct name for this genus is *Discosoma*, although the name *Actinodiscus* has been used incorrectly for many years in the aquarium hobby. Few of the species of mushroom polyps appear to be scientifically described, and identification is difficult, even for experts. These animals thrive under varying conditions and are not particularly demanding.

Discosoma sp.: fluorescent blue-striped corallimorphs.

Discosoma sp.: bright green-striped morphs.

Discosoma sp.: fluorescent-green mushrooms.

Discosoma sp.: metallic blue mushroom.

Rhodactis sp: compare to smooth surfaces of the *Discosoma* spp., above.

Rhodactis sp.: accurate identification of most corallimorphs is impossible.

Discosoma neglecta
Umbrella mushroom polyp

Maximum Size: To about 2.5 in. (6 cm) in diameter.
Range: Caribbean.
Minimum Aquarium Size: Nano tanks, 1 gal. (3.8 L) or more.
Lighting: Moderate lighting; some prefer dim, others bright.
Foods & Feeding: May survive indefinitely on the byproducts of its zooxanthellae, but does better if given the opportunity to feed.
Aquarium Suitability/Reef Compatibility: Good aquarium animals. Often reproduce well. Occasionally overgrow other animals.
Captive Care: This durable species is found in a wide variety of natural habitats, presumably due to a wide tolerance for environmental variables, making it a successful reef aquarium animal. It is not aggressive, but a small clonal group is often very resistant to overgrowth by other animals. Well-fed animals reproduce asexually by pedal laceration, wherein new individuals are produced when the animals bud off small pieces of their pedal discs. The disc is covered with small tentacles that resemble small bumps or tubercles. There are no marginal tentacles, and the column is relatively thick, "bulky," and often brown or green. Disc coloration is variable, ranging from brown to green to blue; streaks of a contrasting color are common.

Discosoma sanctithomae (= Rhodactis sanctithomae)
Warty corallimorph

Maximum Size: To about 2.5 in. (6 cm) in diameter.
Range: Caribbean.
Minimum Aquarium Size: Nano tanks, 1 gal. (3.8 L) or more.
Lighting: Tolerates a wide variety of lighting conditions, from bright to moderate.
Foods & Feeding: Zooxanthellate, but does best if periodically fed small zooplankton, such as enriched brine shrimp.
Aquarium Suitability/Reef Compatibility: Good aquarium animal. Often reproduces well. Occasionally overgrows some other animals.
Captive Care: This relatively common Caribbean corallimorpharian is easily kept and will clone itself repeatedly once settled into good conditions. It is almost intermediate in its morphology between other *Discosoma* and *Rhodactis* and may need a genus of its own. It is a robust animal with a rather stout column. Discs are sub-circular or elliptical. Color is bluish to green to brown. There is a fringe of small marginal tentacles and a region of large, often inflated, disc tentacles surrounding the mouth. It reproduces asexually to form spreading colonies in nature, and will do so in captivity given proper conditions.

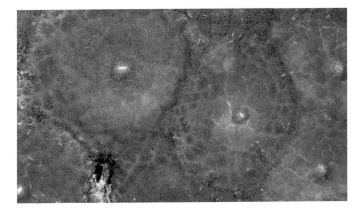

Rhodactis spp.
Rhodactis

Maximum Size: To about 4 in. (10 cm) in diameter.

Range: Indo-Pacific.

Minimum Aquarium Size: Small tanks, 10 gal. (38 L) or more.

Lighting: Generally prefer bright lighting.

Foods & Feeding: They do best in a tank that is well fed. Will occasionally close up and feed on larger particles, but often seem to harvest planktonic material from the water.

Aquarium Suitability/Reef Compatibility: Good aquarium animals, but can be very aggressive. Will overgrow and kill anemones and corals.

Captive Care: If well fed and in good condition, these robust corallimorphs will reproduce asexually by pedal laceration. They generally form large clonal masses in nature; similar masses occur in reef tanks. They are usually larger than *Discosoma* species and are distinguished from them by the presence of branched tentacles on the oral disc. However, in many cases, these branched tentacles are difficult to see. There are many species and color varieties. Tentacles often appear bulbous or relatively large, in contrast to those found on most *Discosoma*. Marginal tentacles are usually relatively large and evident, and often the inside of the mouth is a color that contrasts with the disc.

PSEUDOCORYNACTIS CARIBBEORUM

Pseudocorynactis caribbeorum, Pseudocorynactis spp.
Caribbean corallimorph

Maximum Size: To about 0.5 in. (1.3 cm) in diameter.

Range: Caribbean (similar species found in the Indo-Pacific).

Minimum Aquarium Size: Nano tanks, 1 gal. (3.8 L) or more.

Lighting: Prefer dimly illuminated areas.

Foods & Feeding: They lack zooxanthellae, but do well in reef tanks that are well fed. No target feeding is necessary, but they reproduce more rapidly if fed small pieces of fish.

Aquarium Suitability/Reef Compatibility: Very good aquarium animals.

Captive Care: Looking more like sea anemones than mushroom polyps, these curious-looking animals usually enter the tank on live rock. They do best in areas that are poorly lighted or dark, such as inside caves or under ledges where they form small clonal aggregations. They are usually expanded at night during feeding and are preyed upon by copperband butterflyfishes and numerous shrimps, particularly *Lysmata* species. *Pseudocorynactis caribbeorum* is probably the most abundant, but other indeterminate species, probably of Pacific origin, are also found in captivity. Easily recognized and distinguished by their tentacle tips, which bear colored (*Ps. caribbeorum*) or white (*Ps.* sp.) spherical structures full of nematocysts.

Ricordea florida
Ricordea (Floridian corallimorph)

Maximum Size: To about 2.5 in. (6 cm) in diameter.
Range: Caribbean (a similar species, *Ricordea yuma*, is found in the Indo-Pacific).
Minimum Aquarium Size: Nano tanks, 1 gal. (3.8 L) or more.
Lighting: Prefer moderately illuminated areas.
Foods & Feeding: This species obtains much of its energy from zooxanthellae, but it can be fed plankton or enriched newly hatched *Artemia*.
Aquarium Suitability/Reef Compatibility: Very good aquarium animal.
Captive Care: *Ricordea florida* is a hardy corallimorph that comes in a wide variety of colors, virtually all of them are strikingly pretty. It is an animal that should be kept in moderate light intensity areas: it tends to lose its colors when placed too close to bright lights or in areas that are too dim. Mature individuals have circular to irregular, variably shaped discs, and often have more than one mouth opening. They form large clonal mats, splitting longitudinally. Once overharvested from some reefs, they are becoming a popular aquaculture species, and captive-bred specimens are available. The related *Ricordea yuma* appears in hues of green, purple, and orange.

119

Captivating for reef aquarists and underwater naturalists alike, the thousands of species of stony corals take myriad forms and assume a rainbow of colors.

Introduction to the Stony Corals

Stony corals are a primary motivator for marine aquarists to move beyond fish-only tanks and take up reefkeeping. Having captivated humans for many centuries, these unusual animals exhibit a variety of growth forms and colors, and either directly or indirectly create a habitat for many other animals. All stony corals secrete an exoskeleton of calcium carbonate and organic material from their epidermis. Functionally, there are two types of stony corals—those with and those without zooxanthellae.

Understanding the Zooxanthellae-Coral Symbiosis

Zooxanthellae are photosynthetic, unicellular organisms that are generally put into the group called the dinoflagellates. Often referred to as "algae," dinoflagellates are actually very different from the more typical algal species, such as the kelps, green algae, and coralline red algae, also found in reef tanks. Recent nucleic acid comparisons, along with other morphological treatments, now place the dinoflagellates in a separate Kingdom of life, as different from plants, fungi,

Goniopora djiboutiensis (flowerpot coral) polyps: this species has poor survival rates in aquariums, indicating we have much to learn about its care.

and animals as those groups are from each other.

In corals, zooxanthellae appear as small greenish, golden, or brownish spherical cells living within either the tissues or cells of their hosts. They photosynthesize, using light that passes through their hosts, and in doing so turn carbon dioxide and water into simple sugars. They can also use nitrogenous waste products from their hosts to produce proteins and other organic compounds. Like the more typical algae, dinoflagellates are "leaky" and may lose up to 95 percent of their daily photosynthetic production to their hosts; most of this is in the form of sugars, which the hosts use as food.

Many animals other than corals have entered into a symbiosis with zooxanthellae, but this mutualism is probably more often associated with the stony corals than with any other group. Corals with zooxanthellae are called "hermatypic," or "reef-forming," corals, while those without zooxanthellae are referred to as "ahermatypic" corals. Ahermatypic corals do not form reefs in the tropics, although large reefs of *Lophelia*, a deep-water ahermatype, have been found in the cool waters off Scandinavia.

Additionally, stony coral animals are predatory and require food.

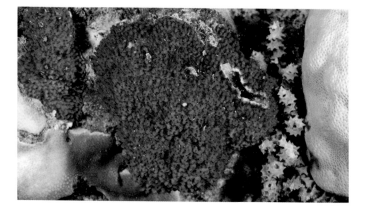

Montipora sp: high-quality live rock may sprout exceptionally attractive encrusting corals, sometimes months after being introduced into the reef aquarium.

They also use the abundant small particulate material from the waters impinging on reefs. The importance of food to corals was first noted anecdotally by C. M. Yonge, one of the first biologists to systematically study coral reef ecology. He determined that of all predators on Earth, corals contain the largest proportion of their body dedicated to the capture of food.

Hermatypic corals represent a zooxanthellae-coral animal mutualism that has evolved to optimize growth and competition for space in coral reef environments. The waters of the Tropics are rich in microzooplankton, but poor in dissolved nutrients. There is also a lack of physical ocean bottom space in shallow waters. These factors have forced significant competition for space, because whatever species can obtain and retain physical space on the shallow ocean bottom will have enough food to thrive. Zooxanthellae provide the means for corals to overgrow and rapidly displace competitors.

Zooxanthellae byproducts are necessary for rapid coral growth and hermatypic coral skeleton secretion, but those materials are not necessary for coral survival. Nitrogen-rich food is necessary for both survival and tissue formation. The coral animal-dinoflagellate mutu-

Montipora sp. (plating montipora): although highly dependent on light to energize their symbiotic zooxanthellae, stony corals also utilize dissolved nutrients.

alism should be thought of as a way to maximize all available nutrient input for combined growth and survival. Such nutrient input comes in two primary forms—as food and as dissolved nutrients. This has profound implications for the captive care of corals and other zooxanthellate animals.

Additional Nutritional Needs

While many stony corals may get the majority of the energy they need for daily metabolism from the photosynthesis of their zooxanthellae, for growth and good health they need additional significant sources of nutrition in the form of some other food. In nature, as an average, corals probably get about 60 to 80 percent of their nutrition from zooxanthellae, 15 to 30 percent from feeding, and 5 to 10 percent from dissolved material. There is much variation in the relative importance of these nutrition sources. The relative contribution may vary from species to species, or within a species from place to place, or even within an individual animal from branch to branch or even polyp to polyp.

The beauty of the system for the coral is that no matter how the

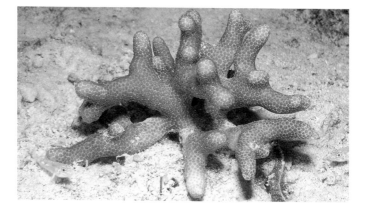

Porites porites (finger coral): a seldom-seen lavender morph of a common Caribbean species. Water quality is a key to maintaining such colors in captivity.

energy sources vary, the coral animal has the means to use them.

For aquarists, this allowable variability means that we can often substitute foods or nutrition sources and still maintain a healthy aquarium inhabitant. Sometimes, whole categories of nutrition can be ignored and the animals still may live, if not thrive. However, for a thriving animal that is more-or-less normal in its growth and behavior, we should attempt to provide a mix of the nutritional and habitat characteristics that are a reasonable approximation of nature. Fortunately, we can now do that for many corals.

Physical Habitat Needs

The physical components of the captive care of corals and other reef animals are primarily water quality, water flow regimes, and light. What many of these conditions are on natural reefs is still open to discussion. In searching through the scientific literature, it becomes evident that many of the factors that aquarists consider important have either never been measured in the reef proper, or very few specifics (of limited utility) are found.

Aquarists and reef scientists alike are very aware of the variability of water flow over and through coral colonies. This variability is exacerbated on real reefs, where the structural heterogeneity of the reef is extremely high, generally far higher than in a reef aquarium. Almost no measurements of important factors within the reef itself yet exist. Most of the parameters are measured in tidal channels or some distance above the reefs. What is happening directly within the reef coral populations themselves is exceptionally hard to assess, as there are too few measurements to provide a good information base.

In point of fact, we simply don't know either the actual values of many of these parameters or how those values vary through time. These unknown parameters include the concentrations of iodine, nitrate, ammonia, strontium, alkalinity, and calcium. While we have data from open ocean situations and, in some cases, data from a few meters above a reef or from sites on either side of a reef, we simply don't know how the chemicals vary on the size scale of the reef that corresponds to an aquarium. Basically, in such situations, we must fall back on a conservative approach based on the knowledge of animal metabolism, in which radical variations from presumed natural conditions are not recommended.

Probably the most important physical parameter is **water quality**. In the ideal world, we would provide water identical to that flowing over a coral reef. This is simply not possible within a closed system. Without constant renewal, the water composition quality fluctuates constantly.

All organisms have a range of conditions within which they may exist. Not everywhere within the range of conditions is equally good. Generally, conditions near the center of a range of physical factors are better than conditions near either extreme. For example, if the tolerable range of natural salinity ranges from about 28 ppt to about 42 ppt, the best salinity at which to maintain the animals would be 35 ppt, and this is indeed the case.

Similar arguments can be made about all physical factors of the reef environment. Recent tabulations of about 1,000 coral reefs have found the average **temperature** range, worldwide, to vary from

Plerogyra sinuosa (bubble coral): it makes sense to maintain captive reefs in the 81 to 84°F (27 to 29°C) range rather than either cooler or warmer.

about 78 to about 86°F (26 to 30°C), with the average at a bit over 81°F (27°C). Complementary studies of coral growth rates show maximum growth is reached at temperatures between 82 to 84°F (28 to 29°C). Consequently, this author believes it makes more sense to maintain captive reefs in the 81 to 84°F (27 to 29°C) range than either cooler or warmer. Some aquarists prefer temperatures in the 78 to 80°F range under the mistaken feeling that it allows a greater margin of safety in avoiding bleaching and disease outbreaks that may occur at higher temperatures. But numerous field studies have shown that corals living at cooler temperatures will bleach at lower temperatures than those maintained at higher temperatures.

In the waters over natural reefs, the concentrations of dissolved mineral nutrients, such as nitrates and phosphates, are normally very low. Natural concentrations of nitrates and phosphates generally would register values of about zero with hobbyist test kits. This is a condition we generally strive for in our artificial reefs. However, in nature, those nutrient concentrations are controlled by the organisms and transient higher values are often noted. The dynamics of the nutrients, their sources, sinks, and utilizations, are not well

Nemenzophyllia turbida (fox coral): contrary to what most hobbyists believe, there is no direct correlation between good water conditions and polyp extension.

understood. We should expect that there will be changes in our appreciation of these nutrient levels as more is learned about coral reef metabolism and ecology. In captivity, most corals and other animals will tolerate high (up to 30 ppm) **nitrate** levels, but measurable **phosphate** concentrations above 0.1 ppm generally have deleterious effects, including failure of polyps to expand and eventual decline and death.

Minor and trace element variability is, if possible, even more poorly known. Virtually none of these factors has been investigated with regard to their effects and physiological pathways within the organisms. It is probably best to try to maintain levels that approach normal offshore seawater concentrations. However, this approach implies being able to adequately assess chemical concentrations in our systems. For many substances, this simply is not within the grasp of hobbyist test kits. However, many of these factors appear to have little biological activity or few metabolic pathways dependent upon them. The utilization amounts of such factors are probably easily met by simple water changes or feedings, and additional supplementation is not necessary. Factors in this category include iodine,

Symphyllia sp.: all stony corals must have calcium supplementation, from kalkwasser or other sources, to support continuous skeletal growth and health.

molybdenum, and iron.

Aquarists often assume that all changes away from natural conditions are negative, but this may not necessarily be the case. Not every material in natural seawater is necessarily beneficial to all organisms, and some are toxic. **Strontium** has been shown to reduce calcium transport in coral tissues, and as such reduces the coral calcification rate. Hobbyists sometimes maintain that strontium additions produce denser coral skeletons, without realizing this simply means that coral growth is stunted. Basically, the epithelium secretes skeletal material, but the animal's growth is retarded and thus there is more calcium carbonate deposited per linear distance of skeleton than would occur under normal conditions. Enzymatic pathways different from calcification pathways exist to shunt strontium into the coral skeletons and out of coral tissue, which contains lower strontium concentrations than the surrounding seawater. Deposition of unwanted materials in exoskeletons is one way of removing potential toxins from the animal's body. Finally, there are no known physiological processes in corals or other cnidarians that require strontium. Strontium is probably one additive that could be left out of seawater

Euphyllia ancora (left) and *Euphyllia paradivisa* (right): lighting requirements of stony corals vary, but most need intense illumination to thrive and grow.

mixes without any deleterious effects.

Outside of water quality, **light** is probably the most important factor in coral husbandry. In natural situations, corals are often stratified by depth. Depth, of course, is correlated to stratification by light. Clear evidence of the effects of differences in light intensity and color on coral growth is widespread and unambiguous. Basically, the aquarist needs to do some homework before purchasing a coral to find out where it would normally be found in its natural environment. This is particularly important for wild-collected animals, which will have little latitude, initially, for adjustment of illumination, either in intensity or quality. For captive-raised animals, this factor is less important, as the aquarist can assume that the aquaculture facility was using more-or-less-standard equipment.

There is a general belief that most corals will benefit by relatively intense illumination. However, there are significant drawbacks to sudden overillumination, including tissue sloughing and death. Although there is agreement that light intensity should match the corals' natural environment, there is also significant argument as to the effects of colored light on corals, and this question is presently unresolved. It is apparent that much of the preference for various colored lights (eg: 6,500°K vs 20,000°K metal halide bulbs) is aesthetic, and is determined by what the aquarist perceives as either attractive or normal. It appears that once a certain threshold of light intensity is reached, any color changes may be irrelevant. On the other hand, some corals do have accessory pigments and adaptations to maximize their utilization of the bluer (higher °K rating) light more characteristic of deeper water.

For most aquarists, particularly novices, a generalized approach is probably best. In such tanks, the light would be moderately intense (VHO fluorescent or power-compact-type bulbs) and there would be some areas in the tank where animals that are unaccustomed to such light can be placed. As the aquarist graduates to keeping the more demanding stony corals, a move to metal halide or bigger arrays of VHO fluorescent lights is usually in order. However, for both high- and low-intensity-requiring corals, specific tanks for just those species are the best solution. Here, the lighting would be tailored for the animals, and both light intensity and light color would be closely monitored.

Water flow influences coral growth and survival in a number of ways. It brings food to the polyps and it moves wastes away. Water flow conditions around natural and cultured corals have been shown to be very important in influencing growth patterns, rates and disease propagation. In many reef situations, the water flow over the reef is far greater than can be provided in captivity. Additionally, such flow is of a different nature than is normally provided for aquariums. Water flow in tanks is generally from a point source, such as a powerhead or water return nozzle. In natural situations, point sources are effectively absent and the whole body of water moves. This provides a very different effect on the organism, and is probably a factor in many of the problems of growing corals in "normal" growth patterns. Any mechanism that more closely approximates the flushing action of waves is probably an improvement in the aquarium. Care must be taken to correlate current flows in tanks with natural flows, as best as they are known or can be estimated.

Porites sp. (possibly *P. nigrescens*): often found in the high-energy zones near the reef crest, "SPS" corals usually require brilliant light and aggressive water motion.

Introduction to "Small-Polyped" Stony Corals

Hobbyists often refer to small-polyped scleractinians (SPS) as if that term is some sort of official biological classification. Unfortunately—and unequivocally—it is not. Within the thousands of species of stony corals, there is a gradient of polyp sizes from very large and fleshy to minute and delicate, and this gradient is effectively continuous. In short, there is no easy way to discern what is a large-polyped vs. a medium-polyped vs. a small-polyped species. Furthermore, corals with polyps of all sizes are found in numerous true evolutionary lineages, so no one type of coral is an SPS species or not.

That said, the term SPS does have some utility as a functional assessment of corals, but it is probably not what most hobbyists think. In cnidarians in general, the sizes of the polyp and tentacles are correlated with the size of the prey. Many of the small-polyped forms that hobbyists focus on are predominantly animals of the reef crest or areas that get flushed with a lot of water, and they are specialized to eat small particulate material, such as larvae, and small

Seriatopora caliendrum (bird's nest coral): farmed or propagated small colonies often survive better and grow faster than large, wild-harvested specimens.

animals, such as larvaceans, small copepods, and small gelatinous zooplankton. They also consume bacterial aggregates, fish feces, and small particulate organic material. These sources of food are necessary as a nitrogen source for the animal. Without them, the corals do not have the capability to build proteins or achieve significant growth.

Aggressiveness of corals is a fact that most hobbyists cheerfully ignore, often to the peril of their other corals and prized invertebrates. These animals have been designed by hundreds of millions of years of evolution to establish themselves in a spot and to hang on to that spot by any means possible. Corals are aggressive animals that fight for space, and if placed too close together they will attack each other. If allowed to continue, such attacks will kill one or the other—or both specimens.

In nature, different individual coral colonies are spaced rather far apart; for mature colonies, spacing may be on the order of meters. The dense "thickets" of corals one sees in pictures of wild reefs are predominantly the result of asexual reproduction by fragmentation and growth of one initial colony.

Turbinaria reniformis (scroll coral): corals must be given room to grow in the aquarium without encroachment by competitors. Crowding can lead to stunting or death.

Putting corals in close proximity in a closed-circuit environment, such as an aquarium, creates stress *immediately*. These animals have chemical scents that other species detect and respond to. These responses include the production of aggressive tentacles, specific aggression polyps on the colony, and accelerated growth either to or away from the other specimen. As the amount of energy available to any coral is finite, this active response to aggression means that the animal must reduce its energy input into other factors, commonly the immune system. Many of the outbreaks of coral disease in aquariums appear to be caused by the stresses generated by too many different animals confined in too small a volume of water. Either the stress allows a disease to spread by reducing the animal's intrinsic means of fighting it, or the "disease" itself is nothing more than a manifestation of severe stress. In the latter case, any bacteria or protozoans present are simply opportunistic and taking advantage of the situation.

Plan ahead, consider potential competitors and try to anticipate the reactions of nearby specimens to every new coral you add. Each system has a finite carrying capacity, and learning to judge this is one of the primary skills that comes with experience. It is *definitely* best

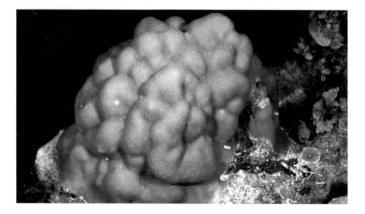

Porites sp.: this boulder-shaped pink specimen illustrates some of the varieties in colors and forms that make species identification of these corals so difficult.

Montipora sp. (possibly *M. digitata*): healthy reef aquariums are usually built one or two corals at a time, with slow stocking and widely spaced placement.

to start slowly and build your reef over many months or years, rather than to stock it up rapidly only to watch it crash in a morass of diseased and dying animals.

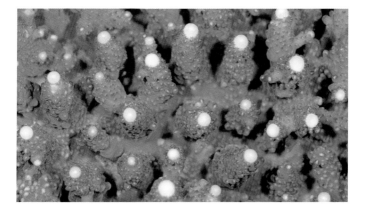

Capable of astonishingly rapid growth, *Acropora* corals are distinguished by axial corallites, or growth tips, seen here in pink on an unidentified Indonesian colony.

Introduction to *Acropora*

Astonishingly successful in the wild, *Acropora* species probably account for more coral biomass than all other coral genera combined. Without a doubt, these are the animals that most people think of when they refer to corals. There are a couple of reasons for this. First, they are exceptionally common, and second, they often dominate in shallow-water communities where they are easily seen.

Corals in this genus have a basic growth form of linear branches. The polyps are found as small cups, or corallites, arranged around the branch. The corallites are typically on small elevations, each of which typically terminates in a polyp. This characteristic gives the genus its name from the Greek roots of *acron*, meaning "on top or extremity" and *por*, meaning "hole or passage." Many hobbyists pronounce *Acropora* "ak-row-POR-a," but this is incorrect. The correct pronunciation is "a-CROP-or-a."

Acropora species may form bushy, tablelike, or even massive colonies. However, in all of these forms, the basic growth form is one of linear branches that may fuse to form either plates or, rarely, solid

Staghorn corals, such as this *Acropora formosa*, are shallow-water, rapidly growing corals that require bright light and constant attention to proper calcium levels.

masses. The polyps are obvious in defined bumps or "houses," and often, especially during rapid growth, have different-sized tentacles.

Acropora is a large genus with hundreds of named species. Additionally, the various species are exceptionally plastic in their morphology, having different shapes and colors under different environmental conditions. Furthermore, this genus is a "poster child" for evolution in action, as it contains many groups of species in the midst of rapid and widespread speciation events, resulting in many exceptionally variable and ill-defined species. These are the "missing-links" that aren't missing. They are the result of one species evolving into one or several daughter species.

Coral taxonomy is based on a number of character sets, but those given the most credence concern the skeleton and the shape and position of the various hard structures. These characters are impossible to examine on living animals. Additionally, these characters were defined and established well before the variability within the genus *Acropora* became well known, and many of the character states may, in fact, be useless at discriminating species.

The intrinsic variability of the group and the problems with the

Acroporids, such as this *A. nobilis*, display highly variable appearances in response to environmental changes. Determining species is a task for specialists.

taxonomy have resulted in deep taxonomic confusion in this ecologically important group. Basically, it is impossible for hobbyists to distinguish species with certainty. Generally, from any single geographic locality, there are a series of names used for the *Acropora* found there. Similar names are used for similar-appearing species from other areas. But there is no certainty that there is any correspondence between any two named species at different locations.

Aquarists have been maintaining, trading, and domesticating various specimens of *Acropora* since the early 1990s. Many names are used in the aquarium trade and may be reasonably consistent within the hobby. However, there is no certainty that these names have any relationship to the wild corals given the same names.

This may cause significant problems with aquarium care. First, it is fundamentally *impossible* to identify many of these corals by comparing them to a photograph of a known type. Most diagnostic characters are invisible in photographs. And, as growth forms vary from place to place or from aquarium to aquarium, we simply have no baseline identification to refer to. Anyone truly serious about identifying *Acropora* will want to refer to the *Corals of the World*

Acropora cerealis (bushy *Acropora*): commonly cultured and easily grown, this species is often available to aquarists as farmed colonies or started fragments.

(Australian Institute of Marine Sciences) by J.E.N. Veron and Mary Stafford-Smith. *Acropora* spp. are found in Volume 1 of this encyclopedic three-volume set.

Because of all the ambiguity about identifications, our best guide for care may be the result of some detective work. If the specimen is a fragment of a cultured or an aquarium-maintained species, the aquarist needs to find out how it has been kept. Specifically, this includes the factors of light and current. If it is a wild-caught species, as much information about its natural habitat as possible should be obtained. If it is possible to ascertain the basic geographic area of its collection, some comparison with photos might be of assistance. In cases such as this, the variables can be reduced: although the scientific name is unimportant, photos of a similar specimen or morphology may give clues regarding depth, currents, and colony orientation. These characters should help to ascertain the initial conditions for colony placement. If the geographic origin of the species is impossible to ascertain, it is best to treat the specimen initially as though it is a deeper-water animal from a low to moderate current regime. These are conservative conditions, but may definitely *not* be

Acropora austera: as with all stony corals having heavy skeletons, this species demands careful attention to calcium and alkalinity levels in the aquarium.

optimal for any given specimen.

Acropora seem to be significantly more prone to transportation and moving stress than most corals. However, once they are in their new environments, they may be shifted gradually without too much damage. Consequently, I consider it most important to get them quickly into their new tanks and into conditions that allow them to recover from transport stress.

Once they have acclimated to their new conditions—generally after a couple of weeks—and they are obviously surviving, then a close observation of the specimen is called for. Ask yourself these questions: Has the color changed? If so, in what manner? A loss of bright colors often means that a change in light intensity has occurred. Often, movement to higher light intensity will improve the color. But note carefully: increases in light intensity, either by varying the illumination or by movement of the colony, ***must*** be done gradually.

The next task would be to assess the specimen for any signs of tissue recession. If there is some, how does it relate to the specimen's water-current orientation? It is possible for recession to be due to too

Shallow-water cluster acroporids, such as this *A. monticulosa,* require bright light, heavy wave action, and strong currents. They are quite difficult to maintain.

much or too little current, and the position of any areas of tissue loss relative to currents will tell which is more likely.

Next, observe the specimen and notice if the polyps are ever fully extended. If so, when? In the absence of any active fish predation, the polyps will generally be out during the day. Notice if you can see the animal feeding by observing it with a hand lens or magnifying glass. Try feeding some enriched newly hatched baby brine shrimp. You may see the active feeding response. If so, the animal is in reasonably good health and food is likely adequate.

Also, observe the colony for signs of growth, particularly new growth zones at the tips of branches. These are evident as pale or colored areas that lack the brownish or gray-green zooxanthellate color that much of the colony may have. Such growth zones indicate that the calcium levels in your tank are adequate and should be maintained at least at current levels. Lack of such new growth generally means that either the calcium levels in the tank water are too low or that the animal has insufficient light or food, or both.

If there is no sign of new growth, but the polyps are extending and there is some tissue recession, the mostly likely cause is lack of

Acropora millepora (cluster *Acropora*): large, wild-collected colonies are often subject to transplant shock. Beginning reef aquarists are urged to buy farmed corals.

sufficient food. This calls for periodic feedings of rotifers, baby brine shrimp, or some other appropriate particulate food.

If there is no sign of new growth, but the polyps are extending and there is no tissue recession, it is likely that the animal has sufficient food, but lacks sufficient calcium. Calcium levels of the system should be assessed and changed, if necessary.

If there is no sign of new growth and the polyps are not extending, and there is some tissue recession, the animal is probably lacking both food and calcium, and conditions need to be changed rapidly or the specimen will perish. Beginning *Acropora* keepers are well-advised to start with fragments from other aquarists or small, captive-propagated colonies rather than colonies from the wild.

Basic Conditions for *Acropora* Husbandry
• Maintain **calcium** concentrations at or near 450 ppm.
• Maintain **alkalinity** at 3.2 to 4.5 meq/L (9 to 12.5 dKH)
• Maintain **phosphate** at undetectable levels.
• The aquarium system must be "mature" (stable for at least a year).
(See *Aquarium Corals*, Borneman [TFH/Microcosm, 2001] for more information.)

Acropora sp. (bottlebrush *Acropora*): while acroporids get much of their energy from light, they absolutely require microplanktonic foods for optimal growth.

Acropora sp: although aquarists often think that good polyp extension is a sign of good health, unfortunately this is not the case. Many abnormal and deleterious conditions may also result in polyp extension.

***Acropora* spp.** (many species, including *A. formosa, A. nobilis, A. yongei*)
Staghorn corals

Maximum Size: Up to 10 ft. (3 m) long; most smaller.
Range: Indo-Pacific.
Minimum Aquarium Size: Large tanks, 100 gal. (380 L) or larger.
Lighting: Bright lighting is essential.
Foods & Feeding: Zooxanthellate; need microplankton or small particulate organic matter for best growth.
Aquarium Suitability/Reef Aquarium Compatibility: Good reef aquarium animals for mature tanks. Will grow too large for small tanks.
Captive Care: Specimens sold as *A. formosa* or *A. yongei* may be good "first" acroporids (see conditions necessary for *Acropora* growth on pages 139-141). In nature, they propagate by fragmentation, resulting in acres of staghorn thickets that are all clones of one individual. This reproductive mode has facilitated their captive propagation and sale as "aquacultured corals." Such clones have undergone physiological adaptation to captivity and survive far better than wild-caught individuals. Many of these corals will show different growth forms in different aquariums.

***Acropora* spp.** (*A. aculeus, A. millepora, A. secale,* many others)
Cluster *Acropora*

Maximum Size: Typically 12 to 24 in. (30 to 61 cm) high, but up to about 6.5 ft. (2 m) in diameter.
Range: Indo-Pacific.
Minimum Aquarium Size: Large tanks, 100 gal. (380 L) or larger.
Lighting: Bright lighting is essential.
Foods & Feeding: Zooxanthellate; need microplankton or small particulate organic matter for best growth.
Aquarium Suitability/Reef Aquarium Compatibility: No *Acropora* should be placed in a tank that is less than a year old. These corals need a stable, "mature" tank with excellent water quality, and must be spaced properly to allow for growth.
Captive Care: Not good beginner corals. They need high, often surging current flow to prevent tissue recession at the base of branches, coupled with very good water quality. They tend to turn brown in tanks with even moderate nutrient levels. Natural ability to propagate by fragmentation allows clonal aquaculturing. Such clones have undergone physiological adaptation to captivity and survive far better than wild-caught individuals. Many of these corals will show different growth forms in different aquariums.

Acropora secale (cluster *Acropora*): a popular favorite among stony coral enthusiasts, this species often has bright-purple branch tips and white polyps.

Acropora nasuta (cluster *Acropora*): these cluster-type *Acropora* need vigorous water movement to keep colonies flushed of debris and to bring in food items.

***Acropora* spp.** (*A. carduus*, *A. echinata*, several others)
Bottlebrush *Acropora*

Maximum Size: May form thickets 12 to 24 in. (30 to 61 cm) deep, but covering a lot of area.
Range: Indo-Pacific.
Minimum Aquarium Size: Large tanks, 100 gal. (380 L) or larger.
Lighting: Bright lighting is essential.
Foods & Feeding: Zooxanthellate; need microplankton or small particulate organic matter for best growth.
Aquarium Suitability/Reef Aquarium Compatibility: No *Acropora* should be placed in a tank that is less than a year old. Need a stable, "mature" tank with excellent water quality and enough space to allow for growth.
Captive Care: Easier to maintain than cluster *Acropora*, they need similar conditions of high, often surging current flow, coupled with very good water quality. Their more open growth form probably allows better water flow than in the cluster *Acropora*, and this allows better survival. Growth slows and colonies tend to turn brown in tanks with even moderate nutrient levels. May be available as "aquacultured" corals. Such clones have undergone physiological adaptation to captivity and survive far better than wild-caught individuals. Many of these corals will show different growth forms in different aquariums.

***Acropora* spp.** (*A. bushyensis*, *A. digitifera*, *A. monticulosa*)
Digitate *Acropora*

Maximum Size: Form clumps to massive colonies to about 10 ft. (3 m) in diameter, but generally less than 12 in. (30 cm) thick.

Range: Indo-Pacific.

Minimum Aquarium Size: Large tanks, 100 gal. (380 L) or larger.

Lighting: Bright lighting is essential.

Foods & Feeding: Zooxanthellate; need microplankton or small particulate organic matter for best growth.

Aquarium Suitability/Reef Aquarium Compatibility: No *Acropora* should be placed in a tank less than a year old. Need a stable, "mature" tank with excellent water quality; must be spaced properly to allow for growth.

Captive Care: Very difficult to maintain, they are rather like cluster *Acropora*, with thicker, more closely set branches that impede water circulation through the colony. They are shallow-water animals used to pounding surf and the resultant surge, coupled with good water quality. Growth slows and colonies tend to turn brown in tanks with even moderate nutrient levels. May be available as "aquacultured" corals. Such clones have undergone physiological adaptation to captivity and survive far better than wild-caught individuals. Many of these corals will show different growth forms in different aquariums.

***Acropora* spp.** (*A. clathrata*, *A. cytherea*, *A. hyacinthus,* others)
Tabulate *Acropora*

Maximum Size: Mushroom-shaped, with the top forming a flat plate; may be several yards (meters) in diameter and height.
Range: Indo-Pacific.
Minimum Aquarium Size: Large tanks, 100 gal. (380 L) or larger.
Lighting: Bright lighting is essential.
Foods & Feeding: Zooxanthellate; need microplankton or small particulate organic matter for best growth.
Aquarium Suitability/Reef Aquarium Compatibility: No *Acropora* should be placed in a tank that is less than a year old. They need a stable, "mature" tank with excellent water quality, and must be spaced properly to allow for growth.
Captive Care: Very difficult to maintain. They need a large tank. These shallow-water animals are from areas of high currents and wave action. Need very high current regimes in aquariums. The tabulate form may be an adaptation to increased exposure to light; need bright lighting. May be available as "aquacultured" corals. Such clones have undergone physiological adaptation to captivity and survive far better than wild-caught individuals. Many of these corals will show different growth forms in different aquariums.

***Acropora* spp.** (*A. austera*, *A. kirstyae*, several others)
Bushy *Acropora*

Maximum Size: Compact clusters of branches radiating from a center. Generally less than 20 in. (51 cm) in diameter.
Range: Indo-Pacific.
Minimum Aquarium Size: Moderate tanks, 50 gal. (190 L) or larger.
Lighting: Bright lighting is essential.
Foods & Feeding: Zooxanthellate; need microplankton or small particulate organic matter for best growth.
Aquarium Suitability/Reef Aquarium Compatibility: No *Acropora* should be placed in a tank less than a year old. Need a stable, "mature" tank with excellent water quality, and proper space to allow for growth.
Captive Care: Easiest of the *Acropora* to maintain. Under good conditions (see pages 139-141), they may grow very rapidly. Branches may grow in length as much as about 0.5 in. (1 cm) a month. Occur in nature from shallow to moderate depths, in areas of variable water flow. May tolerate poorer water conditions than other *Acropora*. May be available as "aquacultured" corals. Such clones have undergone physiological adaptation to captivity and survive far better than wild-caught individuals. Many of these corals will show different growth forms in different aquariums.

Montipora spp.
Montipora

Maximum Size: Highly variable, from compact clumps to widespread colonies many yards (meters) across.

Range: All tropical seas. Most species from the Indo-Pacific.

Minimum Aquarium Size: Small tanks, 10 gal. (38 L) or larger.

Lighting: Generally prefer bright lighting.

Foods & Feeding: Zooxanthellate. Do well in well-fed reef tanks. May be fed with fine particulate foods and tiny plankton.

Aquarium Suitability/Reef Aquarium Compatibility: Excellent reef aquarium animals. Generally not aggressive.

Captive Care: Abundant and ecologically important, *Montipora* species are found throughout and over virtually all reef habitats. Many are vibrantly colored, and numerous species have found their way into the aquarium hobby and are popular with both beginners and advanced hobbyists. Species in this group vary in growth form, from rock-clinging crusts to plates, whorls, shelves, mounds, columns and fingerlike branches. Often, branches will extend from a basal plate or shelf. If conditions are right, they will grow rapidly. The shape of the colony will be significantly determined by the currents, and much variety may be generated in a single aquarium—even within a single

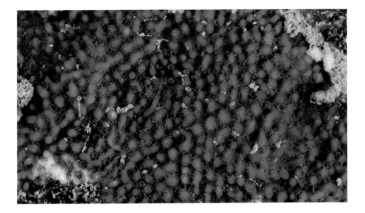

colony. The polyps are small, typically green to brown, but other colors may be found. The polyp tentacles are generally all the same size and, unlike *Acropora*, do not form in the area of most rapid growth, but slightly lateral to it. Polyps are generally retractile into a cavity or hole below the colony surface.

These species fragment easily and may be the best first choice for a novice trying to propagate corals. If a broken fragment is secured in place by a rubber band, and not glue, it will often start to grow rapidly. Small propagated colonies do very well in small tanks.

Montipora colonies respond rapidly to changes in lighting, and in dimmer light, often "brown up" rapidly, a condition that can be reversed by increasing light intensity or repositioning the colony. They will do well in most tanks, as long as the standard conditions for smaller-polyped stony corals are met (see pages 131-134). Maintaining proper calcium and alkalinity levels is a must. They are not particularly aggressive, however, and will often lose aggressive encounters with other corals, sponges, or even algae. This means their position within an aquarium must be chosen with some care.

The problems for determining accurate species names in *Montipora* are just as severe as in *Acropora*. No species names applied in the hobby to *Montipora* should be assumed to be correct.

Montipora sp.: many species of *Montipora* form elegant plates, shelves or whorls. Brown colonies are often reported to shift to brighter colors under strong light.

Plate montiporas, such as this *Montipora tuberculosa*, may form tiers of colorful plates in the aquarium.

Pocillopora spp.
Pocillopora

Maximum Size: Often forms compact clumps but may expand to several yards (meters) across, depending upon the species.

Range: Indo-Pacific.

Minimum Aquarium Size: Small tanks, 10 gal. (38 L) or larger.

Lighting: Generally prefer bright lighting.

Foods & Feeding: Zooxanthellate. Do well in well-fed reef tanks.

Aquarium Suitability/Reef Aquarium Compatibility: Good aquarium animals. Relatively aggressive and may grow to encroach on other corals and sessile invertebrates.

Captive Care: Corals in this genus are characterized by the presence of verrucae, bumps, or warts, on the skeleton. These may be more or less prominent, but are always evident. When the small polyps are extended, the coral may appear as if covered with short, but dense, fur or hair. When disturbed, the polyps will usually withdraw rapidly into their corallites in the skeleton. There is a tendency for the colonies to be compact, massive and "bulky" with relatively short, thick branches. Given good conditions to which they can acclimate, *Pocillopora* species may be fast-growing and aggressive, and will attack other nearby corals. They should be

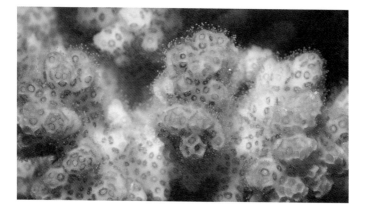

Pocillopora damicornis (cauliflower coral): may be the most widespread Indo-Pacific coral species.

given space for growth when put into an aquarium. The standard conditions for good care of small-polyped stony corals (see pages 131-134) definitely apply to animals in this genus. *Pocillopora* species, particularly the ubiquitous *Pocillopora damicornis*, are ideal beginning corals for a novice aquarist.

Pocillopora damicornis is probably the most widespread hermatypic coral species found throughout the tropical Pacific. It owes this widespread distribution to two characteristics: a long-lived planktonic larval stage that allows it to disperse great distances, and a wide latitude in acceptable conditions. This ability to adapt to different habitats is reflected in growth forms; this is probably the most variable coral in terms of shapes, colors, and general morphological differences. It is also one of the few corals that thrives at temperatures below 79°F (26°C). Unlike most corals, which show a single optimal temperature for growth at about 82°F to 84°F (28°C to 29°C), *Pocillopora damicornis* also has a second growth optimum at 77°F (25°C). This low-temperature growth optimum allows it to exploit, and become dominant in, habitats where most hermatypic corals grow very slowly.

Pocillopora verrucosa (cauliflower coral): branches are typically much thicker and more compact than in the more common *P. damicornis* (see below).

Pocillopora damicornis (cauliflower coral): colors range from brown to yellow, green, and bright pink.

Pocillopora damicornis (cauliflower coral): growth forms vary, depending on light, currents, and other factors.

PORITES CYLINDRICA

Porites spp.
Porites

Maximum Size: Compact clumps to massive colonies spreading over 16 ft. (5 m) in width, depending upon the species.
Range: All tropical seas.
Minimum Aquarium Size: Small tanks, 10 gal. (38 L) or larger.
Lighting: Generally prefer bright lighting.
Foods & Feeding: Zooxanthellate. Do well in well-fed reef tanks.
Aquarium Suitability/Reef Aquarium Compatibility: Excellent aquarium animals. Relatively aggressive.
Captive Care: When people visualize massive corals, *Porites* species are generally what comes to mind. Although many species of *Porites* may form branching colonies, most of species appear as crusts, sheets, or mounding heads. These massive forms are stalwarts among the reef-building corals and may reach very large sizes, although it is important to realize in such cases that only the outer layers are living. *Porites* probably hold the record for known ages of corals, with some living colonies documented as being over 3,500 years old.

In many ways, *Porites* appear similar to *Montipora*, but the two genera may often be distinguished at a glance. Both have polyps that are small and with a uniform tentacle size. Retracted *Porites* polyps,

PORITES NIGRESCENS

however, appear to sit within a meshlike network of small, raised ridges on the colony's surface; no such mesh is found in *Montipora*. When *Porites* polyps are extended, the colonies often appear to be covered with a "velvetlike" plush of tentacles, and discrete polyps may be hard to discern.

Porites are often beautifully colored in pinks, purples, or blues. The brown-green or gray-green coloration of zooxanthellae is very common as well. *Porites* are more demanding in their care than many small-polyped species. They seem to require strong lighting, particularly the brightly colored forms. Relatively high current velocities are often necessary for the animals to thrive. Their care is similar to that of the acroporids (see pages 139-141 for the conditions necessary for good health).

Porites porites (finger coral): this species used to form large beds on many Caribbean reefs. Bleaching events, sea urchin mortalities, and subsequent algal overgrowth are significantly impacting coral distributions in this region.

Porites cylindrica (jeweled finger coral): may be yellow, green, or blue.

Porites sp. (boulder coral): sometimes arrives on healthy live rock.

Seriatopora caliendrum
Brush coral (blunt-tipped bird's nest coral)

Maximum Size: Colonies to about 19 in. (48 cm); most smaller.
Range: Indo-Pacific.
Minimum Aquarium Size: Small tanks, 10 gal. (38 L) or larger.
Lighting: Needs moderate illumination.
Foods & Feeding: Zooxanthellate, but needs microplankton and particulate foods for good growth.
Aquarium Suitability/Reef Aquarium Compatibility: Good reef aquarium animal.
Captive Care: Requirements are similar to those of the *Pocillopora* species. This species is similar in basic shape to the related *Seriatopora hystrix* (page 160), but the branches are not as sharp nor are the polyps found in linear rows. Branches often grow together and fuse to form a "nest" of branches. Colonies are typically some shade of tan to light brown or yellow. Requires moderate currents. Stronger currents may negatively affect them. May do well in dimly lit tanks if well fed.

Seriatopora hystrix
Bird's nest coral

Maximum Size: Colonies to 18 in. (46 cm) in diameter; most smaller.
Range: Indo-Pacific.
Minimum Aquarium Size: Small tanks, 10 gal. (38 L) or larger.
Lighting: Needs bright illumination.
Foods & Feeding: Zooxanthellate. May feed on fine particulate foods.
Aquarium Suitability/Reef Aquarium Compatibility: Excellent reef aquarium animal.
Captive Care: One of the most distinctive corals kept by hobbyists, this species is highly and characteristically branched. The branches often have very sharp (dangerously sharp) points. Because the branches often grow toward one another to form a "nest," this species has been given the common name "bird's nest coral." The branches also often meet and fuse. The basic color may be green, brown, white, yellow, or pink; the coral tends to turn brown under less than ideal aquarium conditions. Rather easy to maintain, it does best under the conditions described for the acroporids (see pages 139-141). In addition to needing bright light, it requires moderate to strong currents. It is not particularly aggressive and will react negatively to nearby corals.

Aquarium specimens of many corals, including the *Seriatopora hystrix* shown here, fluoresce under actinic or metal halide lighting.

Many stony corals, such as *Seriatopora hystrix, Pocillopora damicornis* and the many species of *Acropora* that form cluster-shaped colonies, harbor crabs that live symbiotically in the colony. These crabs are often inadvertently collected along with the coral. There are many species of these crabs, and their behaviors differ significantly from species to species. Some of them, mostly juvenile species of crabs that will grow much larger, feed on the corals and are quite destructive. Other species are truly mutualistic: they feed on coral mucus and actively protect the coral from predation by smaller fishes. Larger coral-eating fishes will eat the coral and the crab together.

One group of cluster coral crabs, the gall crabs, live within cavities, called galls, that are formed by the coral in response to irritation by the crabs. The female gall crabs are often entrapped in the galls, which have a relatively small opening. Here they gain a significant degree of protection from predators. The smaller male crabs can leave the gall and are "roving Romeos," moving from female to female to mate. Gall crabs generally do not persist in captivity, probably due to insufficient planktonic food, but some of the other crabs brought in with these cluster corals may live quite a long time.

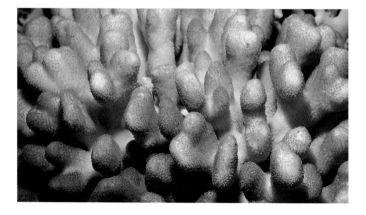

Stylophora spp.
Finger coral (club finger coral)

Maximum Size: Colonies to about 19 in. (48 cm); most smaller.
Range: Indo-Pacific.
Minimum Aquarium Size: Moderate tanks, 50 gal. (190 L) or larger.
Lighting: Need moderate to bright illumination.
Foods & Feeding: Zooxanthellate, but need supplemental microplankton to thrive.
Aquarium Suitability/Reef Aquarium Compatibility: Excellent reef aquarium animals.
Captive Care: Found in diverse habitats, from shallow-water areas with wave action to deeper-water sheltered areas. This habitat plasticity allows them to adapt readily to aquarium conditions. Moderate currents are acceptable, strong ones are better. Colors range from cream to purple, pink, or green. In low-light regimes, brown or tan colors tend to predominate. Brighter lighting will bring out brighter colors, but isn't necessary for survival. Have short sweeper tentacles and secrete noxious chemicals to compete for space. May be available as "aquacultured" corals. Such clones have undergone physiological adaptation to captivity and will survive far better than wild-caught individuals.

Stylophora sp. (club finger coral): green is one of several color morphs seen in this species, which varies in appearance in different habitats.

Stylophora sp. (club finger coral): a juvenile colony with fuzzy polyps extended at night on a reef in Papua New Guinea.

Favia sp: the division between small-polyped and large-polyped stony corals is artificial, but those with bigger polyps are generally able to take large food items.

Introduction to Large-Polyped Stony Corals

The larger-polyped stony corals, like their smaller-polyped cousins, are a grouping of convenience and do not represent any kind of coherent assemblage. Many of them are not truly animals of the reef and are more likely to be found in the lagoonal or sheltered backwater areas of an atoll or fringing reef. Water conditions in such areas are generally more variable than on the reef, and many of these animals appear more tolerant of somewhat degraded environments. Probably as a result of such tolerance, many of them were among the earliest corals that were kept successfully.

Generally in the cnidarians, the prey and tentacle, or polyp, sizes are correlated, and as a result of this "rule," one might expect that these animals would need to be fed larger foods. This appears to indeed be the case. Many of them will eat diced or whole fishes, such as lance fish or silversides, while others will take shrimp or other crustacean prey. A few will eat molluscan foods, such as squid.

It should be emphasized that when offering these food items, the *entire* organism should be fed to the coral. Many essential nutrients

Cynarina lacrymalis (owl eye coral): one of the largest of the single-polyped stony corals, with water-filled lobes and tentacles that come out at night for feeding.

are found in the gut, skin, or exoskeleton. Cutting the food into "bite-size" chunks may help the animal to ingest them, but the pieces should include all parts of the item, not just muscle tissue. Such food should be gently placed on the tentacles, and the animal allowed to choose whether or not to consume it.

In most cases, there are few data about the natural diets of these organisms, and aquarists must try various foods to see what is accepted. Generally, if the food doesn't stick to the tentacles, the animal is not ready to eat or the food is not a good choice. It pays to try different foods, and occasionally to retry rejected foods, all in the name of providing a balanced diet.

Many of these animals may require higher concentrations of bacterial aggregates or dissolved nutrients than are found in reef tanks that are highly filtered and maintained as habitats for reef-crest animals. Because many of these large-polyped stony corals form a relatively massive skeleton, growth is often slower than with some of the more rapidly growing smaller-polyped species.

Blastomussa merleti
Pineapple coral (*Blastomussa*)

Maximum Size: Colonies to 18 in. (46 cm) in diameter; most smaller. Polyps to about 1 in. (2.5 cm) in diameter.
Range: Indo-Pacific.
Minimum Aquarium Size: Moderate tanks, 50 gal. (190 L) or larger.
Lighting: Needs moderate illumination.
Foods & Feeding: Zooxanthellate. Does well in well-fed reef tanks. Will eat crustacean foods, such as small krill or brine shrimp.
Aquarium Suitability/Reef Aquarium Compatibility: Excellent reef aquarium animal.
Captive Care: Corallites are tubular and extend outward from a common base. When the polyps are fully inflated, the colony often appears to be a solid mass. The fleshy polyp is often two-toned, with the oral disc a color that contrasts highly with the edges and sides of the polyp. This species hails from deeper water and often turbid areas, which preadapts it to tanks with low light. Asexual reproduction by budding is common in healthy individuals, and asexual planulae have been implicated by some aquarists who have had small colonies appear all over a reef tank. The tubular corallites are easily broken loose, allowing simple propagation of this species.

Blastomussa wellsi
Wells' pineapple coral (swollen red brain coral)

Maximum Size: Colonies to 18 in. (46 cm) in diameter. Polyps large, fleshy, about 4 to 5 in. (10 to 13 cm) in diameter. Corallites smaller.
Range: Indo-Pacific.
Minimum Aquarium Size: Moderate tanks, 50 gal. (38 L) or larger.
Lighting: Needs moderate illumination; keep lower in a bright tank.
Foods & Feeding: Zooxanthellate. Does well in well-fed reef tanks. Will eat crustacean foods, such as small krill or brine shrimp.
Aquarium Suitability/Reef Aquarium Compatibility: Good tank animal. Not aggressive. Needs careful placement.
Captive Care: Uncommon in nature and relatively uncommon in captivity. Corallites are large and extend outward from a common base. When the polyps are fully inflated, the colony often appears to be a solid mass; may look like a colony of mushroom polyps. Fleshy polyp is predominantly a single color, typically red or green, but is often highlighted or mottled with other contrasting colors. From deeper and often turbid waters. High light and high current levels may be inhibitory. Not a good competitor; will be damaged by contact with many other corals, sea anemones, or mushroom polyps. Even slight contact with a superior competitor may be lethal.

Catalaphyllia jardinei
Elegance coral

Maximum Size: Colonies to about 12 in. (30 cm) in length and 8 in. (20 cm) wide. Tentacles may extend outward another 4 in. (10 cm) in all directions.

Range: Indo-Pacific.

Minimum Aquarium Size: Large tanks, 100 gal. (380 L) or larger.

Lighting: Prefers moderate lighting.

Foods & Feeding: Zooxanthellate. An avid and voracious feeder that needs to be fed. Will eat crustacean foods, such as small krill or brine shrimp. If several types of foods are acceptable, they should be rotated to provide a balanced diet.

Aquarium Suitability/Reef Aquarium Compatibility: While animals collected in the early to mid 1990s were hardy, recent specimens seem to be very delicate and difficult to keep. Often contain parasitic shrimps or crabs burrowed into the tissues and skeleton. Aggressive; needs careful placement. Will be damaged by algae, such as *Caulerpa*, as well as by other large-polyped corals.

Captive Care: Elegance coral is unmistakable. It has a small, almost ridiculously small, laterally compressed, conical base, and the oval

oral disc is large and flattened with a fringe of large, long tentacles. It may contain many mouths. The color is typically a shade of fluorescent green; the tentacles are often the same color as the disc or a contrasting color, such as tan or white, and tipped with pink, blue or lavender.

This species lives in mud or soft sand, and a deep sand bed is absolutely ideal. It normally lives with the skeleton buried in the sediment and the oral disc flush with the sediment, with tentacles extending out laterally over the substrate. It should not be placed on rocks in an aquarium. If it is so placed, the delicate inflated tissue will often become lacerated by contact with the rocks, leading to infection, polyp bail-out, or death.

The sheer size of the polyps indicates that this animal needs a large aquarium: it should not be able to touch another coral even when the polyps are extended fully. *Catalaphyllia jardinei* does not tolerate contact with most soft corals or algae, such as *Caulerpa*. Additionally, although it contains formidable nematocysts, which can irritate human skin, it will lose in any competitive interactions with *Euphyllia* species.

Caulastrea spp.
Torch corals (trumpet corals, candy cane corals)

Maximum Size: Colonies to about 12 in. (30 cm) in length and about the same in width.
Range: Indo-Pacific.
Minimum Aquarium Size: Moderate tanks, 50 gal. (190 L) or larger.
Lighting: Prefer moderate lighting.
Foods & Feeding: Zooxanthellate. Need to be fed, but are avid and voracious feeders. Will eat small krill, brine shrimp, diced fish.
Aquarium Suitability/Reef Aquarium Compatibility: These corals are generally hardy but aggressive, with stinging sweeper tentacles extending up to 2 in. (5 cm) long.
Captive Care: In nature, these corals are often from deeper or turbid regions and may not do well if overly illuminated. If placed in a sheltered area with moderate lighting they tend to do well. These corals seem to benefit from moderate, but not excessive, "flushing" current. If fed well, they will grow rapidly. Larger colonies can be easily fragmented for captive propagation. During feeding, the water motion in the tank should be arrested (shut down) so that the food is allowed to drop onto the discs. The corals will then eagerly feed. After an hour or so, turn the water currents back on.

Nemenzophyllia turbida
Fox coral (ridge coral, jasmine coral)

Maximum Size: Unknown. Probably in excess of 40 in. (1 m). The species is too poorly studied and documented to be definitive.

Range: Indo-Pacific.

Minimum Aquarium Size: Moderate tanks, 50 gal. (190 L) or larger

Lighting: Needs dim to moderate lighting.

Foods & Feeding: Zooxanthellate, but probably needs dissolved nutrients or high levels of particulate organic matter in the water for best health.

Aquarium Suitability/Reef Aquarium Compatibility: Hardy, nonaggressive. Good aquarium animal.

Captive Care: This tan to green coral is a natural for aquarists with its preference for low to moderate currents and without a need for bright lighting. Bright lights are reported to turn the animal brownish (*Aquarium Corals*, Borneman, 2001). It will not do well in a brightly lit high-current reef aquarium maintained for most small-mouthed corals, such as the acroporids. However, it will benefit from their same levels of calcium and alkalinity (see pages 139-141).

Cynarina lacrymalis
Owl eye coral (button coral, donut coral)

Maximum Size: Colonies to 2.5 in. (6 cm) in diameter.
Range: Indo-Pacific.
Minimum Aquarium Size: Moderate tanks, 50 gal. (190 L) or larger.
Lighting: Needs moderate illumination.
Foods & Feeding: Zooxanthellate; needs to be fed. Predatory and will extend long tentacles after dark. An avid and voracious feeder.
Aquarium Suitability/Reef Aquarium Compatibility: Good tank animal.
Captive Care: Solitary polyps; slightly oval with 20 to 25 deep, radiating ridges extending from the center mouth. Found oriented horizontally on flat surfaces, but also vertically on walls. Outer part of the polyp is often a color that contrasts to the inner region. Colors range from browns and greens to pinks and blues or whites. This species moves pieces of fish across its disc and ingests them. Well-fed individuals grow rapidly. It is not an aggressive or good competitor and is negatively impacted by corallimorphs, soft corals, and sea anemones. *Aiptasia* is a particular problem, killing the tissue on the oral disc of the coral. The killed area may be subsequently colonized by small anemones and the process repeated, resulting in the ultimate death of the coral.

Euphyllia spp.
Anchor corals (hammer corals, torch corals, frogspawn corals)

Maximum Size: Colonies to 3.3 ft. (1 m) or more for some species.
Range: Indo-Pacific.
Minimum Aquarium Size: Moderate tanks, 50 gal. (190 L) or larger.
Lighting: Bright, but diffuse illumination; no direct metal halide.
Foods & Feeding: Zooxanthellate. Avid and voracious feeders. Offer meaty foods such as brine shrimp, mysid shrimp, krill and the like.
Aquarium Suitability/Reef Aquarium Compatibility: Good aquarium animals, but very aggressive. Long sweeper tentacles will sting neighboring corals and sessile invertebrates.
Captive Care: This group of large-polyp species have long captivated marine aquarists. The distinctive tentacles are seen in many hues of green, brown, and even pink, often with contrasting tip colors. The shape of the tentacle tips varies with the species. These corals thrive under moderate conditions of current and lighting. Long (up to 16 in. [41 cm]) sweeper tentacles tipped with a sphere containing very potent nematocysts characterize *Euphyllia*. Reducing current flows and relocating neighbors may reduce sweeper tentacle formation. Many animals will be harmed by *Euphyllia* stings. (See *Aquarium Corals*, Borneman [TFH/Microcosm, 2001] for a more complete discussion.)

Euphyllia ancora
Anchor coral

Maximum Size: Individual colonies to about 36 in. (1 m). Sometimes found in large aggregations.
Range: Indo-Pacific.
Minimum Aquarium Size: Moderate tanks, 50 gal. (190 L) or larger.
Lighting: Needs moderate lighting.
Foods & Feeding: Zooxanthellate; voracious feeder, needs meaty foods.
Aquarium Suitability/Reef Aquarium Compatibility: Good aquarium animal, but very aggressive.
Captive Care: This species' common name reflects the shapes at the ends of the generally translucent tentacles, reminiscent of anchors or hammers. The "anchors" are gray, green, tan, or occasionally even shades of blue, red, or orange. As with other deeper-water corals that dwell in soft sediments, anchor corals like some things in moderation, especially currents and lighting. Like other *Euphyllia*, they produce long sweeper tentacles tipped with spheres packed with potent nematocysts, so careful positioning in the aquarium is vital. They are prone to "brown jelly" infections, possibly as a result of injury by hermit crabs and other animals that walk on them. They do well when placed in a deep sand bed.

Euphyllia cristata
Grape coral

Maximum Size: Individual colonies in excess of 18 in. (46 cm) or more.
Range: Indo-Pacific.
Minimum Aquarium Size: Moderate tanks, 50 gal. (190 L) or larger.
Lighting: Needs moderate to bright lighting.
Foods & Feeding: Zooxanthellate, but like all *Euphyllia*, needs meaty foods. Given appropriate foods, it is often a voracious feeder, but in some cases it seems to be very specific about what it will eat, so often periods of trial and error are necessary until the best foods are found.
Aquarium Suitability/Reef Aquarium Compatibility: Good aquarium animal, but very aggressive.
Captive Care: Pale gray to green tentacles in a more-or-less rounded shape is characteristic of this coral. Found in shallower water than most *Euphyllia*, this species does well in bright, but indirect, lighting and needs moderate currents. It produces the standard long *Euphyllia* sweeper tentacles tipped with potent nematocysts, so proper positioning in the aquarium is vital. Will generally do best in aquariums without hermit crabs, which often seem to be able to walk on the coral with impunity, but do damage in the process.

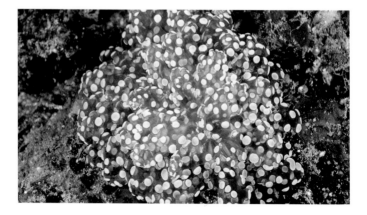

Euphyllia divisa
Frogspawn coral (octopus coral)

Maximum Size: Individual colonies in excess of 3.3 ft. (1 m).
Range: Indo-Pacific.
Minimum Aquarium Size: Moderate tanks, 50 gal. (190 L) or larger.
Lighting: Needs moderate to bright lighting.
Foods & Feeding: Zooxanthellate; voracious feeder on meaty foods.
Aquarium Suitability/Reef Aquarium Compatibility: Good aquarium animal, but very aggressive.
Captive Care: The branched tentacles form spheres at the ends, looking vaguely like a mass of amphibian eggs. The often greenish color of the polyps and tentacles tends to accentuate this resemblance. This species requires about the same aquarium conditions as other *Euphyllia*, but does well in brighter, indirect lighting than does *E. ancora*. Colors range from pinks to tans or greens. Needs moderate currents. It produces the standard long *Euphyllia* sweeper tentacles tipped with potent nematocysts, so careful positioning in the aquarium is vital. Will generally do best in an aquarium without hermit crabs, which often seem to be able to walk on the coral with impunity, but damage it in the process.

Euphyllia glabrescens
Torch coral (pom-pom coral)

Maximum Size: Individual colonies in excess of 19 in. (48 cm).
Range: Indo-Pacific.
Minimum Aquarium Size: Moderate tanks, 50 gal. (190 L) or larger.
Lighting: Needs moderate to bright lighting.
Foods & Feeding: Zooxanthellate, but like all *Euphyllia*, needs meaty foods. Experiment to find acceptable foods.
Aquarium Suitability/Reef Aquarium Compatibility: Good aquarium animal, but very aggressive.
Captive Care: This species is characterized by moderately long, gray, tan, green, or beige tentacles tipped with a sphere of white, bright green, or sometimes yellow. It almost looks like an anemone, except that there is no obvious oral disc. It shares the requirements for physical conditions with other *Euphyllia*, although this species does well in brighter, indirect, lighting than does *E. ancora*. It needs moderate currents. It produces the standard long *Euphyllia* sweeper tentacles tipped with potent nematocysts, so proper positioning in the aquarium is vital. Will generally do best in an aquarium without hermit crabs, which often seem to be able to walk on the coral with impunity, but will damage it in the process.

Euphyllia paradivisa
Branching frogspawn coral

Maximum Size: Individual colonies in excess of 19 in. (48 cm).
Range: Indo-Pacific.
Minimum Aquarium Size: Moderate tanks, 50 gal. (190 L) or larger.
Lighting: Needs moderate to bright lighting.
Foods & Feeding: Zooxanthellate, but like all *Euphyllia*, needs meaty foods. Experiment to find acceptable foods.
Aquarium Suitability/Reef Aquarium Compatibility: Good aquarium animal, but very aggressive.
Captive Care: The branching basis of the skeleton results in clusters of tentacles similar in shape to those found in frogspawn corals. Tentacles are often translucent, pale green or gray, while the tentacle tips are often brightly contrasting. This species shares the requirements for physical conditions with other *Euphyllia*, although it does well in brighter, indirect, lighting than does *E. ancora*. It needs moderate currents. It produces the standard long *Euphyllia* sweeper tentacles tipped with potent nematocysts, so proper positioning in the aquarium is vital. Will generally do best in an aquarium without hermit crabs, which often seem to be able to walk on the coral with impunity, but damages it in the process.

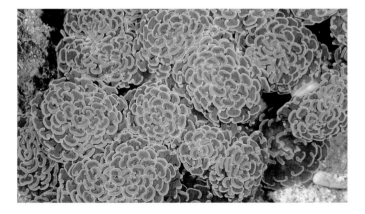

Euphyllia parancora
Branching hammer coral (branching anchor coral)

Maximum Size: Individual colonies to about 36 in. (1 m).
Range: Indo-Pacific.
Minimum Aquarium Size: Moderate tanks, 50 gal. (190 L) or larger.
Lighting: Needs moderate lighting.
Foods & Feeding: Zooxanthellate, but like all *Euphyllia*, needs meaty foods. Experiment to find acceptable foods.
Aquarium Suitability/Reef Aquarium Compatibility: Good aquarium animal, but very aggressive.
Captive Care: The colony is branched to produce clusters of tan to brilliant green polyps. This coral species likes things in moderation, especially currents and lighting. Like other *Euphyllia*, it produces long sweeper tentacles tipped with spheres packed with potent nematocysts, so proper positioning in the aquarium is vital. It is prone to "brown jelly" infection, possibly as a result of injury by hermit crabs and other animals that walk on it. It will do well when placed in a deep sand bed.

Favia spp., _Favites_ spp., _Platygyra_ spp., many others
Moon corals (closed brain corals, brain corals, maze corals)

Maximum Size: Some species reach in excess of several yards (meters) in diameter. Many are smaller.
Range: Tropical seas.
Minimum Aquarium Size: Moderate tanks, 50 gal. (190 L) or larger.
Lighting: Moderately bright lighting.
Foods & Feeding: Zooxanthellate. Need to be fed. Feed at night for best results. Will take meaty foods, including mysids and diced fish.
Aquarium Suitability/Reef Aquarium Compatibility: Excellent reef aquarium animals. Can be aggressive with sweeper tentacles.
Captive Care: Generally known as "closed brain corals," species from these genera are very difficult to tell apart. _Favia_ individuals appear separate on the colony surface and have discrete grooves between individuals. In _Favites_, the corallites of adjacent individuals share a common wall. _Platygyra_ have a mazelike surface, with meandering corallite walls. These animals are really quite easy to maintain. Their feeding tentacles are found as a fringe inside the edge of the polyp and are extended at night. These animals will reward being fed by growing well. They are effectively aggressive, extending long, thin sweeper tentacles at night; give them room to sweep and grow.

Favia sp.: one of the most widespread of coral genera in tropical seas, *Favia* colonies typically form massive or dome shapes.

Favia sp.: note the distinctly separate corallites, a usual *Favia* characteristic, with no sharing of common walls.

Favites sp. (pineapple coral): closely related to and easily confused with the *Favia*, this genus displays shared corallite walls.

Favites sp. (pineapple coral): like other brain corals, *Favites* are remarkably hardy and often tolerate different lighting schemes.

Platygyra daedalea (maze coral): note meandering corallite walls with valleys in a contrasting color, a characteristic of this genus.

Diploria labyrinthiformis (grooved brain coral): a beautiful Caribbean species, not usually available to aquarists.

Fungia spp.
Plate corals

Maximum Size: To about 12 in. (30 cm).
Range: Indo-Pacific.
Minimum Aquarium Size: Moderate tanks, 50 gal. (190 L) or larger.
Lighting: Must have bright illumination.
Foods & Feeding: Zooxanthellate, but need significant feeding to stay healthy or grow. Will eat small pieces of fish, shrimp, or squid placed on the oral disc.
Aquarium Suitability/Reef Aquarium Compatibility: Good aquarium animals. Can be aggressive.
Captive Care: Normally found on sand or coral rubble, they should be placed on similar substrates in a reef aquarium. *Fungia* are able to climb significant slopes, as well as turn themselves over. Mobile *Fungia* are rather fascinating animals, but they do have a drawback: both their nematocysts and copious chemically laden mucus secretions pack quite a punch. As they move, they may bump into other corals or animals in the tank and cause significant damage. Care must be taken with their placement. Colors range from tan to pink to green. Numerous small tentacles are found over the surface of the animal. They generally retract during the day.

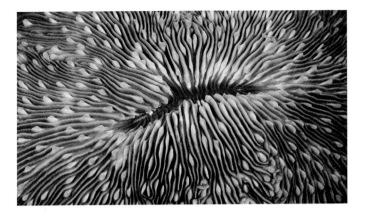

Fungia sp.: note distinctly colored central mouth opening. Feeding with bits of marine protein (fish or shrimp) is highly recommended.

Fungia sp: these are bottom-dwellers, resting on sand or coral rubble in the wild.

Fungia fungites: species identification within the Family Fungiidae is highly challenging.

Galaxea spp.
Star corals

Maximum Size: Colonies to about 3.3 ft. (1 m) across; most smaller.
Range: Indo-Pacific.
Minimum Aquarium Size: Moderate tanks, 50 gal. (190 L) or larger.
Lighting: Must have bright illumination.
Foods & Feeding: Zooxanthellate, but will benefit from feeding of small zooplankton or particulate material.
Aquarium Suitability/Reef Aquarium Compatibility: Good aquarium animals. Extend long sweeper tentacles that sting other corals.
Captive Care: *Galaxea* species are beautiful but very fragile, with a delicate skeleton extending upward beyond the oral disc as paper-thin walls topped by minute fingerlike spikes. The corallites are long, thin cylinders and are prone to fracture. Once established in an aquarium, they can grow substantially. They require frequent cleaning of the colony with a blast from a turkey baster, or place them in surge or turbulent water areas. *Galaxea* are notorious for their ability to sting other invertebrates by extending long sweeper tentacles that can exceed 12 in. (30 cm). A new colony is typically placed in the upper level of the reef to get maximum illumination and given plenty of room to expand. Colonies are typically gray to green.

Goniopora spp.
Flowerpot corals

Maximum Size: Some to about 20 in. (51 cm) across; most smaller.

Range: Indo-Pacific, in low-current, turbid, lagoonal backwaters.

Minimum Aquarium Size: Moderate tanks, 50 gal. (190 L) or larger.

Lighting: Need bright illumination; don't do well under dim lighting.

Foods & Feeding: Zooxanthellate, but will benefit from being fed small zooplankton.

Aquarium Suitability/Reef Aquarium Compatibility: Not suitable for most aquariums; colonies usually die within a year. Aggressive.

Captive Care: There are several species of *Goniopora*, all attractive but difficult to keep alive. Calcium levels must be high (450+ ppm), but even this does not ensure long-term survival. They do not do well in high current, but reportedly can thrive in systems with refugiums and no protein skimming. Potent nematocysts are capable of inflicting severe damage to nearby corals. Colonies are roughly spherical and covered by tissue. Polyps are large, more than 0.5 in. (13 mm) across, with 24 tentacles, and may extend 4 to 12 in. (10 to 30 cm) from the skeleton. Light green to tan. Polyps are often pink or lavender around the mouth, situated on a cone. Some clownfishes "adopt" *Goniopora* as a surrogate host, which may cause the coral's death.

Heliofungia spp.
Large-tentacled plate corals (long-tentacled plate corals)

Maximum Size: Colonies to about 8 in. (20 cm) across.
Range: Indo-Pacific.
Minimum Aquarium Size: Moderate tanks, 50 gal. (190 L) or larger.
Lighting: Need bright illumination; don't do well under dim lighting.
Foods & Feeding: Zooxanthellate, but must be fed. Probably prey on small fishes in nature and prefer fishes to crustacean food in captivity. Large pieces of fish can be placed on the tentacles and will be rapidly eaten.
Aquarium Suitability/Reef Aquarium Compatibility: Easily kept if well fed with frequent feedings of whole fish.
Captive Care: *Heliofungia* are good aquarium animals that, when fully inflated, resemble anemones. They live on sand or coral gravel and need the same substrate in an aquarium. Not as mobile as *Fungia*, not as aggressive. Often do not recover from being stung, so place them where this is not likely to happen. Do best in moderate currents. Each disc is a large, single polyp with long tentacles. Tentacle length may exceed 8 in. (20 cm). Disc is gray, green, or brown with radial stripes extending out from the mouth. Tentacles are usually green or brown and have white, yellow, or pink tips.

Hydnophora **spp.**
Horn corals (furry corals)

Maximum Size: Some species with colonies to about 3.3 ft. (1 m) across; most smaller.
Range: Indo-Pacific.
Minimum Aquarium Size: Moderate tanks, 50 gal. (190 L) or larger.
Lighting: Need bright illumination; don't do well under dim lighting.
Foods & Feeding: Zooxanthellate, but must be fed; will eat a lot of food if it is offered.
Aquarium Suitability/Reef Aquarium Compatibility: Reasonably good reef aquarium animals. Aggressive; occasionally form sweeper tentacles. They are seldom damaged, but other corals may be.
Captive Care: This genus has numerous species, all characterized by a skeletal feature called a "hydnophore," the small conical bump or pimple formed when two adjacent corallites meet and merge. Tentacles are tapering and often short. The appearance of the tentacles and hydnophores together gives these corals a rather untidy, disheveled appearance. They do well with moderate current, but don't tolerate disturbance well and may bleach, recede, or die if conditions change. Colors range from browns to fluorescent greens. Both encrusting and branching species are collected and propagated.

Lobophyllia spp.
Lobed brain corals (open brain corals)

Maximum Size: Some species with colonies to about 3.3 ft. (1 m) across or high; most smaller.

Range: Indo-Pacific.

Minimum Aquarium Size: Moderate tanks, 50 gal. (190 L) or larger.

Lighting: Tolerant of most lighting conditions, but prefer bright.

Foods & Feeding: Zooxanthellate, but must be fed; will eat a lot of food if it is offered.

Aquarium Suitability/Reef Aquarium Compatibility: Good reef aquarium animals; not aggressive or terribly demanding of water conditions.

Captive Care: Impressive additions to the reef aquarium, *Lobophyllia* species are characterized by deep grooves surrounded by thick fleshy tissue. Tentacles are usually hidden out of sight on the inner margins of the fleshy edges and emerge only at night when food is offered. Prefer low to moderate currents. Do not fare well in coral-to-coral interactions, so care should be taken to place them in situations that will not result in contact with other corals when they expand significantly at night. The underlying skeleton is relatively massive; the coral tissue is usually a dark shade of green, brown, bronze, or red, with the papillae on the surface a lighter contrasting color.

MAIN PHOTO, POLYPS EXTENDED; INSET, POLYPS RETRACTED

Physogyra lichtensteini
Pearl coral (grape coral, small bubble coral)

Maximum Size: Colonies to about 12 in. (30 cm) in diameter; most smaller.

Range: Indo-Pacific.

Minimum Aquarium Size: Moderate tanks, 50 gal. (190 L) or larger.

Lighting: Prefers low light intensity; avoid areas of strong illumination.

Foods & Feeding: Zooxanthellate, but must be fed; will eat lots of food if it is offered.

Aquarium Suitability/Reef Aquarium Compatibility: This is a good reef aquarium animal, but it is aggressive and will form sweeper tentacles. Somewhat fragile and prone to disease and damage.

Captive Care: Similar to bubble coral (page 192), this animal is characterized by the presence of small (3-5 mm in diameter) vesicles or tissue "bubbles" that arise from the polyps. These are zooxanthellae "accommodators" and, by inflation, expose their internal zooxanthellae to much more light. Prefers weak currents. Does not tolerate disturbance by hermit crabs; if the tank contains large numbers of them, the coral may not be a good choice. Colonies, green to greenish white, tend to form massive heads in the wild. Vesicles inflate during the day and deflate at night when the tentacles are extended.

Plerogyra sinuosa
Bubble coral (grape coral, octobubble coral)

Maximum Size: Colonies to about 12 in. (30 cm) in diameter; most smaller.
Range: Indo-Pacific.
Minimum Aquarium Size: Moderate tanks, 50 gal. (190 L) or larger.
Lighting: Prefers low light intensity; avoid areas of strong illumination.
Foods & Feeding: Zooxanthellate, but must be fed; will eat lots of food if it is offered.
Aquarium Suitability/Reef Aquarium Compatibility: Good reef aquarium animal, but aggressive and will form sweeper tentacles. Somewhat fragile and prone to disease and damage.
Captive Care: Related to the small bubble coral *Physogyra* (page 191). Colors range from white to green, blue, or tan. Characterized by the presence of large (up to 0.75 in. [2 cm] in diameter) vesicles or bubbles that arise from the polyps. Prefers weak current. Avoid areas of strong illumination. Does not tolerate disturbance by hermit crabs. Once established, it tends to be relatively hardy if not disturbed. Bubbles are zooxanthellae "accommodators" that, by inflation, expose their internal zooxanthellae to much more light. Bubbles inflate during the day and deflate at night during tentacle extension.

TRACHYPHYLLIA GEOFFROYI

Trachyphyllia spp.
Open brain corals

Maximum Size: Colonies to about 18 in. (46 cm) in diameter; most smaller.

Range: Indo-Pacific.

Minimum Aquarium Size: Moderate tanks, 50 gal. (190 L) or larger.

Lighting: Will tolerate bright lighting, if gradually adapted to it.

Foods & Feeding: Zooxanthellate, but must be fed; will eat lots of food if it is offered.

Aquarium Suitability/Reef Aquarium Compatibility: Good reef aquarium animals, but may eat smaller fishes.

Captive Care: *Trachyphyllia* are solitary, often truly spectacular corals whose colors fluoresce under actinic lighting. They start life attached to the substrate and become free-living with maturity. Place on sand or in a sediment bed. These are voracious feeders that are often adept at capturing small fishes. *Centropyge* angelfishes and tangs will often nip at and can kill them. They do not tolerate hermit crabs. Skeleton is usually oblong and irregular. The colony usually has a conical spike on the bottom, which is buried in the substrate. Often two or more colors are found in one colony, and the furrows and walls of the valleys are differently colored.

TUBASTRAEA AUREA

Tubastraea aurea, Tubastraea faulkneri
Yellow sun corals

Maximum Size: Colonies to about 5 in. (13 cm) in diameter.
Range: Indo-Pacific.
Minimum Aquarium Size: Small tanks, 10 gal. (38 L) or larger.
Lighting: Prefer dim lighting. Too much light results in overgrowth by algae.
Foods & Feeding: Because they lack zooxanthellae, they must be oriented where feeding them is easy, as they must be fed a lot. Suitable foods include adult brine shrimp, mysids, diced fish, meaty plankton. Never feed them less than twice a week.
Aquarium Suitability/Reef Aquarium Compatibility: Not suitable for most tanks, where insufficient food or too much light is provided.
Captive Care: These glorious corals are best reserved for more advanced aquarists willing to feed them regularly. When well-fed, they appear "bloated," the polyps increase in size, and new polyps form. If in good condition, they reproduce by the use of asexual planulae. When this occurs, small yellow polyps appear in various areas around the tank. They prefer high-current areas. Their polyps are normally retracted during the day, but the animals can be acclimated to feed during the day and remain open.

Tubastraea micrantha
Black sun coral

Maximum Size: Colonies to about 10 ft. (3 m) in height.
Range: Indo-Pacific.
Minimum Aquarium Size: Large tanks, 100 gal. (380 L) or larger.
Lighting: Prefers dim lighting. Too much lighting results in overgrowth by algae.
Foods & Feeding: Must be oriented where feeding them is easy, as they must be fed regularly. Acceptable foods include adult brine shrimp, mysids, diced fish, and zooplankton. Feed daily; each polyp in the colony should get food.
Aquarium Suitability/Reef Aquarium Compatibility: Not suitable for most tanks in which too much light or not enough food is offered.
Captive Care: Although not easy to keep, this is a striking black to deep green coral that provides a beautiful contrast to the pastel shades of hermatypic corals. Rarely acclimates to feeding in the light. Does best in high-current areas and is resistant to most aquarium problems except malnutrition. It forms treelike, upright colonies lined with large polyps, often more than 1 in. (2.5 cm) across. When the polyps are extended, they have hints of orange in the black, often with orange or light greenish orange tentacles.

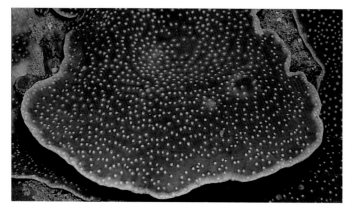

TURBINARIA RENIFORMIS

Turbinaria spp.
Cup corals (pagoda corals)

Maximum Size: Colonies to about 36 in. (91 cm) in diameter; most smaller.

Range: Indo-Pacific.

Minimum Aquarium Size: Large tanks, 100 gal. (380 L) or larger.

Lighting: Bright lighting is good, but lighting isn't overly important.

Foods & Feeding: Zooxanthellate, but must be fed with enriched baby brine shrimp, along with occasional adult *Artemia* and other foods such as diced silversides.

Aquarium Suitability/Reef Aquarium Compatibility: Good reef aquarium animals. Not aggressive; will be damaged by sweeper tentacles.

Captive Care: These corals need good current flow to flush away mucus. Supplemental flushing with a turkey baster may be necessary if waste materials accumulate. If they are in good condition, the polyps extend regularly and well. Watching the polyps is a good indicator of tank conditions, as they are very susceptible to changes in water quality. There are numerous species and growth forms. May grow as massive plates, heads, or as flattened branches. The evenly spaced, 1 cm in diameter polyps face upward or into currents; may be quite bushy and appear to have two or more whorls of tentacles.

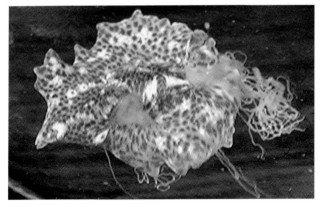

UNIDENTIFIED SESSILE COMB JELLY; TENTACLES PARTIALLY RETRACTED.

Astricola spp., *Coeloplana* spp.
Sessile comb jellies

Maximum Size: Individuals to about 1 in. (2.5 cm) long.

Range: All tropical seas.

Minimum Aquarium Size: Small tanks, 10 gal. (38 L) or larger.

Lighting: Immaterial.

Foods & Feeding: Must be fed foods such as enriched baby *Artemia*, along with occasional feedings of adult *Artemia*.

Aquarium Suitability/Reef Aquarium Compatibility: Good reef aquarium animals. Rarely become overly abundant. May irritate corals or other sessile invertebrates.

Captive Care: Even among the oddest of the invertebrates, these are rather bizarre animals. Most comb jellies (ctenophores) are wholly planktonic, although one small group has sessile adults. They look like flatworms with elevated ridges on their upper surfaces that may appear to have been outlined with a very fine white or colored pen. They are introduced to aquariums on their host (e.g., sea stars, soft corals, gorgonians, sea urchins). They feed by extending two fine hairlike tentacles into the water column and become instantly recognizable as ctenophores, as they have branched or fringed tentacles. If the tank is well fed with small planktonic foods, they may persist or even thrive.

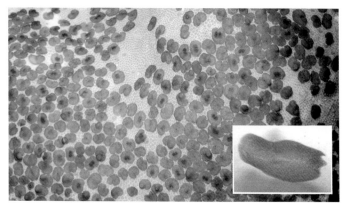

PLANARIAN PLAGUE IN A TANK; INSET: CLOSEUP OF *CONVOLUTRILOBA RETROGEMMA*

Convolutriloba retrogemma
Planaria (red flatworm, red menace)

Maximum Size: Individuals to about 0.25 in. (6 mm) long.
Range: All tropical seas.
Minimum Aquarium Size: Nano tanks, 1 gal. (3.8 L) or larger.
Lighting: Zooxanthellate. Dim light may assist in controlling this pest.
Foods & Feeding: Detritus or algae feeders.
Aquarium Suitability/Reef Aquarium Compatibility: Significant pests. Can reach plague proportions. Difficult to eradicate.
Captive Care: Planaria enter aquariums as hitchhikers. They range in color from deep wine red to light tan or green. Under 10x magnification, the front end appears gently rounded, while the tail has three trailing points or lobes, one on each edge and one in the middle. In some aquariums, small populations persist for long periods without causing problems, while in others they rapidly reproduce by fission. They may literally be everywhere in the tank. Control of this pest is difficult, as its requirements are similar to those of most desirable animals in the system. Reduce the intensity and duration of lighting for a couple of weeks; feeding should also be reduced. The headshield slug *Chelidonura varians* may also be effective in reducing the population. Commercial chemical treatments may eradicate them.

198

PSEUDOCEROS SP.

Pseudoceros spp., *Pseudobiceros* spp.
Polyclad flatworms

Maximum Size: Large species to 10 in. (25 cm); usually reach lengths of 2 in. (5 cm) and widths of about 0.5 in. (1.3 cm).

Range: All seas.

Minimum Aquarium Size: Nano tanks, 1 gal. (3.8 L) or larger.

Lighting: Immaterial.

Foods & Feeding: Predatory; need specific prey for survival. Diets of most are unknown.

Aquarium Suitability/Reef Aquarium Compatibility: Predatory; prey largely unknown; short-lived in captivity.

Captive Care: These common hitchhikers often have frilly edges that undulate in waves down the animal as it moves. They often have two small tentacles at the front end, with C-shaped eye spots near the tentacles. Polyclads are thin (most less than 1 mm thick), oval, rectangular, or somewhat teardrop-shaped. Over 100 described species are some of the most strikingly colored and beautiful marine animals. Most appear to be predators on tunicates or other sessile animals, and as we are unable to maintain tunicates in the aquarium, we have a long way to go before we can maintain their flatworm predators. Some species, common in reef tanks, prey on snails.

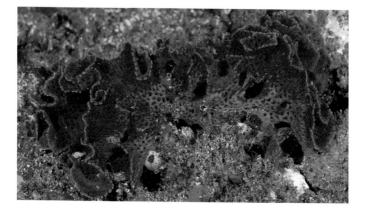

Iodictyum sp.: a reddish-purple bryozoan colony growing in the wild, where these so-called "moss animals" often occur in areas swept by strong currents.

Introduction to Bryozoans

Bryozoans are some of the most difficult animals for amateur aquarists, and even some professionals, to identify. In many ways, they are superficially like hydroids or some corals in that they consist of a polyplike animal that lives in a skeleton. However, they are significantly more advanced animals than corals, having a complete gut and other organ systems that are lacking in the cnidarians. They also lack the stinging capsules, or nematocysts, found in, and characteristic of, the Cnidaria.

There are a great many species of bryozoans, sometimes given the common label "moss animals," and many are common on coral reefs. They may exist as erect branching colonies that look like small delicate corals, as calcareous encrusting sheets, or as flexible colonies that appear very similar in structure to some algae. Regardless of their colony shape, they may be distinguished by several characteristics.

• First, although the colonies may be quite large, the polyps are very small, often less than 0.1 mm across the tentacle span. A hand lens or powerful magnifying glass is needed to see them. Species with giant polyps 10 times as large as normal may be found, but these are the very rare exception rather than the rule.

• Second, the polyps are arranged in linear, regular rows, with precisely repeated distances between the polyps. This will serve to distinguish them from the sponges, corals, and hydrocorals, where any small holes are rather haphazardly distributed.

• Finally, under magnification, if the colony is disturbed, the polyps withdraw very rapidly, which is in contrast to the slow withdrawal of hydrozoan polyps.

Identification to species level requires microscopic examination, so a hobbyist can only be confident of the genus level. Maintaining bryozoan species in captivity is not easy. As might be expected from animals with such small feeding polyps, bryozoans generally feed on very small particulate material, often bacterial aggregates in the water column. Such food cannot be added to the marine aquarium, but in some cases it may be generated internally in the aquarium, particularly if the aquarium has a good, functional sand bed filter. This particulate matter may be present in sufficient amounts to allow bryozoan survival.

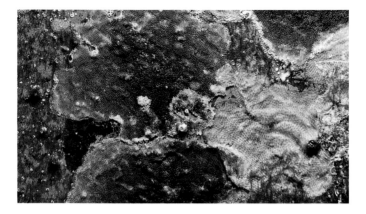

Schizoporella spp.
Purple encrusting bryozoans

Maximum Size: Large colonies to 10 in. (25 cm) in diameter; most smaller.

Range: Caribbean.

Minimum Aquarium Size: Nano tanks, 1 gal. (3.8 L) or larger.

Lighting: Immaterial.

Foods & Feeding: Need very small particulate material, bacterial aggregates in the water column. Such foods cannot be added, but may be generated internally by a good, functional sand bed.

Aquarium Suitability/Reef Aquarium Compatibility: Difficult to maintain, probably due to a lack of appropriate foods.

Captive Care: Purple encrusting bryozoans are common throughout the Caribbean and illustrate some of the common properties of the bryozoan group. They can be recognized as a purple calcareous crust, not unlike some coralline algae in appearance. The surface of the crust is spotted with minute holes, one per feeding polyp, which are spread regularly across the surface. The polyps are not usually visible without magnification. Identification to species level requires microscopic examination.

Triphyllozoon spp.
Lace bryozoans

Maximum Size: Large colonies to 12 in. (30 cm) or more in height.
Range: Indo-Pacific.
Minimum Aquarium Size: Nano tanks, 1 gal. (3.8 L) or larger.
Lighting: Immaterial. Dim lighting may prevent algal overgrowth.
Foods & Feeding: Need very small particulate material, bacterial aggregates in the water column. Such foods cannot be added, but may be generated internally by a good, functional sand bed.
Aquarium Suitability/Reef Aquarium Compatibility: Difficult to maintain, probably due to a lack of appropriate foods.
Captive Care: These animals grow as a colony, forming a white calcareous mesh with more-or-less diamond-shaped holes a few millimeters on a side. The mesh network and white calcareous skeleton identify this genus. Individual polyps live in small holes regularly arrayed along the edges. When the animal is at ease, the polyps extend from the surface. Colonies are roughly rectangular and usually about half as wide as long. Prefer lots of current. May do well in tanks with a healthy sand bed; presently no reports of long-term success with them. Often have symbiotic hydrozoans living on them, seen above as small white dots a short distance from the mesh.

PHORONIS AUSTRALIS

Phoronis spp., *Phoronopsis* spp.
Phoronids

Maximum Size: Tentacles span to about 1 in. (2.5 cm) in width.

Range: All seas.

Minimum Aquarium Size: Small tanks, 10 gal. (38 L) or larger.

Lighting: Immaterial. Dim lighting may prevent algal overgrowth.

Foods & Feeding: Will feed on very small particulate material, bacterial aggregates in the water column. Such foods cannot be added, but may be generated internally via a good functional sand bed.

Aquarium Suitability/Reef Aquarium Compatibility: Easy to maintain; good aquarium animals.

Captive Care: Phoronids are interesting, beneficial worms. They have distinctive white, translucent gray, green, brown, or black horseshoe-shaped tentacle crowns; tentacles lack side branches. They may enter an aquarium via live rock or in association with other animals and occasionally are found living with other animals (e.g., *Phoronis australis* is found living in the tubes of tropical cerianthids, or tube anemones). They should be kept with their associated animals or rock and not be manipulated, as their tubes and the worm inside tend to break easily. Hermit crabs and shrimps will kill them.

Y-SHAPED PROBOSCIS MOVING OVER SUBSTRATE; BODY HIDDEN IN ROCKS

Achaetobonellia spp., *Bonellia* spp.,
Echiurid worms (bonellid worms)

Maximum Size: Bodies 1 to 2 in. (2.5 to 5 cm) long; may have a proboscis that stretches out to 3.3 ft. (1 m) or more.
Range: All seas.
Minimum Aquarium Size: Small tanks, 10 gal. (38 L) or larger.
Lighting: Immaterial.
Foods & Feeding: Feed on detritus.
Aquarium Suitability/Reef Aquarium Compatibility: Easy to maintain; good aquarium animals.
Captive Care: These harmless and interesting animals sometimes appear in reef tanks, most likely imported with live rock or live sand. The only visible part of these worms is the long, thin, branched proboscis that extends out of the burrow to collect particulate material. It forms two equal lobes at the tip that appear to be T- or Y-shaped. The small saclike body stays buried in the rocks. Bonellids have a pigment, bonellin, that colors all body parts deep green. If the animal is threatened or disturbed, it may sever its proboscis, which later regrows. These worms do well in reef tanks as long as the tank is well fed. They may be preyed upon by fishes, some snails, and some sea stars.

Eunice sp. (bobbit worm): sometimes more exotic than commonly known, the annelid worms can make fascinating, in this case fearsome, subjects for aquarists.

Introduction to the Segmented Worms (Phylum Annelida)

The annelids are called segmented worms, as their body appears to be made of similar, repeated body regions called segments. Probably the most familiar annelid is the common earthworm. Although there are significant internal variations from segment to segment, externally the earthworm's segments appear very similar to one another, and the body appears to be composed of a series of rings or annuli. These annuli give the phylum its name.

The three major classes within this phylum are Oligochaeta, Hirudinea, and Polychaeta or, respectively, earthworms, leeches, and bristleworms. All three may be found in marine aquariums at least occasionally, and a number of them are absolutely vital to the health of reef systems. Additionally, there are a number of smaller annelid groups whose members may occasionally appear in a reef system. The three major classes are distinguished as follows:

• Marine earthworms, members of the **Class Oligochaeta**, are typically small and spend all of their lives living within the sediments.

Terebellid or spaghetti worm: often unexpectedly appearing in established aquariums, worms often enter with live substrates or attached to other invertebrates.

Although earthworms are abundant and common within most terrestrial or freshwater sediments, they are relatively rare in our marine tanks. Unless you have access to a microscope, they are difficult to distinguish from some of the bristleworms.

• Members of the **Class Hirudinea**, the leeches, are abundant in marine ecosystems where they are either ectoparasites or predators on fishes or some of the invertebrates. Occasionally, they enter our systems attached to a fish, but this is really rather rare. They are characterized by the presence of a sucker at both ends, and are generally good swimmers. Some are very brightly colored and may be quite attractive. Nonetheless, as they are generally easily removed from fish and disposed of, they do not need further discussion.

• The remaining large group, **Class Polychaeta**, or bristleworms, is very diverse. There are easily 10,000 species of polychaetes, and a rather large number of varieties are commonly found in reef aquariums. Polychaetes are characterized by the presence of an appendage, called a parapodium, on either side of each segment. These parapo-

Chloeia sp. fireworm eating dead fish: this is one of many highly beneficial polychaete worms that inhabit and scavenge the nether regions of reef tanks.

dia are often modified, depending on the mode of life of the particular species. Extending from the ends of each parapodium are the bristles that give this class its name. The term "polychaete" is derived from the Greek root words *poly* and *chaeta*, meaning "many" and "hairs" or "bristles," so the aquarist's use of "bristleworm" is quite appropriate as a common name for the group.

Although worms are often thought of as being simple, the polychaetes tend to have complicated internal structures. The gut is complex, with various regions devoted to the processes of digestion. Their circulatory system is entirely within vessels, and the animals often have hemoglobin as a respiratory pigment, and often have multiple hearts. They commonly have kidneys in many of the segments. The nervous system is also complex, and these supposedly "simple" animals often have some very sophisticated behaviors.

The number of shapes and forms of polychaete worms is immense; most invertebrate zoology students are amazed at just how many different ways there are to make worms. This diversity is evident in the next level of classification, the family. Families of worms are groupings of species with similar morphologies and lifestyles.

Chloeia viridis (Caribbean fireworm): this highly predatory worm forages on debris but also swims to catch slow-moving fishes. Note stinging bristles.

The Class Polychaeta is generally subdivided into some 75 to 100 different families, and these are the groups that biologists generally use when discussing the varieties of polychaetes and how they live.

Within each family, the various species all share some common morphological attributes. These characteristic structures and shapes are correlated with certain specific lifestyles. This means that if you can determine the family of the worm, you can know a lot about its natural history and behavior. This is fortunate, because relatively few of the species common in captivity have been studied in the natural reef.

Identification of polychaete annelids to the species level is difficult, except in a few instances. It often requires comparative examination of the parapodia and setae.

Protula magnifica (magnificent hard-tube feather duster): true to its name, but a species demanding more care and feeding than most aquarists can give.

Introduction to Feather Duster Worms

The many varieties of segmented worms that may appear from time to time in reef aquariums arrive in one of two ways. They may be purchased for their beauty or filter-feeding abilities, or they may arrive as hitchhikers on live rock or in live sand. Feather duster worms are from four common families within the Class Polychaeta, one of the three major classes of the annelids (segmented worms). Although species from each family have some unique attributes, there are many similarities in the biology of all feather duster worms.

Common Characteristics
• All worms in this group have crowns of tentacles used in feeding—these arrangements are the so-called "feather dusters."
• These crowns are comprised of branched tentacles, with each tentacle's branches arranged like the filaments along a feather.
• All feather dusters feed on fine particulate organic material, such as phytoplankton and bacterial aggregates, suspended in the water.
• All have mechanisms and structural modifications in the tentacles

Unidentified feather duster: exact feeding requirements of many species of feather dusters are not known, but include phytoplankton and small particulate matter.

that allow sorting of the filtered particles.

There are differences between the individual species, presumably related to their specific diets. However, as hobbyists, we do not have sources for any worm's specific foods. Feeding small particulate material, such as phytoplankton, should provide enough nutrition for any species of feather duster. The presence of bacterial particulates produced by sand bed fauna also helps provide these animals with balanced nutrition.

Generally, feather duster worms will do best in areas with moderate to high currents. Lighting is immaterial to their health. All feather dusters are attacked and eaten by certain fishes, such as the copperbanded butterflyfish (*Chelmon rostratus*), some wrasses, many hermit crabs (if larger than the aperture of the worm tube), many true crabs, and several species of predatory snails, including many of the whelks. Some feather dusters, particularly the smaller species, may reproduce asexually by fission or budding, but most do not.

Identification of these worms to family is easy—basically it involves examining the tube. Identification to species is also easy for a few common large species. Small species are difficult to identify, as

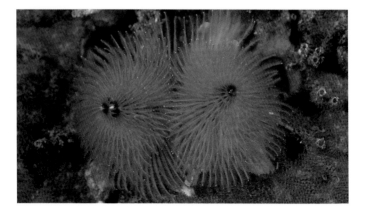

Spirobranchus sp.: the tentacles are used by these worms for respiration and filter-feeding on microplankton and perhaps suspended bacterial matter.

the shapes of the bristles on the hind part of the body are important characteristics, and few hobbyists have the equipment necessary to examine these.

Family Differences

Family Sabellidae: Tubes are made of a relatively soft material, which may be very flexible or about as stiff as cardboard. Sabellid worms range from very small to quite large. The biggest are over 36 in. (91 cm) long, with tentacle crowns over 5 in. (13 cm) in diameter. In the aquarium world, these are the animals commonly called "feather duster worms," although the other families have similar feathery crowns. Some smaller species reproduce asexually very well in captivity, forming large colonies.

Family Serpulidae: Tubes are made of calcium carbonate and are often attached to rocks or other substrate material. They frequently have a doubled crown of tentacles, sometimes forming a doubled, tapered helix. The often have an operculum, or plug, that fits into the tube and seals it when the worm has withdrawn. In the aquarium

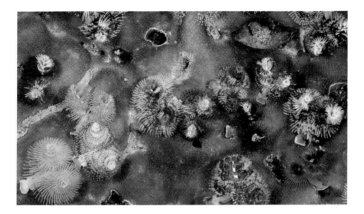

Spirobranchus giganteus (Christmas tree worm): embedded in a colony of *Porites* coral. The reef aquarist must meet the needs of both worms and coral.

world, these are commonly called "hard-tubed feather dusters," "Christmas tree worms," or "Coco worms."

Family Spirorbidae: These diminutive worms live in small tubes often found attached to rocks or growing on the sides of the aquarium. The tightly spiraled tube is seldom over 0.2 in. (5 mm) in diameter. The tentacle crown is bright red or red-orange, but is clearly seen only with magnification. They are common and reproduce well in captivity, but are probably never intentionally purchased.

Family Sabellaridae: Tubes are made of cemented sand or other substrate grains. The tentacle crown is generally smaller and less brightly colored than in the other families. The individual worms seldom exceed 4 in. (10 cm) in length, but collectively they may form reefs of cemented worm tubes that are hundreds of yards long and up to 66 ft. (20 m) high. These worms are seldom seen in captivity because the aggregations of tubes are simply too difficult to break for the animals to be easily collected. However, individuals may enter tanks attached to live rock.

Bispira spp.
Spiraled feather dusters

Maximum Size: Tentacle crown to 2 in. (5 cm) in diameter.

Range: Tropical seas.

Minimum Aquarium Size: Small tanks, 10 gal. (38 L) or larger.

Lighting: Immaterial.

Foods & Feeding: Feed on particulate organic material and phytoplankton. Need target feeding in most tanks to survive.

Aquarium Suitability/Reef Aquarium Compatibility: Difficult to maintain; most starve to death after a few months.

Captive Care: These delicate, beautiful sabellids have a brownish, parchmentlike tube. Unfortunately, they are likely to starve in most reef aquariums. They prefer moderate currents and may be sustained with feedings of microplankton. The tubes should be buried in the sediment or in cracks or crevices of rocks, with the large end of the tube about 0.4 in. (10 mm) out of the substrate. They are characterized by having a one-to-several-tentacled whorled helical crown. In the most complex forms, the crown resembles that of the Christmas tree worm (*Spirobranchus giganteus*), in having a tapered helix of three or more whorls. Tentacle side branches are usually white, with a red, pink, orange, blue, or black central stem.

Sabellid species
Dwarf feather dusters

Maximum Size: Tentacle crown to 0.4 in. (10 mm) in diameter.

Range: Tropical seas.

Minimum Aquarium Size: Small tanks, 10 gal. (38 L) or larger.

Lighting: Immaterial, although they thrive in low-light conditions.

Foods & Feeding: Feed on particulate organic material and phytoplankton. Possibly absorb dissolved nutrients.

Aquarium Suitability/Reef Aquarium Compatibility: Easy to maintain. Good aquarium animals.

Captive Care: These small sabellids are found from time to time for sale as "dwarf" or "small" feather dusters, but most hitchhike their way into tanks. They often grow well in aquariums without specific care, although individuals of many hermit crab species will kill and eat them. It is likely that they are able to feed on dissolved nutrients to a greater extent than most sabellids. They reproduce in captivity, probably by fission in the tube of the parent, resulting in one or more offspring. They seem to prefer living on substrates rather than in them, and are found growing on rocks or aquarium walls. They prefer moderate current. The tentacle crown is typically white, with a brown or gray parchmentlike tube.

Sabellastarte indica
Giant feather duster worm

Maximum Size: Tentacle crown to about 4 in. (10 cm) in diameter.
Range: Indo-Pacific; similar species in all tropical seas.
Minimum Aquarium Size: Small tanks, 10 gal. (38 L) or larger.
Lighting: Immaterial.
Foods & Feeding: Feeds on particulate organic material and phytoplankton. Requires regular target feeding.
Aquarium Suitability/Reef Aquarium Compatibility: Needs a lot more planktonic food than is commonly found in captivity and generally will starve to death over a period of about six months to a year.
Captive Care: Unfortunately, long-term survival of this handsome worm in captivity is poor, due to lack of food. It does somewhat better in tanks with a good sand bed, but still needs the addition of phytoplankton. If food is insufficient, it will starve for a while and then shed the tentacle crown. A new, smaller crown is regenerated within a couple of weeks and the smaller animal attempts to feed. If food is still insufficient, and the crown sheds a second and maybe even a third time, the animal eventually dies. In nature, it lives buried in sediments with about 0.5 in. (1.3 cm) of the tube projecting above the surface. The horseshoe-shaped crown is orange, black, or brown.

Sabellastarte magnifica
Giant feather duster worm

Maximum Size: Tentacle crown to about 4 in. (10 cm) in diameter.
Range: Caribbean; similar species in all tropical seas.
Minimum Aquarium Size: Small tanks, 10 gal. (38 L) or larger.
Lighting: Immaterial.
Foods & Feeding: Feeds on particulate organic material and phytoplankton. Needs regular target feeding.
Aquarium Suitability/Reef Aquarium Compatibility: Best avoided by most aquarists. Generally will starve to death over a period of about six months to a year.
Captive Care: Long-term survival in captivity is poor, because it needs a lot more planktonic food than is commonly found in captive systems. Will do somewhat better with a good sand bed, but still needs the addition of phytoplankton. If food is insufficient, it will starve for a while and then shed the tentacle crown. If food is still insufficient, and the crown sheds a second and maybe a third time, the animal eventually dies. In the wild, this species lives buried in sediments with about 0.5 in. (1.3 cm) of the tube projecting above the surface. Characterized by a doubled row of tentacles in the crown. Often has unbanded tentacles, with white fringe and dark stalks.

Sabellastarte sanctijosephi
Giant feather duster worm

Maximum Size: Tentacle crown to about 4 in. (10 cm) in diameter.
Range: Indo-Pacific; similar species in all tropical seas.
Minimum Aquarium Size: Small tanks, 10 gal. (38 L) or larger.
Lighting: Immaterial.
Foods & Feeding: Feeds on particulate organic material and phyto-plankton. Needs a lot of hard-to-provide food.
Aquarium Suitability/Reef Aquarium Compatibility: Not a good choice for most aquariums, as it typically starves to death over a period of about six months to a year.
Captive Care: As with other large feather dusters, this eye-catching species fares poorly in captivity, where it is difficult to feed. It does somewhat better with a good sand bed, but still needs the addition of phytoplankton. If food is insufficient, it will starve for a while and then shed its tentacle crown. If food is still insufficient, and the crown sheds a second and maybe a third time, eventually the animal dies. Characterized by a doubled row of tentacles in the crown. Often has unbanded tentacles, with white fringe and dark stalks. In the wild, it lives buried in sediments with about 0.5 in. (1.3 cm) of the tube projecting above the surface.

Protula magnifica
Magnificent hard-tube feather duster (coco worm)

Maximum Size: Tentacle crown to 3 in. (7.6 cm) in diameter; large tube to almost 1 in. (2.5 cm) in diameter in a large adult; may be more than 24 in. (61 cm) long.

Range: Tropical seas.

Minimum Aquarium Size: Small tanks, 10 gal. (38 L) or larger.

Lighting: Immaterial.

Foods & Feeding: Feeds on particulate organic material and phytoplankton. Need a lot of hard-to-provide food.

Aquarium Suitability/Reef Aquarium Compatibility: Best kept only by advanced aquarists, as captive specimens generally will starve to death over a period of about six months to a year.

Captive Care: This species needs an aquarium that has high levels of calcium and regular infusions of small phytoplankton. Given these conditions, it is capable of a long life. Strong to moderate currents are necessary. The tentacle crown is comprised of two helices of 3 or 4 whorls. The tentacle stalks and the shafts of each "feather" tend to be red, hot pink, or rose-peach. The feather filaments are usually white or occasionally pink. It lacks the plug, or operculum, common to many serpulids.

Spirobranchus giganteus
Christmas tree worm

Maximum Size: Indo-Pacific tentacle crowns are about 0.5 in. (1.3 cm) in diameter and 0.75 in. (1.9 cm) long; Caribbean animals can be two times as large.

Range: Tropical seas.

Minimum Aquarium Size: Small tanks, 10 gal. (38 L) or larger.

Lighting: Immaterial.

Foods & Feeding: Feeds on particulate organic material and phytoplankton, which must be supplied on a regular basis.

Aquarium Suitability/Reef Aquarium Compatibility: Should be kept only by the expert reef aquarist willing and able to provide planktonic food. Otherwise, the animal generally will slowly starve to death.

Captive Care: This glorious species lives in a tube excavated within a living coral head. Until recently, both coral and worm would almost always perish in captivity, although the coral had a better chance. With the addition of live phytoplankton, the animals can now do well in captivity. They require moderate to strong, but not buffeting, current flow to bring food to them. Caribbean specimens are usually brown, mottled, or violet; Pacific forms are mostly blue, pure white, or pure yellow. Pacific specimens are found in pieces of *Porites*.

Spirorbis spp.
Spiral tube feather dusters (spirorbids)

Maximum Size: About 0.25 in. (6 mm) in diameter or larger.
Range: Tropical seas.
Minimum Aquarium Size: Small tanks, 10 gal. (38 L) or larger.
Lighting: Immaterial.
Foods & Feeding: Feed on particulate organic material and phytoplankton. Probably survive on dissolved nutrients in many tanks.
Aquarium Suitability/Reef Aquarium Compatibility: Easy to maintain; harmless.
Captive Care: These are the tiniest of the feather dusters and make their way into virtually all marine aquariums. Tubes are usually spirally coiled about 1⅓ to 1½ whorls and often first spotted on the walls of the tank. The minuscule crown is generally brilliant red or blaze orange, but tentacles are difficult to see because of their small size. Spirorbids are simultaneous, self-fertilizing hermaphrodites. The larval period is short and the adults brood the larvae in their tubes. Juveniles exit the parent's tube and crawl a short distance before starting to secrete their own tubes. Once the tube is started, they remain in place for the rest of their lives. No special care is needed to maintain these harmless animals. Eaten by copperband butterflyfish.

LOIMIAMEDUSA SP.

Terebellidae species
Spaghetti worms

Maximum Size: Body about 12 in. (30 cm) long in a large species; tentacles may extend another 36 in. (1 m). Most aquarium species are less than 1 in. (2.5 cm) long.

Range: All seas.

Minimum Aquarium Size: Small tanks, 10 gal. (38 L) or larger.

Lighting: Immaterial.

Foods & Feeding: Feed on particulate organic material, detritus.

Aquarium Suitability/Reef Aquarium Compatibility: Good scavengers. Easy to maintain and harmless.

Captive Care: These tube-building polychaetes have a body that is almost never seen, with a telltale crown of unbranched long, thin feeding tentacles, colored white, tan, or gray. When feeding, these cryptic animals extend their tentacles—resembling overcooked vermicelli noodles—over the substrate. These worms live in tubes secreted between or under rocks, in rock cracks or crevices, or in sediments. They are good at collecting and removing small particulate debris from rocks, particularly from crevices and small cavities. Hermit crabs and other crabs, some shrimps, some whelks, and numerous fishes, such as many wrasses and some butterflyfishes, prey on them.

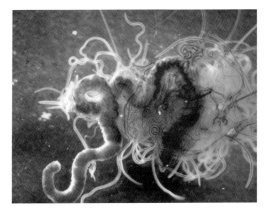

Cirratulid species
Hair worms

Maximum Size: Body less than 2 in. (5 cm) long.
Range: All seas.
Minimum Aquarium Size: Small tanks, 10 gal. (38 L) or larger.
Lighting: Immaterial.
Foods & Feeding: Feed on particulate organic material, detritus.
Aquarium Suitability/Reef Aquarium Compatibility: Good scavengers. Easy to maintain; harmless.
Captive Care: Commonly misidentified as spaghetti worms or terebellids (see facing page), cirratulids are often available as part of sediment fauna booster kits and may enter a tank in live sand. Usually red, orange, dark brown or black, featureless except for several long, spaghetti-like yellow, tan, or red gills arising from various body segments, and a few feeding tentacles from the head. Generally, only one or two gills arise per segment. The worms lie in the sediment with their gills passing up through the sediment particles until they reach the surface. They process sediment and will help ensure that the sediment detritus load remains stable. One or two worms every couple of centimeters is a reasonably healthy concentration. They are eaten by nipping fishes, hermit crabs, crabs, and cleaner shrimps.

Eurythoe sp.
Aquarium fireworm

Maximum Size: Up to about 18 in. (60 cm); most smaller.
Range: Tropical seas.
Minimum Aquarium Size: Small tanks, 10 gal. (38 L) or larger.
Lighting: Immaterial.
Foods & Feeding: Scavenger on most foods or carrion.
Aquarium Suitability/Reef Aquarium Compatibility: Exceptionally beneficial scavenger; harmless to healthy animals. Dangerous to touch; bristles are venom-tipped and can deliver a painful sting. These stings can lead to inflammation.
Captive Care: This scavenger usually arrives on live rock or in the base of a coral and helpfully consumes dead or dying animals, food remains, and other waste matter. It lives in crevices or holes in the rockwork and comes out to scavenge after dark or after food has been introduced to the tank. Generally reproduces well and can establish large populations. Oval to almost rectangular in cross section; has one large tuft of white, calcareous bristles on each side of each segment. Frilly pink or orange gills located above each bristle tuft may be hard to see. Basic color is pink, pinkish orange, or tan. A beneficial scavenger such as this species should not be removed from the aquarium.

Hermodice carunculata
Coral-eating fireworm (bearded fireworm)

Maximum Size: Up to about 12 in. (30 cm) long.
Range: Caribbean; similar species are found in the Indo-Pacific.
Minimum Aquarium Size: Small tanks, 10 gal. (38 L) or larger.
Lighting: Immaterial.
Foods & Feeding: Will eat corals, soft corals, zoanthids, and other cnidarians.
Aquarium Suitability/Reef Aquarium Compatibility: Preys on corals, soft corals and sea anemones. It is dangerous to the touch, as the chaetae (bristles) are filled with venom.
Captive Care: This fireworm is predatory on many potential reef tank inhabitants, such as many soft corals, anemones and polypoid animals. It is generally smaller than *Eurythoe* (page 224) and can be distinguished by its reddish to silver-gray body color, the presence of blood-red frilly gills above each tuft of chaetae, and the presence of frilled appendages (the "beard") on the back of the head. Fortunately, this species is rare in marine reef tanks and is probably collected only infrequently. If there were sufficient food for *Hermodice* in a tank, it would probably reproduce as well as *Eurythoe*, but there are no reports of this occurring.

Eunice spp.
Eunicid worms (bobbit worms)

Maximum Size: Huge; longest collected is about 20 ft. (6 m); may reach lengths of 50 ft. (15 m) and a diameter of 1 in. (2.5 cm).
Range: All seas.
Minimum Aquarium Size: Moderate tanks, 50 gal. (190 L) or larger.
Lighting: Immaterial.
Foods & Feeding: Scavengers on large chunks of meaty foods; predatory.
Aquarium Suitability/Reef Aquarium Compatibility: Very efficient at eating carrion. Predatory forms can eat aquarium fishes, sessile animals.
Captive Care: Although a model for certain sci-fi aliens (see photo, page 206) and unwelcome in most aquariums, some eunicids may be efficient and beneficial scavengers, as well as being quite attractive. They are robust and can grow quite large. Common in fresh live rock. All have well-developed heads characterized by 5 large tentacle-like projections, one of which always arises from the center of the "forehead." They usually live in burrows and extend out to obtain food. Most are predators, with 3 to 5 pairs of large, chitinous, pincer-like jaws. The largest are capable of catching and eating fish up to 4 in. (10 cm) in length. They have excellent predator-avoidance responses; to remove one, its burrow must be found and the worm extracted.

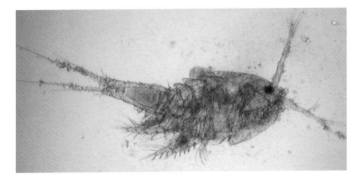

Harpacticoid copepods (copepods, pods)

Maximum Size: To about 1 mm long.
Range: Tropical seas.
Minimum Aquarium Size: Small tanks, 10 gal. (38 L) or larger.
Lighting: Immaterial.
Foods & Feeding: Microalgae, small particulate matter.
Aquarium Suitability/Reef Aquarium Compatibility: Common, detritivores, food for fishes, quite desirable.
Captive Care: The tiny crustaceans that scuttle around ocean bottoms and in aquariums are likely all harpacticoid copepods. Most aquarists notice them about a week or 10 days after setting up a tank. They appear as small white specks moving on the glass, or swarms of tiny white dots in the water. Small, teardrop-shaped animals, they move in jerky spurts. They enter tanks on live rock or in live sand. They feed by scraping small algae or bacteria off rocks. They reproduce rapidly and are excellent food for many aquarium animals. No special care is necessary. They thrive in reef tanks and do especially well in tanks with a good sand bed. They are particularly good food for mandarinfishes and a good population of them may be necessary for the survival of these fishes.

Acorn barnacles

Maximum Size: To about 4 in. (10 cm) across; most about 0.5 in. (13 mm) or less.

Range: All seas.

Minimum Aquarium Size: Small tanks, 10 gal. (38 L) or larger.

Lighting: Immaterial.

Foods & Feeding: Can be fed enriched *Artemia* or some other moderately large high-energy foods. Phytoplankton are too small.

Aquarium Suitability/Reef Aquarium Compatibility: Harmless; difficult to feed, so they generally die of starvation in captivity.

Captive Care: Accidental arrivals in most reef aquariums, these barnacles secrete a secondary covering of calcareous plates, creating their characteristic volcanolike structure, but inside this is a shrimplike animal that has its feet modified as a filtering fan. They fasten themselves to hard substrates for life, and consequently are often brought in incidentally on corals, live rock, or some other hard-shelled organism. Most are capable of living several years if they are not eaten by a predator. In reef systems, if given enough food, there is no reason that some individuals should not reach this potential longevity.

Pyrgomatid or coral barnacles

Maximum Size: To about 1.2 in. (3 cm) across.
Range: Tropical seas.
Minimum Aquarium Size: Small tanks, 10 gal. (38 L) or larger.
Lighting: Immaterial.
Foods & Feeding: Can be fed enriched *Artemia* or some other moderately large high-energy foods. Phytoplankton are too small.
Aquarium Suitability/Reef Aquarium Compatibility: Harmless; difficult to provide with enough food.
Captive Care: These barnacles are specialized to live on scleractinian corals and hydrocorals. They attach to, and then bore into, the coral. They secrete a single shell around themselves that is often covered by subsequent coral growth, so all that is seen is a rounded or conical bump on the surface of the coral with a slit or oval opening at the top. A typical barnacle filtering fan extends from this opening to feed on plankton. They don't really do harm to the coral, although their activities may slightly weaken the coral's skeleton and/or they may intercept food before it gets to the coral. When the barnacle dies, the coral often grows over its shell and all evidence that a barnacle was once there disappears, except for a rather odd lump on the coral's surface.

Mysis spp.
Possum shrimps (mysid shrimps)

Maximum Size: To about 12 in. (30 cm) long; most much smaller.
Range: Tropical seas.
Minimum Aquarium Size: Small tanks, 10 gal. (38 L) or larger.
Lighting: Immaterial.
Foods & Feeding: They may be fed using phytoplankton.
Aquarium Suitability/Reef Aquarium Compatibility: Highly desirable as a self-replenishing live food source in reef aquariums.
Captive Care: Mysid shrimp are often abundant in a reef aquarium or refugium, although it takes a sharp eye to see them. Because they feed on microalgae, their refugium needs enough light to allow algae to thrive. Mysids make excellent food for small fishes; if they are in a refugium with access to the main tank, enough escapees make it into the tank to provide supplemental nutrition between scheduled feedings. They most often enter the aquarium with algae, such as *Chaetomorpha*, which forms dense mats of wirelike strands within which the mysids may be protected from predation. Distantly related to true shrimps, mysids have a decidedly shrimplike shape and are largely transparent. They lack the thoracic walking legs seen in most shrimps and instead have slender paddlelike appendages.

CAPRELLID AMPHIPOD ON GORGONIAN

Caprellid amphipods
Skeleton shrimps

Maximum Size: To about 2 in. (5 cm) long; most much smaller. Aquarium forms are usually less than 0.4 in. (10 mm) long.
Range: All seas.
Minimum Aquarium Size: Small tanks, 10 gal. (38 L) or larger.
Lighting: Immaterial.
Foods & Feeding: All feeding modes are found in this group as a whole, but those found on live rock in captivity are generally predatory. Foods include crustaceans, hydrozoans, coral polyps, and worms.
Aquarium Suitability/Reef Aquarium Compatibility: Generally harmless. Good food for other animals, but difficult to maintain.
Captive Care: Like pale amber or transparent walking-stick animals, herbivorous skeleton shrimps may be cultured in a refugium when provided with appropriate food, generally some algae. The long tubular body terminates in a small but bulbous head with two pairs of long antennae that may be as long as the rest of the body. Large appendages end in claws that close like a jackknife. Anterior appendages can reach a span as wide as the animal's length. They will sit on a rock promontory or a piece of algae that they grip with their hind legs. Carnivorous forms can be removed using forceps.

Gammaridean amphipods
Scuds (side shrimps, *Gammarus* shrimps)

Maximum Size: To about 2 in. (5 cm) long; aquarium forms are usually less than 0.4 in. (1 mm) long.
Range: All seas.
Minimum Aquarium Size: Small tanks, 10 gal. (38 L) or larger.
Lighting: Immaterial.
Foods & Feeding: Aquarium forms are usually detritivores.
Aquarium Suitability/Reef Aquarium Compatibility: Harmless; good food for other animals. Easy to raise in a refugium.
Captive Care: Common in most marine tanks with live rock or sand. These highly successful crustaceans lack a carapace. Unlike shrimps, all body segments are visible. Colors vary from colorless to browns or greens. Flattened a bit from side to side. Hindmost visible appendages tend to be longer than the anterior ones, and the terminal segments are splayed out to the side, allowing the animal to stand upright like a bicycle with training wheels. Most in our tanks live by scraping algae off the substrate. They are good fish food and seem to know it, so they are seldom visible during the day. They can be cultured in a refugium. *Chaetomorpha crassa* algae is a good species for amphipod culture, as are the various filamentous green algae referred to as "hair algae."

CIROLANIDS ON THE HEAD OF A BATFISH

Cirolanidae, cf. *Lironeca*
Cirolanids (cirolanid isopods, fish lice)

Maximum Size: To about 3 in. (7.5 cm) long; most about 0.4 to 1 in. (1 to 2.5 cm) long.
Range: All seas.
Minimum Aquarium Size: Small tanks, 10 gal. (38 L) or larger.
Lighting: Immaterial.
Foods & Feeding: Large family of species that are scavengers, parasites, and predators. The latter two groups attack live fishes.
Aquarium Suitability/Reef Aquarium Compatibility: Predatory and parasitic forms are extremely dangerous. Will even attack and suck the blood of aquarists.
Captive Care: Cirolanid isopods have a pointed front end, a streamlined tapered body, short antennae, and big eyes on the front of the head. Generally white or mottled gray. Enter tanks riding on a fish or in a piece of live rock. If you spot one on a fish, it must be removed with forceps; transfer the fish to a hospital tank treated with antibiotics until the fish's wound heals. If the isopod leaves the fish you can 1) remove the fish and wait 2-3 months until you are sure the isopod is gone 2) remove all live rock and sand and discard it. If you do nothing, it is likely that the isopods will kill off your fishes one by one.

LEBBEUS GRANDIMANUS, A TEMPERATE SHRIMP, WITH A WHITE TUMOR ISOPOD

Epicaridae species
Shrimp tumor isopods

Maximum Size: To about 1 in. (2.5 cm) long; most smaller.
Range: All seas.
Minimum Aquarium Size: Small tanks, 10 gal. (38 L) or larger.
Lighting: Immaterial.
Foods & Feeding: These isopods are blood suckers that parasitize shrimp.
Aquarium Suitability/Reef Aquarium Compatibility: Pests. Occasionally found in captivity on shrimps.
Captive Care: These isopods appear as large, often whitish, lumps on the sides of shrimp. They are difficult or impossible to remove. The first isopod to infect the shrimp host becomes female. It attaches to the upper part of the shrimp's legs under the carapace, then alters its shape to grow over them. Subsequent isopods turn into small males fastened to the female. As the female grows, sucking the blood of the host, she loses most of her pill-bug shape and grows into a large white mass that may render its host sterile. As the host shrimp grows, the isopod molts along with it and grows as well. The original infection occurs through an intermediate host not found in captivity; a tumor isopod on a shrimp will not infect other shrimps in the aquarium.

Odontodactylus scyllarus (peacock mantis shrimp): adult female bearing a large mass of reddish-colored eggs. Note large, mobile eyes on blue stalks.

Introduction to Mantis Shrimps

Mantis shrimps sometimes go by their subclass name Hoplocarida, a name that is particularly apt. *Hoplites* were the soldiers of ancient Greece who carried long spears, and *carida* are shrimps. So the name "hoplocarid" would be translated as "spear-carrying soldier shrimps." It fits.

Mantis shrimps are unmistakable. They have what appears to be a lobster's abdomen attached to a preying mantis's thorax, topped by a head all their own. The main characteristic of the head is the presence of large, very mobile eyes. Clasped to the front of the thorax are a pair of large, raptorial appendages. These are tipped with a claw, whose tip points backward and closes like a jackknife. Because there are many species, the color varies considerably, but the most common ones in captivity are generally studies in greens and browns. Some may be very brightly colored, even dazzling, like *Odontodactylus scyllarus* (above and on pages 236 and 238).

These are predatory, highly territorial, and reasonably intelligent crustaceans. Most of them appear to be predators on fishes or other

Odontodactylus scyllarus (peacock mantis shrimp): exceptionally eyecatching but a menace to other reef animals, this predator deserves a species tank of its own.

crustaceans, but our data about their natural history is fairly limited. The largest mantises may be the size of a small lobster, but most in aquariums are on the order of 1 to 2 inches (2.5 to 5 cm) long, and maybe 0.2 to 0.4 inches (5 to 10 mm) wide. These animals live in burrows, caves, or holes. Often the first indication that an aquarist has a mantis shrimp is the appearance of a couple of eyes staring back at him or her from a hole in the live rock. Another indication is the unexplained loss of fishes, snails, or hermit crabs in their systems.

Mantis shrimps catch their prey with large, clawed appendages. There are basically two types of mantis shrimps, distinguished primarily by the way they kill their prey. In one lineage, the claws are exceptionally sharp, and the shrimps capture their prey by a slicing strike. Even a moderately sized slicing mantis shrimp is capable of slicing a fish the size of a damselfish in half. Biologists find this rather impressive.

The other lineage kills its prey by striking a forceful blow with the claws. The force of the strike is generally sufficient to kill the prey outright, and in some large striking mantis shrimps, it is roughly equivalent to the force of a .22 caliber bullet as it exits the muzzle of a gun. They have been known to shatter the glass walls of a large aquarium. Aquarists find this quite impressive.

Fisherfolk familiar with these shrimps know them as "thumb-splitters." The same force that can dispatch a fish in a single blow or break aquarium glass can inflict deep, painful wounds on incautious hands. Treat these animals with respect.

In general, most reefkeepers do not want to discover a mantis shrimp in their tanks. This may seem reasonable in some ways, but in actuality, most small mantis shrimps are not a problem. If the tank is well fed, the mantis shrimps may simply eat the food put in by the aquarist, just like all the other inhabitants. If there are no noticeable mortalities, these shrimps can probably be left in the system indefinitely.

However, some mantis shrimps are not reef-safe and must be removed. Various traps are available commercially, but the shrimps are often not attracted to the trap. Perhaps the easiest way to rid your tank of a mantis shrimp is to note where its hole or den is, then remove that rock. Once out of the aquarium, the rock can be held over a pail, and carbonated water (which will not harm most of the animals on the rock) can be poured into the hole. This often causes the mantis to abandon the hole and fall into the bucket.

If you need to remove such an animal from your system and want to collect it rather than kill it, I would urge you to set it up in a small aquarium of its own. These are fascinating animals, fully capable of learning to know their keepers and respond to them. They make very interesting pets that thrive under standard reef conditions if given a cave of their own and sufficient food.

Odontodactylus scyllarus
Peacock mantis shrimp

Maximum Size: To about 6 in. (15 cm) long; most smaller.
Range: Indo-Pacific.
Minimum Aquarium Size: Moderate tanks, 20 gal. (76 L) or larger.
Lighting: Prefers dim lighting.
Foods & Feeding: Requires meaty foods. Will eat snails, fishes, or other crustaceans. Will take diced fish, krill, and some prepared foods. Feed regularly.
Aquarium Suitability/Reef Aquarium Compatibility: Not a community tank animal, but is an exceptionally good pet in a species tank. Handle with care; it can inflict deep wounds.
Captive Care: Among the most colorful reef animals, this is a bottom-living, nocturnal carnivore and is a "smash-strike" mantis shrimp. Needs rocks arranged as a burrow or cave, but will do a lot of remodeling. A fully grown peacock mantis is capable of shattering the glass walls of most aquariums, but it can be kept in acrylic tanks. They are among the most intelligent, if not *the* most intelligent, of the arthropods. It will soon learn to recognize different people and respond to them differently. Has a lot of "personality" and makes an engaging aquarium resident. It will feed heavily and requires good filtration.

Alpheus spp.
Pistol shrimps

Maximum Size: To about 3 in. (7.6 cm) long; most smaller.
Range: All tropical seas.
Minimum Aquarium Size: Small tanks, 10 gal. (38 L) or larger.
Lighting: Prefer dim lighting.
Foods & Feeding: Some take live foods like snails, fishes, or other crustaceans. Most will take diced fish, krill, and some prepared foods.
Aquarium Suitability/Reef Aquarium Compatibility: Some are good community animals, others are not. Generally, those without a symbiont are short-lived.
Captive Care: Generally symbiotic, these small shrimps live curious lives with various partners from gobies to crinoids. Several are found living with burrowing gobies, where they share the fish's burrow. If both the shrimp and goby are available, they make an attractive aquarium display. Burrowing gobies need a deep sand bed for the construction of their home. Many *Alpheus* species appear to be primarily nocturnal and do best in a dimly lit aquarium. These shrimps have a pair of dissimilarly sized claws. Their name comes from their ability to produce a loud cracking or snapping noise with their large "clicker claw," which may be as big as their thorax.

Hymenocera picta
Harlequin shrimp

Maximum Size: To about 2 in. (5 cm) long; most smaller.
Range: Indo-Pacific.
Minimum Aquarium Size: Small tanks, 10 gal. (38 L) or larger.
Lighting: Normal reef lighting.
Foods & Feeding: Needs live sea stars as food. Almost any star will do. The chocolate-chip star (*Protoreaster nodosus*) is commonly used.
Aquarium Suitability/Reef Aquarium Compatibility: Does well in a standard reef tank if provided with live sea stars to eat. This kind of feeding may result in significant water fouling; good filtration is a must.
Captive Care: This is a small, bizarrely shaped animal. The claws are enlarged and almost circular in outline. Body color is white to tan or yellow, and the body and all appendages are mottled with large red, magenta, or pink spots. It is surprisingly cryptic against a background of coralline algae-covered rubble. Its diet is specific; nothing else will do but live sea stars. It has been observed to dine on the legs first, leaving the oral disc for last, and in the process keeping the star alive as long as possible. This species is eaten by some larger fishes and presumably its color pattern developed under natural selection for protection.

Lysmata amboinensis
Pacific scarlet cleaner shrimp (skunk cleaner shrimp)

Maximum Size: To about 2 in. (5 cm) long.
Range: Indo-Pacific.
Minimum Aquarium Size: Small tanks, 10 gal. (38 L) or larger.
Lighting: Normal reef lighting.
Foods & Feeding: Efficient scavenger; will eat most aquarium foods.
Aquarium Suitability/Reef Aquarium Compatibility: Suitable aquarium animal. May take food from corals, sea anemones, and other slower creatures and may have a deleterious effect on them.
Captive Care: This animal will groom parasites and debris from fishes and make for an interesting display of reef behavior. Do not add excess iodine as it may cause premature molting and lower life expectancy. It normally lives two to three years in captivity. There is a bright white stripe running the length of the top of the body, from the front of the animal to the tip of the tail fan. This mid-back white stripe terminates at a wide white spot at the end of the body in front of the tail fan. There is also a discrete red gap between it and a wedge of white on the tail fan, and there is no white edging on the tail fan; however, there are white dots at the front and rear of the fan on each edge.

Lysmata californica
Peppermint shrimp (Catalina cleaner shrimp)

Maximum Size: To about 2 in. (5 cm) long.
Range: From the subtropical eastern Pacific.
Minimum Aquarium Size: Small tanks, 10 gal. (38 L) or larger.
Lighting: Normal reef lighting.
Foods & Feeding: Efficient scavenger; will eat most aquarium foods.
Aquarium Suitability/Reef Aquarium Compatibility: Suitable for cool water aquariums only. May take food from corals, sea anemones, and other slower creatures and may have a deleterious effect on them.
Captive Care: Although sometimes collected and sold without proper labeling, this is not a tropical animal and will not survive long in tanks kept at normal reef temperatures. The only special care *Lysmata californica* needs is a cool-water tank: 50 to 68°F (10 to 20°C). This animal is nocturnal and reclusive—it is often never seen after it is added to a tank. Tends to eat small polyps; may attack small soft coral polyps, such as *Clavularia*, zoanthids, and both small- and large-polyped stony corals. Sometimes this predation is significant. It will not eat *Aiptasia*. It has a pale white, yellow, or amber body with numerous longitudinal stripes running from the front of the body to the end of the abdomen.

Lysmata debelius
Fire shrimp (scarlet cleaner shrimp, blood shrimp)

Maximum Size: To about 1.2 in. (3 cm) long.
Range: Indo-Pacific.
Minimum Aquarium Size: Small tanks, 10 gal. (38 L) or larger.
Lighting: Prefers dim lighting.
Foods & Feeding: Efficient scavenger; will eat most aquarium foods.
Aquarium Suitability/Reef Aquarium Compatibility: Nocturnal, reclusive, often not visible. Some may eat only polyps, such as soft corals, zoanthids, and small stony corals.
Captive Care: Regarded by many as the most beautiful of the many attractive *Lysmata* species, *L. debelius* has a scarlet or blood-red body with only a few white freckles on the anterior end. Antennae and legs are brilliant white, and true to this type of advertisement, it is, at least occasionally, a cleaner shrimp. Some fire shrimp reportedly prey primarily on polyps. A single individual in a small reef may seriously impact soft corals, small-polyped stony corals, or zoanthid colonies. Needs no special care, although it should have some sort of cave or hole in the rockwork in which to take shelter. In a low-light tank, this shrimp may even be visible during the day, whereas in a normal reef tank, it may never be seen.

Lysmata grabhami
Caribbean scarlet cleaner shrimp

Maximum Size: To about 2 in. (5 cm) long.
Range: Caribbean.
Minimum Aquarium Size: Small tanks, 10 gal. (38 L) or larger.
Lighting: Normal reef lighting.
Foods & Feeding: Efficient scavenger; will eat most aquarium foods.
Aquarium Suitability/Reef Aquarium Compatibility: Suitable aquarium animal. May take food from corals, sea anemones, and other slower creatures, and may have a deleterious effect on them.
Captive Care: Both in the wild and in the reef aquarium, this attractive shrimp cleans fishes and may climb all over them, picking at and removing parasites, dead tissue, and debris. It may be very useful in preventing disease. Not bothered by most other animals, with the exception of the banded coral shrimp (*Stenopus hispidus*). Does best in pairs or small groups. Do not add excess iodine, which will cause premature molting and lower life expectancy. Normally lives two to three years in captivity. The antennae (feelers) and some anterior appendages are brilliant white. There is a white stripe running the length of the top of the body; the tail fan has a thin white stripe along each outer edge.

Lysmata wurdemanni
Peppermint shrimp

Maximum Size: To about 1.5 in. (4 cm) long.
Range: Caribbean.
Minimum Aquarium Size: Small tanks, 10 gal. (38 L) or larger.
Lighting: Normal reef lighting.
Foods & Feeding: Efficient scavenger; will eat most aquarium foods.
Aquarium Suitability/Reef Aquarium Compatibility: Suitable aquarium animal. May take food from corals, sea anemones, and other slower creatures and may have a deleterious effect on them.
Captive Care: This shrimp has a tendency to eat small polyps and may thus may benefit the hobbyist who is plagued with a case of the pest anemone *Aiptasia*, which this shrimp is reputed to eat. *Lysmata wurdemanni* is nocturnal and reclusive and lives up to four years. The only special care needed is a cave or space in the rockwork for shelter. Aquarists may never see it once it is added to the tank. Has a pale white, yellow, or amber body with numerous longitudinal stripes about 0.25 to 0.5 mm in width running from the front of the body to the end of the abdomen. Legs and body are pale orange; the legs have no yellow or white stripes. May change color significantly over a short time, depending on its physiological condition and stress state.

FEMALE WITH PINK EGG MASS UNDER ABDOMEN

Periclimenes holthuisi
Purple-spotted commensal shrimp

Maximum Size: To about 2 in. (5 cm) long.
Range: Tropical Indo-Pacific.
Minimum Aquarium Size: Small tanks, 10 gal. (38 L) or larger.
Lighting: Immaterial.
Foods & Feeding: Symbiotic on various corals and anemones. May eat tentacles or other bits of anemone flesh; may also eat mucus or scavenge carrion.
Aquarium Suitability/Reef Aquarium Compatibility: Generally interesting and harmless. Occasionally may cause problems to their hosts.
Captive Care: This shrimp is an ectoparasite or commensal on a number of different hosts, including anemones and corals. It always does best under the conditions that support the best growth of its host, which it may need both for protection and nutrition. It tends to do best on a larger anemone or coral, as the host may need to be large enough to withstand the low-level but continual predation by the shrimp. This shrimp has a transparent body with deep blue or purple spots trimmed with white, and red eyes. The chelipeds (claw-bearing appendages) are blue, banded with purple.

Periclimenes venustus
Venustus commensal shrimp

Maximum Size: To about 2 in. (5 cm) long.
Range: Tropical Indo-Pacific.
Minimum Aquarium Size: Small tanks, 10 gal. (38 L) or larger.
Lighting: Immaterial.
Foods & Feeding: Symbiotic on various anemones worldwide in the Tropics. Some eat tentacles or other bits of anemone flesh; may also eat anemone mucus or scavenge carrion.
Aquarium Suitability/Reef Aquarium Compatibility: Some are fine in captivity. Others, particularly those from the Indo-Pacific, may cause problems to their host anemones.
Captive Care: This delicate and beautiful shrimp lives in a possibly ectoparasitic relationship with an anemone (or occasionally a coral, as in the photograph above). Will do best under the conditions that support the best growth of its host. Should not be kept in a tank without its host, as this will cause stress and make the shrimp prone to disease. May need its host for proper nutrition as well, and always tends to do best on a larger anemone, as the anemone needs to be large enough to withstand the low-level but continual predation by the shrimp. This is a slender shrimp, mostly transparent, with long white antennae.

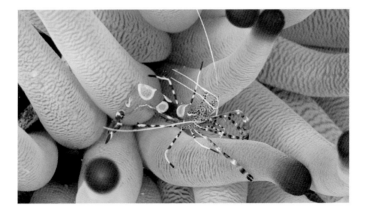

Periclimenes yucatanicus
Spotted commensal shrimp (spotted cleaner shrimp)

Maximum Size: To about 2 in. (5 cm) long.
Range: Caribbean.
Minimum Aquarium Size: Small tanks, 10 gal. (38 L) or larger.
Lighting: Immaterial.
Foods & Feeding: Symbiotic on various anemones. Some eat tentacles or other bits of anemone flesh; may also eat anemone mucus or scavenge carrion.
Aquarium Suitability/Reef Aquarium Compatibility: Generally only slightly damage host. May be fine if there is enough food to scavenge.
Captive Care: Found on several anemones and originally considered a harmless commensal, it may, in fact, be ectoparasitic, feeding on the anemone's tissues. Has the long, white antennae characteristic of cleaner shrimps and may be a cleaner as well. Its cryptic color and behavior of hiding on its host leaves no doubt that it gets protection from its host. The host anemone must be large enough to withstand the low-level but continual predation by the shrimp. The shrimp will do best under the same conditions that support its host. Should not be kept without its host as this will stress the shrimp and leave it prone to disease. May need its host for proper nutrition as well.

RHYNCHOCINETES DURBANENSIS

Rhynchocinetes **spp.** (*R. brucei, R. durbanensis, R. hiatti, R. rigens, R. rugulosus, R. uritai*)
Camelback shrimps (hinge-beak prawns)

Maximum Size: To about 1.6 in. (4 cm) long.
Range: Tropical seas.
Minimum Aquarium Size: Small tanks, 10 gal. (38 L) or larger.
Lighting: Immaterial.
Foods & Feeding: Feed on small polyps. Scavenge food.
Aquarium Suitability/Reef Aquarium Compatibility: Prey on corals and other polyps. Not reef aquarium safe, except in very large tanks with a healthy growing population of various polyps. Nocturnal.
Captive Care: These small shrimps are attractive, with bright white stripes or spots surrounded by maraschino-cherry-red lines, but are a mixed blessing for most aquariums. They are very active at night and can be seen gleaning materials off rocks and other hard substrates, and a few in a tank will reduce the net growth of zoanthids or star polyp colonies to zero. Named for the pronounced "hump" on their abdomens, these species are exceptionally similar in color pattern and general morphological features. They all have large compound eyes that reflect a brilliant copper or red light in the beam of a flashlight at night.

Rhynchocinetes uritai (camelback shrimp): note characteristic body shape for which this group is named. Males have larger pincers.

Rhynchocinetes hiatti (camelback shrimp): the prominent upward tilt of the rostrum (the foremost extension of the carapace) is typical of this genus.

Rhynchocinetes sp. (camelback shrimp): a mixed blessing in reef tanks, they prey on polyps, including noxious *Aiptasia* anemones but also many desirable species.

Rhynchocinetes hiatti (camelback shrimp): note large eyes, typical of this group of shrimps, also known as hinge-beak prawns.

Saron marmoratus, Saron spp.
Saron shrimps

Maximum Size: To about 4 in. (10 cm) long.
Range: Indo-Pacific.
Minimum Aquarium Size: Moderate tanks, 50 gal. (190 L) or larger.
Lighting: Immaterial.
Foods & Feeding: Feed on small polyps. Scavenge food.
Aquarium Suitability/Reef Aquarium Compatibility: Prey on corals and other polyps. Not reef aquarium safe. Will do well in their own system.
Captive Care: These large, attractive shrimps need plenty of hiding places. If added to an established aquarium with lots of live rock, they do well but are seldom seen, except at night. They do best in typical reef conditions, but they prey on small animals, including small polyps, such as zoanthids, star polyps, and perhaps small corals. They will eat most aquarium foods; without polyps to eat, they are reasonably good scavengers. Given their habits, they may be more appropriate for reef tanks featuring primarily fishes, rather than corals. Probably the most common species seen in the aquarium trade is *Saron marmoratus*, a large shrimp with mottled red and white on a greenish or gray background. They have a pair of exceptionally well-developed clawed appendages located anteriorly on the thorax.

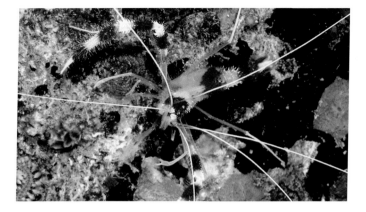

Stenopus hispidus
Banded coral shrimp

Maximum Size: To about 4 in. (10 cm) long.
Range: Tropical seas.
Minimum Aquarium Size: Moderate tanks, 50 gal. (190 L) or larger.
Lighting: Immaterial.
Foods & Feeding: Scavenger. Most meaty foods are fine.
Aquarium Suitability/Reef Aquarium Compatibility: Aggressive; may attack other shrimps and crustaceans. Preys on snails and worms.
Captive Care: *Stenopus hispidus* is a hardy animal that is often a first invertebrate for many beginning aquarists. It will actively clean fishes, but is a facultative predator on other animals, as well as being a scavenger. Will eat polychaete worms and will sometimes decimate a population of these helpful animals. Tends to be very aggressive toward other crustaceans, and may attack and kill scarlet cleaner shrimps, camelback shrimps, or hermit crabs. This shrimp is best kept singly or in mated pairs to avoid deadly battles between individuals. It is generally harmless to other reef aquarium inhabitants, although it will sometimes remove food from corals or sea anemones. Its antennae are white in the manner of other cleaner shrimps, and the body and legs are distinguished by violet or red bands.

STENOPUS SCUTELLATUS

Stenopus scutellatus = Golden coral shrimp
Stenopus zanzibaricus = Yellow banded coral shrimp

Maximum Size: To about 2 in. (5 cm) long.
Range: *S. scutellatus*, Caribbean; *S. zanzibaricus*: Indo-Pacific.
Minimum Aquarium Size: Moderate tanks, 50 gal. (190 L) or larger.
Lighting: Immaterial.
Foods & Feeding: Scavenger. Most meaty foods are fine.
Aquarium Suitability/Reef Aquarium Compatibility: Aggressive; may attack other shrimps and crustaceans. Predatory on snails and worms.
Captive Care: These species are cleaner shrimps as well as scavengers and, at times, facultative predators on smaller animals. They will eat polychaete worms and will sometimes decimate a population of these helpful animals. Tend to be very aggressive toward other crustaceans, and may attack and kill other cleaner shrimps, camelback shrimps, or hermit crabs. Generally harmless to other reef inhabitants except bristleworms and the occasional snail, although they will sometimes remove food from corals or sea anemones. Both are yellow to amber with bands of red and white on the abdomen and chelipeds (pincer claws). *Stenopus scutellatus* has long white antennae; those of *Stenopus zanzibaricus* are red. Often fight to the death with *Stenopus hispidus* and generally lose these battles.

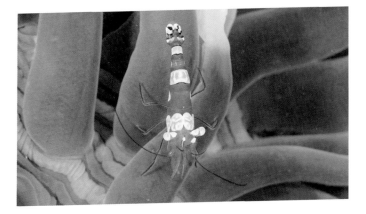

Thor amboinensis
Anemone shrimp (sexy shrimp)

Maximum Size: To about 0.75 in. (2 cm) long.
Range: Tropical seas.
Minimum Aquarium Size: Small tanks, 10 gal. (38 L) or larger.
Lighting: Immaterial.
Foods & Feeding: Scavenger. Most meaty foods are fine. Probably grazes on its host anemone's tissues.
Aquarium Suitability/Reef Aquarium Compatibility: Good aquarium animal. Harmless to most reef aquarium animals.
Captive Care: This tiny shrimp commonly lives on larger anemones. In the Caribbean, it is often found on the Caribbean carpet anemone (*Stichodactyla helianthus*, page 97); in the Indo-Pacific, it may be found on most of the larger anemones. It is a gregarious shrimp, living in groups of several individuals on an anemone, and should be kept in groups of three or more. Characterized by its small size, white patches, and green or tan basic color, it is easily recognizable. Aggressive clownfishes, such as *Amphiprion clarkii*, do not tolerate them well and often kill them. This shrimp may eat anemone tissues or mucus but is relatively harmless and may make an interesting aquarium specimen if left alone by the resident fishes.

Enoplometopus spp.
Flame lobsters (reef lobsters)

Maximum Size: Larger species to 6 in. (15 cm) long; most smaller.
Range: Tropical seas.
Minimum Aquarium Size: Moderate tanks, 50 gal. (190 L) or larger.
Lighting: Immaterial.
Foods & Feeding: Scavengers. Will accept most meaty foods.
Aquarium Suitability/Reef Aquarium Compatibility: Good aquarium animals. Harmless to most reef aquarium inhabitants. Need vigorous water movement.
Captive Care: About the size and shape of crayfish, these lobsters are much more strikingly colored. Reds and oranges are dominant, but some species have prominent purple and lavender markings. Because they are from the more energy-intensive parts of the reef, they need good water movement. They are facultative predators/scavengers, but despite their rather awesome claws, they are relatively harmless in a reef tank. Will do best in a species tank, but because of their size, they should not be confined to a tank much smaller than 50 gallons. In a community tank, they should be given much more room to diffuse their "picking" tendencies. They are primarily nocturnal and will be reclusive during the day.

Palinurellus wieneckii
Mole lobster

Maximum Size: To about 6 in. (15 cm) long.
Range: Indo-Pacific.
Minimum Aquarium Size: Moderate tanks, 50 gal. (190 L) or larger.
Lighting: Immaterial.
Foods & Feeding: Scavenger. Accepts most meaty foods. Preys on some reef aquarium animals.
Aquarium Suitability/Reef Aquarium Compatibility: Will eat shrimps, clams, and snails, but is an otherwise attractive aquarium animal.
Captive Care: This unusual animal lacks large claws and is related to the large spiny lobsters found most frequently on restaurant platters. Lives in caves or rock piles and may burrow into sediments. May also construct a burrow in the sand of an aquarium bottom. Reclusive and nocturnal, but in its own tank it will often learn to be out during the day. Needs a moderate to large tank of its own, or a large reef aquarium that is sufficiently productive to allow low-level continuous predation. Will not bother corals or soft corals, but often associates with large anemones and attempts to live around the base, causing clownfishes that live with the anemone to become very stressed. Generally orange, covered with fine spines and hairs.

Panulirus versicolor
Blue spiny lobster

Maximum Size: Including antennae, to about 40 in. (1 m) long.
Range: Tropical seas.
Minimum Aquarium Size: Large tanks, 100 gal. (380 L) or larger.
Lighting: Immaterial.
Foods & Feeding: Scavenger. Accepts most meaty foods. Preys on some reef aquarium animals.
Aquarium Suitability/Reef Aquarium Compatibility: Will eat fishes, shrimps, clams, and snails; otherwise an attractive aquarium animal.
Captive Care: This is a large, commercially important species, but juveniles make surprisingly good aquarium inhabitants, with brilliant blue and white markings and long white antennae. It is a good scavenger, but will eat small snails, clams, hermit crabs, or sea urchins. Nocturnal feeder; reclusive during the day and will hide in caves. Requires good water movement as well as caves or sand in which to burrow. If well fed, its predatory needs seem to be largely defused; small ones of less than 3 in. (8 cm) will grow rapidly, molting frequently. Will not bother cnidarians, but fishes, particularly those that hide in caves at night, are at risk when the lobster is small. When the lobster is fully grown, all mobile animals are at risk.

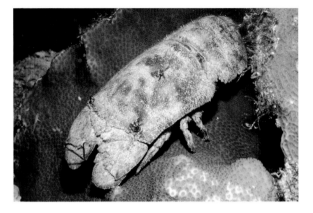

Arctides spp., *Parribacus* spp.
Slipper lobsters (bulldozer lobsters)

Maximum Size: Including antennae, to about 12 in. (30 cm) long.
Range: Tropical seas.
Minimum Aquarium Size: Large tanks, 100 gal. (380 L) or larger.
Lighting: Immaterial.
Foods & Feeding: Scavengers. Most meaty foods are fine. Prey on some reef aquarium animals.
Aquarium Suitability/Reef Aquarium Compatibility: Fascinating aquarium animals, but will eat fishes, shrimps, clams, and snails.
Captive Care: Slipper lobsters may be thought of as spiny lobsters with small, flat, shovel-shaped antennae instead of the usual long, tapering spines. They tend to be somewhat duller in coloration than the spiny lobsters. They are predators on smaller invertebrates. They do well in a tank devoted to them or in a very large reef tank. In a normal reef tank, they will eat snail populations, many worms, and other animals. Corals and soft corals are generally safe with them, but they tend to grow too large for many crowded reefs. There are a number of genera and probably a couple of dozen species from tropical or subtropical seas worldwide.

CALAPPA CALAPPA

Calappa spp.
Shameface crabs

Maximum Size: To about 12 in. (30 cm) across the carapace.
Range: Tropical seas.
Minimum Aquarium Size: Large tanks, 100 gal. (380 L) or larger.
Lighting: Immaterial.
Foods & Feeding: Predatory on snails; must be fed live large snails.
Aquarium Suitability/Reef Aquarium Compatibility: Not reef aquarium animals, but will do well in a species tank devoted to them. Handle with care to avoid injury from their powerful claws.
Captive Care: *Calappa* species are easily identified by the large, flattened claws that are held in front. These make them appear as though they are hiding behind the claws in "shame"—hence the common name. They prey on snails—their claws are very well designed for the destruction of snail shells. One claw holds the shell and the other is used to open it like an old-fashioned can opener. They must be provided with a deep sand bed, as most species live on or bury into sand. Given the mechanical advantage inherent in their claws, it is best if the aquarist takes care not to be grabbed by them. They also use their claws to bury themselves and may disappear into a deep sand bed with surprising rapidity.

CYCLOCOELOMA TUBERCULATA

Majidae species
Decorator crabs (spider crabs)

Maximum Size: To about 12 in. (30 cm) across the leg span.
Range: Tropical seas.
Minimum Aquarium Size: Moderate tanks, 50 gal. (190 L) or larger.
Lighting: Immaterial.
Foods & Feeding: Prey on small animals. Scavenge aquarium foods.
Aquarium Suitability/Reef Aquarium Compatibility: Not reef-safe, although they make an interesting display in a tank of their own.
Captive Care: Decorator and spider crabs are closely related, decorator crabs differing primarily in having groups of hooklike spines located at various places on their bodies. They attach bits of debris, sponges, algae, tunicates, or other animals to these hooks, becoming quite camouflaged. Novice aquarists often think that having a decorator crab in their tank is a good thing, but it soon becomes apparent that they prey on many sessile or slow-moving invertebrates like hermit crabs, clams, and feather dusters, and the crab often rearranges its camouflage to match its new home by tearing off pieces of soft corals, zoanthids, sponges, and other decorative items to attach to its body. Can easily devastate a tank.

Mithrax sculptus
Emerald crab

Maximum Size: To about 2 in. (5 cm) across the leg span.
Range: Caribbean.
Minimum Aquarium Size: Small tanks, 10 gal. (38 L) or larger.
Lighting: Immaterial.
Foods & Feeding: Mostly herbivorous on algae, but also preys on small animals and will scavenge aquarium foods.
Aquarium Suitability/Reef Aquarium Compatibility: Relatively safe herbivore, but there have been occasional reports of it attacking sessile animals.
Captive Care: This small spider crab is, true to its name, predominantly green. Unlike most of its kin, it neither decorates itself nor preys very often on living animals. Truly an oddity among crabs, it is mostly herbivorous. It seems to prefer adherent fleshy green algae, but will eat other types. This is one of the few aquarium animals that will eat bubble algae, which may occasionally reach plague proportions in some tanks. *Mithrax sculptus* requires normal reef aquarium conditions, plenty of algae, and some rockwork, but is otherwise undemanding.

Percnon gibbesi
Sally Lightfoot crab

Maximum Size: To about 4 in. (10 cm) across the leg span.
Range: Caribbean, Indo-Pacific.
Minimum Aquarium Size: Moderate tanks, 50 gal. (190 L) or larger.
Lighting: Immaterial.
Foods & Feeding: Small ones are somewhat herbivorous; larger specimens are distinctly predatory. Will scavenge if appropriate prey are not present in the tank.
Aquarium Suitability/Reef Aquarium Compatibility: Not reef safe. Large specimens get aggressive, predatory, and destructive.
Captive Care: This speedy, flattened spider crab has a small body, long legs, and an endearing common name. A better name for it might be "Jekyll and Hyde crab"—it will seem to be a benign aquarium inhabitant for several months and then will undergo a personality shift, probably due to sexual maturity. The male's claws enlarge and their bases swell to accommodate the larger muscle mass. The crab lunges at and often catches fishes. Large ones will tear apart sea anemones and corals to get their gut contents, and they will feast on small hermit crabs. These crabs are very fast and nearly impossible to catch, except in baited traps.

Stenorhynchus seticornis
Arrow crab

Maximum Size: To about 6 in. (15 cm) across the leg span.
Range: Caribbean.
Minimum Aquarium Size: Large tanks, 100 gal. (380 L) or larger.
Lighting: Immaterial.
Foods & Feeding: Will scavenge most aquarium foods. Also preys on many smaller animals.
Aquarium Suitability/Reef Aquarium Compatibility: Very aggressive. Does well under normal reef aquarium conditions, but will do best in tanks over 150 gal. (570 L).
Captive Care: The arrow crab is an unusual, interesting animal, but with a mixed, even nasty reputation in reef tanks. It will attack other crustaceans, such as banded coral shrimps. Its claws are small, and while is does not usually bother most sessile invertebrates, it will destroy polychaete annelid populations, which are some of the better reef aquarium scavengers. Predation on these annelids will be significantly deleterious. Arrow crabs also scavenge on excess food, but not as much as on the polychaetes they kill. If a lot of caves are provided in the tank, they will survive, but will not thrive. They are not bothered by most fishes.

NEOPETROLISTHES MACULATA

Neopetrolisthes maculata, Neopetrolisthes ohshimai, Neopetrolisthes spp.

Anemone crabs (porcelain crabs)

Maximum Size: To about 2 in. (5 cm) across the leg span.
Range: Indo-Pacific, Caribbean.
Minimum Aquarium Size: Small tanks, 10 gal. (38 L) or larger.
Lighting: Immaterial.
Foods & Feeding: Feed on larger particulate foods suspended in the water column. Some also scavenge aquarium foods.
Aquarium Suitability/Reef Aquarium Compatibility: Good aquarium animals. Most starve to death due to a lack of sufficient planktonic foods.
Captive Care: These crabs are commensals that live on large anemones, particularly clownfish-host anemones in the Indo-Pacific. They differ from "standard" crabs in having only three pairs of thoracic walking legs. The last (fourth) pair is reduced and folded up over the back of the thorax. Their claws are large, flattened, and roughly elliptical. A pair of large appendages is located on the front underside of the thorax and remains out of sight until the animal feeds. Looking like large, frilled baskets, these mouthparts are like nets waved through the water to catch particulates, such as zooplankton. Clownfishes may drive these crabs off their anemone, resulting in the crab's death.

Petrolisthes spp.
Porcelain crabs

Maximum Size: To about 2 in. (5 cm) across the leg span.
Range: All seas.
Minimum Aquarium Size: Small tanks, 10 gal. (38 L) or larger.
Lighting: Immaterial.
Foods & Feeding: Suspension feeders or scavengers. Will eat most meaty aquarium foods.
Aquarium Suitability/Reef Aquarium Compatibility: Good aquarium animals. Scavengers.
Captive Care: Porcelain crabs that do not live on anemones are common and intriguing. They are slower than most of the "standard" crabs, and probably because of this, many of them have adapted a rather startling defense: If stressed, as they back away, they will drop off one or both of their big claws, which continue to move and presumably keep the predator's attention while the crab scuttles away to safety. They are reclusive and nocturnal. Provide plenty of rockwork as they shelter in rock crevices. Often a shade of tan, brown, dark green, or black, they are flattened, have three pairs of walking legs and large diamond-shaped or elliptical claws. Claws held on the ends of their folded appendages are often larger than the rest of the crab.

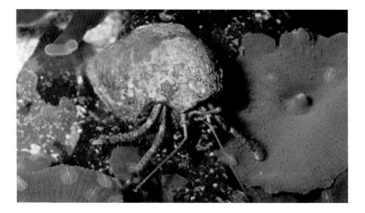

Clibanarius tricolor
Blue leg hermit crab

Maximum Size: About 0.75 in. (1.9 cm) across the leg span.
Range: Caribbean.
Minimum Aquarium Size: Small tanks, 10 gal. (38 L) or larger.
Lighting: Immaterial.
Foods & Feeding: Will scavenge on most aquarium foods. Prefers meaty items and will prey on many smaller animals.
Aquarium Suitability/Reef Aquarium Compatibility: Reef aquarium safe only in concentrations of one crab or fewer per 10 gallons.
Captive Care: This is a "busy" species, constantly moving or plucking at rocks or substrate, eating small snails, small polyps, or other minute animals. Will attack, kill, and eat snails and wear their shells. Removes food from sessile invertebrates, such as corals, sea anemones, and soft corals. In nature, it is relatively rare on reefs, often being more common in sandy areas near the reef. Does well in standard reef temperatures and conditions. Provide it with a good supply of empty snail shells of various sizes to accommodate growth (shells should be larger than the one the crab has when it is added to the tank). In large numbers, this species can do a lot of damage in a reef tank.

Paguristes cadenati
Scarlet hermit crab

Maximum Size: About 1.5 in. (3.8 cm) across the leg span.
Range: Caribbean.
Minimum Aquarium Size: Small tanks, 10 gal. (38 L) or larger.
Lighting: Immaterial.
Foods & Feeding: Will scavenge most aquarium foods. Prefers meaty items and also preys on many smaller animals.
Aquarium Suitability/Reef Aquarium Compatibility: Reef aquarium safe only in concentrations of 1 crab or fewer per 10 gallons.
Captive Care: Often recommended as a reef scavenger, this bright red or red-orange crab can do significant damage if introduced in large numbers. Will eat small snails, small polyps, or other minute animals. Will attack, kill, and eat snails and wear their shells. Will attack and remove food from sessile invertebrates like corals, sea anemones, and soft corals. May significantly and negatively impact many other animals found in the system. In nature, it is relatively rare on the reef, being more common in sandy areas near the reef. Needs a good supply of empty snail shells in the tank. To accommodate growth, these shells should be larger than the one the crab has when it is put into the tank.

Paguristes digueti
Red leg hermit crab

Maximum Size: About 2.5 in. (6.4 cm) across the leg span.
Range: Gulf of California.
Minimum Aquarium Size: Small tanks, 10 gal. (38 L) or larger.
Lighting: Immaterial.
Foods & Feeding: Will scavenge most aquarium foods. Also preys on many smaller animals.
Aquarium Suitability/Reef Aquarium Compatibility: Reef aquarium safe only in concentrations of 1 crab or fewer per 10 gallons.
Captive Care: This dull red or scarlet hermit is often sold as a beneficial scavenger, but in large numbers it can do a lot of damage in a reef aquarium. It prefers animal flesh and will eat small snails, small polyps, or other minute animals. Will attack, kill, and eat snails and wear their shells. Will attack and remove food from sessile invertebrates like corals, sea anemones, and soft corals. May significantly and negatively impact many other animals found in the system. In nature, it is relatively rare on the reef, being more common in sandy areas near the reef. Provide it with a good supply of empty snail shells to accommodate growth (shells should be larger than the crab's current shell).

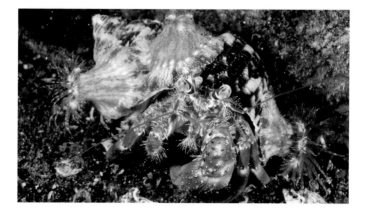

Dardanus pedunculatus
Anemone hermit crab

Maximum Size: About 4 in. (10 cm) across the leg span.
Range: Indo-Pacific.
Minimum Aquarium Size: Large tanks, 100 gal. (380 L) or larger.
Lighting: Immaterial.
Foods & Feeding: Will scavenge most aquarium foods. Also preys on many smaller animals.
Aquarium Suitability/Reef Aquarium Compatibility: Reef aquarium safe only in large tanks.
Captive Care: The anemone hermit crab is readily identified by its green eyes and claws with spines on the outer surface. The body is red, orange, and white, but the color pattern varies a bit with age and the animal's condition. It covers its snail shell with sea anemones (from the genus *Calliactis*, see page 99). The anemones provide both camouflage and protection for the crab. This crab is too large and potentially predatory for long-term survival in a small or moderate-sized coral reef tank. It needs normal reef conditions and, as with other hermit crabs, it will eat most anything. Because of its size, it may be able to catch and eat "sleeping" fishes during the night, although there are no confirmed reports of this behavior.

Petrochirus diogenes
Giant hermit crab

Maximum Size: About 12 in. (30 cm) across the leg span.
Range: Caribbean.
Minimum Aquarium Size: Large tanks, 100 gal. (380 L) or larger.
Lighting: Immaterial.
Foods & Feeding: Will scavenge most aquarium foods. Also preys on many smaller animals.
Aquarium Suitability/Reef Aquarium Compatibility: Neither appropriate for nor safe in a reef aquarium.
Captive Care: Probably the largest hermit crab in the Caribbean, this species is found inhabiting queen conch (*Strombus gigas*) shells. (It is rumored to kill and eat full-grown queen conchs.) It is distinguished by its large size, green or blue eyes, and the "scaly" appearance of the appendages created by a covering of numerous short spines. Like all large hermit crabs, it will eat whatever it can catch or scavenge, but this crab is not herbivorous. Crabs this size are capable of killing fishes or eating even well-protected animals like sea urchins. Seldom found on reefs, but common in nearby sandy areas. It is occasionally collected and will do well if given a large tank with a good sand bed. Requires normal conditions of salinity and temperature.

Pycnogonid species
Sea spiders

Maximum Size: About 12 in. (30 cm) across the leg span; aquarium forms seldom exceed 1 in. (2.5 cm) in leg span.
Range: All seas.
Minimum Aquarium Size: Small tanks, 10 gal. (38 L) or larger.
Lighting: Immaterial.
Foods & Feeding: Prey on many desirable animals, such as bryozoans, hydroids, corals, zoanthids, etc.
Aquarium Suitability/Reef Aquarium Compatibility: Not reef tank safe. Not venomous.
Captive Care: These odd, spiderlike animals hitchhike into systems on new livestock they had been preying upon. They may move slowly and deliberately, with a body that is long and thin like a soda straw and seems to function as nothing more than a hinge for the leg attachments. They generally have simple eyes located on a tubercle (a rounded protrusion) on the trunk. The number of legs—four, five, or six pairs—varies with species and gender. Males always have an extra pair of legs they use to carry egg masses that the female deposits. There is no separate head; the front of the body is elongated into a proboscis, a long tube terminating in a small mouth with three jaws.

LIMULUS POLYPHEMUS

Carcinoscorpio **spp.,** *Limulus polyphemus,* *Tachypleus* **spp.**
Horseshoe crabs

Maximum Size: About 24 in. (61 cm) long.
Range: Eastern Atlantic, Eastern Pacific.
Minimum Aquarium Size: Large tanks, 100 gal. (380 L) or larger.
Lighting: Immaterial.
Foods & Feeding: Their preferred prey are animals living in a deep sand bed. Will scavenge most meaty aquarium foods.
Aquarium Suitability/Reef Aquarium Compatibility: Not suited to most home aquariums. Tend to starve in most systems.
Captive Care: These are true living fossils with a complex and thoroughly alien appearance. They are bulldozers capable of significantly rearranging a tank. They can strip a sand bed of noticeable life, after which they starve. They can easily become wedged in live rock formations, and are simply not suited to most reef tanks. Viewed from above, there are three parts to the body: a large, rounded, shield-shaped prosoma; a squarish middle opisthosoma; and a long, narrow tail spike. Horseshoe crabs have large compound eyes, and midway between the front eyes lies a small group of single eyes. Six pairs of appendages are found under the prosoma. The mouth faces the rear between the bases of the anterior appendages.

Sipunculid species
Peanut worms

Maximum Size: About 6 in. (15 cm) long; most smaller.
Range: All seas, buried deep in burrows.
Minimum Aquarium Size: Small tanks, 10 gal. (38 L) or larger.
Lighting: Immaterial.
Foods & Feeding: Detritus feeders.
Aquarium Suitability/Reef Aquarium Compatibility: Good reef aquarium scavengers. Harmless.
Captive Care: Found in live rock, these urn-shaped worms have a long, tapered front end and lack a head or segments. They do well in normal reef conditions, but their populations dwindle as they suffer occasional mortality from hermit crabs or fishes. May be about the size of a peanut, but most are smaller. The long, tapered end typically bears a cluster of small, moplike tentacles, and the mouth is between their bases. When it feeds, it contracts its body and the internal pressure forces a long tapered end, called an "introvert," to expand. It unrolls from the inside out, like pushing out the finger of a glove. It will expand outward and begin to daub the substrate, collecting particulate material to be eaten. When the worm is startled or finished eating, powerful retractor muscles pull back the introvert.

Polyplacophora
Chitons (coat-of-mail shells)

Maximum Size: About 12 in. (30 cm) long; most far smaller.
Range: All seas.
Minimum Aquarium Size: Small tanks, 10 gal. (38 L) or larger.
Lighting: Immaterial.
Foods & Feeding: Grazing herbivores.
Aquarium Suitability/Reef Aquarium Compatibility: Good reef aquarium animals. Harmless.
Captive Care: Chitons are extreme algae eaters that can even harvest the hard, green, calcareous algae that sometimes predominates on aquarium walls. They can easily rasp sandstone to pieces and have even been reported to rasp grooves in acrylic tanks. They are flattened, oval mollusks with eight shells on their backs. Around the edge of the animal is a tissue flap, called the "girdle," enclosing the shells. They fasten to the substrate with a large foot located on the bottom surface. There are no eyes, and other sensory structures are "obscure." When feeding, a strong toothed structure, the "radula," is pushed out of the mouth and pulled across the substrate, rasping algae or sponges and other sessile invertebrates. The strength of the teeth on the radula is legendary: they are hardened with iron oxide salts (hematite).

Tridacna crocea (crocea clam): the smallest of the giant clams, but one of the most flamboyantly pigmented invertebrates on the coral reef.

Introduction to Giant Clams
(Class Bivalvia; Family Tridacnidae)

Giant clams, or tridacnids, are favorite reef animals, and many aquarists are able to keep them successfully—growing impressively large specimens and witnessing spawning events in their aquariums.

These often stunningly pigmented clams have a symbiotic association with zooxanthellae, which provide much of the energy the clam needs to survive and thrive. The zooxanthellae are found living in the mantle of the clam, which in normal clams faces downward. Through evolution, the tridacnid body has rotated so that the mantle and shell gape are positioned upward. Presumably, this allows maximum irradiation of the zooxanthellae. Contrary to popular opinion, it is not the zooxanthellae that give the clams their sometimes brilliant colors. The credit goes to iridophores, pigment holding cells that protect the clam against UV radiation.

The two shells of the tridacnid are hinged together, and near the hinge is a region where the shells do not meet. The foot will extend

Tridacna maxima (maxima clam): heavily overharvested in the wild for the Asian restaurant trade, giant clams for aquarists are now sustainably aquacultured.

through this hole, referred to as the byssal hole, or gape, allowing the animal to move or to cling to the substrate by the use of fibers (byssal threads) secreted by the foot.

As adults, these are all large clams. Indeed, *Tridacna gigas* is the largest clam, and may reach lengths well in excess of 4.25 feet (1.3 m). Tridacnids generally require a lot of light, often quite a bit more than some hobbyists are willing or able to provide.

In nature, some *Tridacna* species, particularly *T. crocea* and *T. squamosa*, are found in the shallowest—and brightest—of reef areas. Aquarium lighting must correspond to this intensity for good clam health. Some of the other species are capable of living in lower-light regimes, but with tridacnids, the more light, the better. Temperature and salinity should be within normal reef aquarium conditions. Calcium levels must be kept high, as for stony corals, in the 400 ppm+ range to support shell grow. Some experienced clam keepers recommend maintaining pH no higher than 8.3.

Additionally, these are suspension-feeding animals, and they need a lot of food to survive, particularly as juveniles. In nature, until their shell length exceeds about 4 inches (10 cm), the majority of

Tridacna squamosa (squamosa or fluted clam): giant clams are difficult to identify with certainty by their colorful mantles alone. This may be a *squamosa* hybrid.

their nutrition comes from feeding. When the clam is smaller, the volume of the mantle tissue is simply not large enough to provide space for enough zooxanthellae to keep the clam going. Even after that point, food in the form of phytoplankton or dissolved organic matter such as ammonium nitrate is necessary to supplement the production of algal photosynthate from the zooxanthellae. Fortunately, with the advent of phytoplankton foods, feeding of the clams is relatively easy, but it must be done on a regular schedule for the animals to thrive.

Healthy clams will respond to stimuli by closing their shells or withdrawing their mantles. Clam hinges are held together by a proteinaceous ligament that tends to force the clam to open. Consequently, closing is an active process, while gaping is passive. If a clam is injured or dying, the closure response is often weak or slow. If a clam does not voluntarily close its shell or attempt to after it has been stimulated, it has died and should be removed from the tank. Before buying any clam, be sure it reacts to a hand passing over it, throwing a shadow. It the clam fails to close quickly, leave it where it is. Any clam that appears to be gaping open with no closing reflex

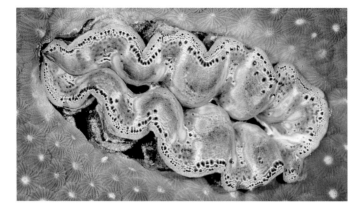

Tridacna crocea (crocea clam): when purchasing a clam, be sure it is healthy and reacts by closing its shell rapidly when your hand casts a sudden shadow over it.

is probably never going to recover.

These clams are also subject to parasitism from a couple of sources. The most dangerous parasites are the small, pyramidellid snails in the genera *Tathrella*, *Pyrgiscus*, and possibly some others. These are small snails, about the size of a grain of rice or smaller. They are found around the edges of the mantle tissue or around the byssal gape. Pyramidellids punch holes in the clam's tissues and suck blood. In nature, each clam probably has a few of these bloodsuckers and can tolerate them. In an aquarium, however, they do not disperse and will accumulate on the clams. The numbers become great enough that they may easily overwhelm a clam. To prevent their occurrence, all clams should be well scrubbed with a toothbrush (to remove snails and adherent snail egg masses) prior to placing them in an aquarium. Subsequently, the clams should be inspected regularly for a couple of months, and any visible snails removed.

These large bivalves may also contain small shrimps and crabs that live in the mantle cavity and are ectoparasites or commensals. Although these can be removed from the clams, they will probably do no harm to healthy animals.

Hippopus hippopus
Hippopus clam (horse-hoof clam)

Maximum Size: About 16 in. (41 cm) long.
Range: Indo-Pacific.
Minimum Aquarium Size: Moderate tanks, 50 gal. (190 L) or larger.
Lighting: Needs brightly illuminated conditions.
Foods & Feeding: Zooxanthellate, but needs to feed for growth. Small juveniles, under 2 to 4 in. (5 to 10 cm), can be difficult to keep, needing phytoplankton and special feeding to grow.
Aquarium Suitability/Reef Aquarium Compatibility: Excellent reef aquarium animal.
Captive Care: This clam may have coloration that is muted compared to some *Tridacna*, but it is still attractive, with mantle colors ranging from light tan or brown through green. The byssal opening is small. This species is easy to keep and, as with all giant clams, gains grandeur with increasing size. The mantle typically bears thin linear markings. The shell is asymmetrical, without scutes or flutes, and has thin brown or reddish stripes parallel to the outer edges. Shells can close tightly in mature specimens. Place in a bed of sand or coral rubble with room to grow. As with all tridacnids, buy farm-raised specimens rather than wild-caught.

Tridacna crocea
Crocea clam

Maximum Size: About 6 in. (15 cm) long.
Range: Indo-Pacific.
Minimum Aquarium Size: Moderate tanks, 50 gal. (190 L) or larger.
Lighting: Needs brightly illuminated conditions.
Foods & Feeding: Zooxanthellate, but needs to feed for growth. Small juveniles, under 2 to 4 in. (5 to 10 cm), can be difficult to keep, needing phytoplankton and special feeding to grow.
Aquarium Suitability/Reef Aquarium Compatibility: Excellent reef aquarium animal.
Captive Care: This is the smallest of the giant clams. Brilliant blues and greens are typical mantle colors. This can be a challenging clam to keep, having a large byssal opening under the animal, where parasites can enter and problems can start. On the reef, these clams occupy crevices and holes, presumably for protection, and should be placed on a hard substrate in the aquarium. They are found in very shallow water in equatorial regions, so bright lighting is a must. This clam has shells with a concentric sculpture of numerous small, projecting blades.

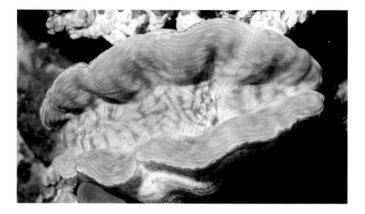

Tridacna derasa
Derasa clam (smooth giant clam)

Maximum Size: About 18 in. (46 cm) long.

Range: Indo-Pacific.

Minimum Aquarium Size: Moderate tanks, 50 gal. (190 L) or larger.

Lighting: Needs brightly illuminated conditions.

Foods & Feeding: Zooxanthellate, but needs to feed for growth. Small juveniles, under 2 to 4 in. (5 to 10 cm), can be difficult to keep, needing phytoplankton and special feeding to grow.

Aquarium Suitability/Reef Aquarium Compatibility: Excellent reef aquarium animal.

Captive Care: One of the larger *Tridacna*, this species can make a dramatic display in an aquarium. It is characterized by a mantle often colored with greens and blues, but brown individuals tend to predominate in the reef hobby. The shell is without concentric sculpture or has low ridges or blades. Most individuals in nature are found on hardpan substrates, but some are found in sand. Small individuals with a shell length of less than 4 in. (10 cm) get most of their nutrition from phytoplankton filtered from the water, so the clam needs consistent feedings of phytoplankton, preferably of different types. This species is aquacultured and commonly available.

Tridacna gigas
Gigas clam (giant clam)

Maximum Size: Over 4.25 ft. (1.3 m) long. Large specimens are very rare due to overfishing.

Range: Indo-Pacific.

Minimum Aquarium Size: Large tanks, 100 gal. (380 L) or larger.

Lighting: Does well under bright illumination but not required.

Foods & Feeding: Zooxanthellate, but needs to feed for growth. Small juveniles, under 2 to 4 in. (5 to 10 cm), can be difficult to keep, needing phytoplankton and special feeding to grow.

Aquarium Suitability/Reef Aquarium Compatibility: Excellent reef aquarium animal.

Captive Care: This is the largest living clam species; the shell may weigh in excess of 500 lbs. (227 kg). Shell lacks prominent concentric sculpture and is deeply folded. Mantle is usually brown to black, occasionally green, with blue spots or rings surrounding lenses that reflect light into zooxanthellate chambers. Typically found on sand, coral rubble, or hard substrates in deeper waters, it is less demanding of intense light. Small clams (less than 4 in. [10 cm] long) get most of their nutrition from phytoplankton filtered from the water, so they need consistent feedings with phytoplankton.

Tridacna maxima
Maxima clam

Maximum Size: About 16 in. (41 cm) long.

Range: Indo-Pacific.

Minimum Aquarium Size: Large tanks, 100 gal. (380 L) or larger.

Lighting: Needs brightly illuminated conditions.

Foods & Feeding: Zooxanthellate, but needs to feed for growth. Small juveniles, under 2 to 4 in. (5 to 10 cm), can be difficult to keep, needing phytoplankton and special feeding to grow.

Aquarium Suitability/Reef Aquarium Compatibility: Excellent aquarium animal. Somewhat more challenging to keep than *T. gigas*, *T. derasa*.

Captive Care: The most widespread of the tridacnids. Closely related to *T. crocea*, this species has many of the same dramatic colors in the mantle; however, it has a wider range of base colors. Recorded colors literally range from black to white. Mantle coloration varies with locality. Most natural specimens lack the iridescence prized by aquarists. When fully extended, a prominent row of hyaline organs (mistakenly called eyespots) is found around the edge of the mantle. Shell has concentric sculpture of numerous low blades or plates; small individuals may be distinguished from *T. crocea* only by dissection. Needs to be placed on hard substrates.

Tridacna maxima (maxima clam): no two are exactly alike, and aquarists covet rare specimens such as this. Note hyaline organs dotting the edge of the mantle.

Tridacna maxima (maxima clam): the most widespread of the giant clams, it often embeds itself in reef fissures or even within stony coral colonies, as here.

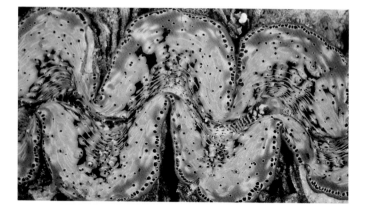

Tridacna maxima (maxima clam): hyaline organs (lenticular openings that focus light on the zooxanthellae) are clearly visible as black dots lining the mantle edge.

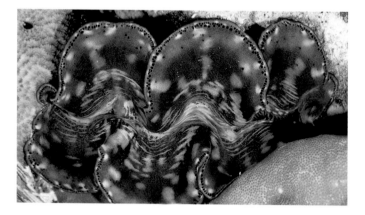

Tridacna maxima (maxima clam): colors are mostly a function of genetics, and clam farms in the Indo-Pacific select for alluring pigmentation such as this.

Tridacna squamosa
Squamosa clam (fluted clam)

Maximum Size: About 16 in. (41 cm) long.
Range: Indo-Pacific.
Minimum Aquarium Size: Large tanks, 100 gal. (380 L) or larger.
Lighting: Needs brightly illuminated conditions.
Foods & Feeding: Zooxanthellate. For small juveniles, phytoplankton is necessary for good health and good growth.
Aquarium Suitability/Reef Aquarium Compatibility: Excellent reef aquarium animal. Small juveniles, under 2 to 4 in. (5 to 10 cm), can be difficult to keep, needing phytoplankton and special feeding to grow.
Captive Care: Highly variable in color and mantle patterning, *T. squamosa* is relatively hardy and often a long-lived addition to a reef aquarium. This clam has shells with a distinctive concentric sculpture of numerous scutes, blades, or plates. The shell is folded radially, but not as much as with *Tridacna gigas* (page 283). Small individuals with a shell length of less than 4 in. (10 cm) get most of their nutrition from phytoplankton that they filter from the water, so the animal needs consistent feedings with phytoplankton, preferably of several different types. Older clams are easier to keep. This species lives in crevices, so place it on firm substrate, not sand.

LIMA SCABRA

Lima lima, Lima scabra
Flame scallops

Maximum Size: About 3.5 in. (9 cm) in diameter.

Range: Caribbean, Indo-Pacific.

Minimum Aquarium Size: Small tanks, 10 gal. (38 L) or larger.

Lighting: Prefer dim lighting, and seek out dim areas, such as caves.

Foods & Feeding: Substantial amounts of phytoplankton are necessary for good health and good growth.

Aquarium Suitability/Reef Aquarium Compatibility: Good reef aquarium animals. Impossible to maintain without phytoplankton additions.

Captive Care: White shells shaped as rounded triangles. Ridges radiate from the hinge to the bottom of the shell. These are crossed by concentric rings of small spines, giving the shell surface an appearance and texture like a rasp. The tissues are blaze orange to red; many long sensory tentacles extend outward from the mantle. Do well under normal reef salinity and temperature, but need lots of food for good health. Are reclusive and will hide. The brilliant beauty of the tentacles extending from a cave may make keeping them worthwhile. Should not be kept with mobile predators like whelks, large sea stars, hermit crabs, or true crabs. Many fishes will also pluck at and kill them.

Lopha cristagalli
Zig-zag oyster (cockscomb oyster, sawtooth oyster)

Maximum Size: Up to 3.5 in. (9 cm) in length.
Range: Indo-Pacific.
Minimum Aquarium Size: Moderate tanks, 50 gal. (190 L) or larger.
Lighting: Immaterial.
Foods & Feeding: Substantial amounts of phytoplankton are necessary for good health and good growth.
Aquarium Suitability/Reef Aquarium Compatibility: Good reef aquarium animals. Impossible to maintain without phytoplankton additions.
Captive Care: Striking in its zig-zag growth pattern. Imported occasionally into the aquarium hobby on its own, it shows up more frequently attached to a gorgonian as a small animal. It grows rapidly if given good amounts of phytoplankton and normal reef conditions of temperature and salinity. Predatory fishes, crabs, hermit crabs, and some shrimps will impact the animal, feeding on its exposed tissues. Some whelks will bore holes into such clams and eat them. Without predators, and if the clams are given the appropriate food, they should do well and make an attractive addition to a tank. Bright lighting is unnecessary and probably a negative influence.

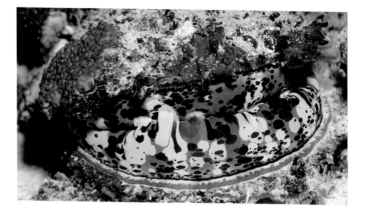

Spondylus spp.
Thorny oysters

Maximum Size: Up to 8 in. (20 cm) across the spines; most smaller.
Range: Tropical seas.
Minimum Aquarium Size: Moderate tanks, 50 gal. (190 L) or larger.
Lighting: Immaterial.
Foods & Feeding: Substantial amounts of phytoplankton are necessary for good health and good growth.
Aquarium Suitability/Reef Aquarium Compatibility: Good reef aquarium animals. Impossible to maintain without phytoplankton additions.
Captive Care: Shells are round and "inflated," covered with long calcareous spines formed from radial sculpturing on both shells; spines are longer on the more exposed upper shell. Immobile as adults. Must be oriented in the position they had when collected, as they have good balance sensory organs and will become stressed if positioned upside down or at odd angles. Under such stress they may not feed and will die. Exposed mantle tissue is often brilliant red, yellow, orange. Do well under reef normal conditions. Perfect animals for a tank where the low-light intensity would help prevent algal fouling. Predatory animals, such as shrimps, crabs, hermit crabs, whelks, and "nipping" fishes should be excluded from the tank.

Cypraea tigris (tiger cowrie): grazing snails that arrive in marine aquariums range from very plain and inconspicuous to highly ornamental, such as this cowrie.

Introduction to Grazing Snails

Some of the most commonly kept and badly mistreated animals in the reef hobby belong to the group of snails that can be loosely called top and turban shells. Taxonomically, these are placed in the Families Trochidae and Turbinidae, of the Phylum Mollusca, Class Gastropoda. There are several hundred species in each family, and there is much overlap in general shape. All have conical coiled shells, with no anterior spout or tube. The aperture tends to be circular, and the outside coil of the shell tends to have smooth or slightly rounded edges. Only a few species show some other shell sculpturing, and these few are generally in the genus *Astraea* and its near relatives. If viewed from above, shells of some of these animals tend to exhibit a multi-arm star shape, giving *Astraea* species the common name "star shells." However, most species in the rest of the grazing snail group are bereft of much obvious sculpturing.

The body of these animals extends out of the circular aperture and is often strikingly colored. There are two eyes, each located at the base of a large tentacle on either side of the head. Numerous

Astraea sp. (star shell): although popular and very useful as algae grazers, many snails are overstocked by inexperienced aquarists and tend to starve in captivity.

small sensory tentacles (typically eight), extend out from the shell aperture on each side and behind the animal. The basic natural history is relatively similar throughout all the groups. These are almost all grazing herbivores that tend to eat small adherent algae, such as diatoms, dinoflagellates, or macroalgal sporelings that they can dislodge from the substrate. Most cannot cut algal tissues, so they cannot eat macroalgae.

The two groups differ regarding one easily discernable characteristic. Animals in the Family Turbinidae, which contains the *Turbo* and *Astraea* species, have a white calcareous operculum, or plug, to the shell's aperture. The animals in the Family Trochidae, which includes *Tegula* and several other lineages, have a brown, proteinaceous or horny operculum.

There are differences of natural habitat as well. The *Turbo* and *Astraea* spp. collected for the reef hobby tend to come from rubble or reef-flat areas. This makes a difference in their acceptability as aquarium wall grazers. Some of these, particularly *Astraea* spp., are never in natural environments where they are likely to be dislodged and land on their backs on the sand. Hence, they have never devel-

Ovula costellata (egg cowrie): egg cowries graze on soft corals and not on algae. Most aquarists would probably not wish to keep such predators in their reef tanks.

oped a righting reflex and will not be able to turn over. Some hobbyists claim that their snails are too "stupid" to turn over. It isn't the snails that are stupid, it is the hobbyist who puts the animals in foreign and inappropriate situations. Trochids tend to come from areas of reef walls and prominence where, if they are dislodged, they must turn over or be eaten by fishes. These have good righting reflexes.

These grazing snails are probably the most commonly imported animals for the aquarium trade. Literally millions are imported, only to be shipped under inadequate conditions and sent home with aquarists who promptly kill them by treating them poorly.

This is a real shame. These are sophisticated, advanced animals capable of long lives, and it is simply not acceptable to kill them because of a lack of understanding of their care. All snails have complex circulatory systems that require slow acclimation to changes in salinity. If otherwise stressed, as in the transport and movement from their home environments to an aquarium, even rapid minor changes in salinity can result in death. They need to be acclimated slowly over several hours, and if this is done well, they will survive.

Additionally, many dealers, distributors and hobbyists keep the salinities of their tanks far too low. Transporting these animals through and into such tanks will simply result in their demise. Such mortality is simply unacceptable and inhumane. Furthermore, these animals are often plunked into a tank with the idea that they will control all the algal problems that hobbyists have. In fact, all most of them can do is eat diatoms.

Additionally, they tend to need a lot of algal food to stay healthy. The standard aquarium practice of throwing a few dozen into a tank and then watching as they all die slowly over a few weeks from starvation certainly ranks right up there on the idiocy scale. If the hobbyist takes the time to introduce a few snails at a time, and then adds more if they are needed, a lot less mortality will result and the system will reach equilibrium more easily.

Provided there is enough food, once acclimated to a system these animals tend to do well and may live a long time. Some temperate turbinids will live more than 50 years. For tropical species, lifespans of a couple of decades should not be unusual.

If they are kept well, they will often reward the aquarist by reproducing. The males puff out quantities of white, smoky sperm, and the females may deposit quantities of tiny white, yellow, or orange eggs, often in a gelatinous mass that will dissolve over a couple of hours. Fertilization will occur in the tank's water, and an embryo will develop within a few hours. They pass through a rapid nonfeeding larval period of a few days, and will often survive this in a reef tank. Juveniles are sometimes seen a few weeks after spawning events. Some fishes, shrimps, crabs, hermit crabs, and brittle stars will eat these small snails, but occasionally a few make it to adulthood. Other potential pests or predators of adults include nipping fishes, such as copperbanded butterflyfishes (*Chelmon rostratus*), some *Centropyge* angelfishes, and virtually all hermit crabs. All of these animals will impact the snails to some degree.

Haliotis spp.
Abalones

Maximum Size: Variable from 0.8 in. (2.0 cm) to 7.8 in. (20.0 cm).
Range: Indo-Pacific.
Minimum Aquarium Size: Moderate, 50 gal. (190 L) to large tanks, 100 gal. (380 L) or larger, depending on the species.
Lighting: Must be sufficient to support healthy algal growth.
Foods & Feeding: These wholly herbivorous grazing animals need a tank with a good growth of various algae, diatoms.
Aquarium Suitability/Reef Aquarium Compatibility: Good reef aquarium animals. Harmless.
Captive Care: Abalones are related to limpets and are good, active grazers, with a radula (scraping mouthpart) that functions as a whisk broom, sweeping the substrate for food. They are very effective at removing diatoms, small algae, and detritus. Will not tolerate changes in salinity; abalones need full-strength saltwater. They acclimate very slowly to new water conditions—treat them accordingly. Shells are oval to elongate, shaped like an ear, with small breathing holes for exhaling water. The broad, flat foot adheres so strongly to the substrate that the shell will rip free of the body before it pulls free of the substrate. Some species are captive-bred.

Turbo spp.
Turban shells (*Turbo* grazers)

Maximum Size: Up to 6 in. (15 cm) long and wide; aquarium forms much smaller.
Range: All seas.
Minimum Aquarium Size: Nano tanks, 1 gal. (3.8 L) or larger.
Lighting: Must be sufficient to support healthy algal growth.
Foods & Feeding: These are wholly herbivorous grazing animals that need a tank with a good growth of diatoms and microalgae.
Aquarium Suitability/Reef Aquarium Compatibility: Good choice for reef aquariums, but some snails offered for sale, particularly those collected in Mexico, are subtropical animals and do not survive well when housed in normal reef temperatures.
Captive Care: Tropical *Turbo* spp. are good reef aquarium animals. They have conical, coiled shells and lack an anterior spout or tube. The aperture from which the body extends is circular. A white calcareous operculum, or plug, closes the aperture during retraction. The outside coil tends to have smooth or slightly rounded edges. Eyes are located at the base of a large tentacle on either side of the head. Numerous small and several (typically eight) sensory tentacles extend from the aperture on each side and behind the animal.

Astraea spp., *Lithopoma* spp.
Star shells

Maximum Size: Up to 4 in. (10 cm) long and wide; aquarium forms much smaller.

Range: All seas.

Minimum Aquarium Size: Nano tanks, 1 gal. (3.8 L) or larger.

Lighting: Must be sufficient to support healthy algal growth.

Foods & Feeding: These are wholly herbivorous grazing animals that need a tank with a good growth of diatoms and microalgae.

Aquarium Suitability/Reef Aquarium Compatibility: Tropical *Astraea* spp. and *Lithopoma* spp. are good reef aquarium animals.

Captive Care: Excellent grazing animals if not overstocked and allowed to starve slowly. Have conical, coiled shells with a circular aperture. Lack an anterior spout or tube; a white calcareous operculum (plug) seals the aperture during retraction. Circumference of the shell tends to have longitudinal ridges or raised spikes at regular intervals; viewed from above, they give the shell a star shape. In some species, this sculpturing is not prominent. White, tan, or beige body extends out of the circular aperture. Eyes are located at the base of a large tentacle on either side of the head. See pages 291-294 for advice about their proper stocking levels and care.

Grazing on algal films, diatoms, and cyanobacteria, *Astraea* and *Lithopoma* spp. function as good cleaners if not overstocked.

Astraea and *Lithopoma* spp. are often introduced by aquarists at the rate of one per gallon to control algae. This is a recipe for unnecessary snail deaths.

LIVE *COLONISTA* RETRACTED; NOTE PIT AT CENTER OF OPERCULUM.

Collonista spp.
Mini turbos (baby grazing snails)

Maximum Size: Up to 0.25 in. (6 mm) long and wide.

Range: Indo-Pacific.

Minimum Aquarium Size: Nano tanks, 1 gal. (3.8 L) or larger.

Lighting: Must be sufficient to support healthy algal growth.

Foods & Feeding: These are wholly herbivorous grazing animals that need a tank with a good growth of diatoms and microalgae.

Aquarium Suitability/Reef Aquarium Compatibility: Beneficial algal grazing reef aquarium animals.

Captive Care: True to their common name, these tiny grazers resemble baby or miniature *Turbo* snails. They are common hitchhikers into reef aquariums and do well in many tanks. They have conical, coiled white or mottled white and brown shells with a circular aperture; a white calcareous operculum, or plug, seals the aperture during retraction. They lack an anterior spot or tube. The shell is smooth with low spiral ridges or grooves. White, tan, or beige body extends out of the circular aperture. Eyes are located at the base of a large tentacle on either side of the head. Numerous small and several (typically eight) sensory tentacles extend from the aperture on each side and behind the animal. Reproduce well in some systems.

Tegula funebralis
Margarita snail (margarite snail)

Maximum Size: Up to 0.75 in. (1.9 cm) long and wide; most smaller.
Range: Eastern Pacific, from Central Alaska to Baja California.
Minimum Aquarium Size: Nano tanks, 1 gal. (3.8 L) or larger.
Lighting: Must be sufficient to support healthy algal growth.
Foods & Feeding: This is a wholly herbivorous grazing animal that needs a tank with a good growth of diatoms and microalgae.
Aquarium Suitability/Reef Aquarium Compatibility: Unsuitable for reef aquariums.
Captive Care: This snail has a conical, coiled black shell. Often the outer layer of the shell flakes off, showing the mother-of-pearl layer beneath. Shells have a circular aperture; lack an anterior spot or tube; have a calcareous operculum, or plug, to seal the aperture during retraction. Shell may or may not have low spiral ridges or grooves, and low radial annulations may be present; otherwise it is smooth. They come from the rocky intertidal of the Pacific coast of North America. Can tolerate short periods of warm water in the summer in nature. Can survive a few weeks or months in reef tanks, then they die from being slowly "cooked." Annual rings on the shell indicate they may live well over 100 years in their natural habitat.

Trochus spp.
Trochus **snails** (turban snails, top shells)

Maximum Size: Up to 3 in. (7.6 cm) long and wide; most smaller.
Range: Tropical seas.
Minimum Aquarium Size: Nano tanks, 1 gal. (3.8 L) or larger.
Lighting: Must be sufficient to support healthy algal growth.
Foods & Feeding: Wholly herbivorous grazers that must have a tank with a good growth of diatoms and microalgae.
Aquarium Suitability/Reef Aquarium Compatibility: Beneficial reef aquarium animals. Harmless to other invertebrates.
Captive Care: In an aquarium with enough algal growth to sustain them, these snails are good, long-lived grazers. Add only a few snails at a time; they will starve if overstocked. They have conical, coiled shells that resemble a child's top or a pyramid. Have a circular aperture; lack an anterior spot or tube. Shell often with spiral ridges, radial ridges, bumps, or a combination. Body may be strikingly or drably colored, depending on the species, and extends out of the circular aperture. Eyes located at the base of a large tentacle on either side of the head. Numerous small and several larger (typically eight) sensory tentacles extend from the aperture on each side and behind. Reproduce well in some systems. Will not eat macroalgae.

Tectus spp.
Pyramid top shells (*Tectus* snails)

Maximum Size: Up to 3 in. (7.6 cm) long and wide; most smaller.
Range: Tropical seas.
Minimum Aquarium Size: Nano tanks, 1 gal. (3.8 L) or larger.
Lighting: Must be sufficient to support healthy algal growth.
Foods & Feeding: Wholly herbivorous grazers that must have a tank with a good growth of diatoms and microalgae.
Aquarium Suitability/Reef Aquarium Compatibility: Beneficial reef aquarium animals.
Captive Care: These are active grazers and good reef aquarium animals. Add a few at a time. If overstocked, they will starve. Shells are conical, coiled, various colors, generally tans or browns; often with fine spiral ridges and beading. Have a circular aperture; lack an anterior spout or tube. Have a brown, horny operculum to seal aperture during retraction. Shell whorls lack noticeable swelling, so shell forms a smooth-sided cone. Eyes located at the base of a large tentacle on either side of the head. Numerous small and several larger (typically eight) sensory tentacles extend from the aperture on each side and behind. These snails will reproduce well in some systems.

Nerita spp.
Nerites

Maximum Size: Up to 1.5 in. (3.8 cm) long.
Range: Tropical seas.
Minimum Aquarium Size: Nano tanks, 1 gal. (3.8 L) or larger.
Lighting: Must be sufficient to support healthy algal growth.
Foods & Feeding: Feed on adherent microalgae.
Aquarium Suitability/Reef Aquarium Compatibility: Common reef aquarium animals. Harmless to beneficial.
Captive Care: There are many species in the genus *Nerita* and its close relatives, all grazers on algae. Some are nocturnal and others are creatures of tidepools and will move up on the aquarium walls above the water level—or even leave the tank. They can be hardy and good reef animals. Shells are rounded with a low apex; the aperture is semicircular and the inside edge often has several distinct "teeth" or folds in the calcareous shell material. Typically, the outer shell has spiral grooves or ridges. Shells are drab; black and browns predominate. A few are white with attractive striping. Nerites are harmless to other tank inhabitants. With sufficient food, they will lay many egg capsules on the aquarium walls. Reproduction and survival to recognizable juveniles is uncommon, but has occurred.

CERITHIUM LITTERATUM

Cerithium spp.
Ceriths

Maximum Size: Up to 6 in. (15 cm) long; most less than 1 in. (2.5 cm).
Range: All seas.
Minimum Aquarium Size: Moderate tanks, 50 gal. (190 L) or larger.
Lighting: Immaterial.
Foods & Feeding: Feed on detritus and algae or eat sediments to digest the resident organic material and bacteria.
Aquarium Suitability/Reef Aquarium Compatibility: Common reef aquarium animals. Harmless to beneficial. Need a deep sand bed.
Captive Care: *Cerithium* spp. have elongate, conical shells. Some species may form massive aggregations in the wild. They will plow through the substrate, eating detritus and sediments. They are tolerant of variation in water conditions, but do best in normal reef settings. If oriented with the aperture at the bottom, the spire may have seven or more whorls. Have a ridge or series of bumps where a whorl covers over the bottom of the whorl above it. Have a small brown or amber operculum for the aperture, which is oval and inclined outward from the shell's long axis. Another small notch occurs in the upper outer edge of the aperture where the whorl contacts the whorl above.

Cypraea tigris
Tiger cowrie

Maximum Size: Up to 4 in. (10 cm) long; most smaller.
Range: Indo-Pacific.
Minimum Aquarium Size: Large tanks, 100 gal. (380 L) or larger.
Lighting: Must be sufficient to support healthy algal growth.
Foods & Feeding: Need sufficient micro- and macroalgae growth to do well. May eat filamentous green (e.g., hair) algae.
Aquarium Suitability/Reef Aquarium Compatibility: Herbivorous—harmless to other invertebrates.
Captive Care: Tiger cowries are strikingly beautiful, active herbivores. In a well-secured tank, they will be an attractive and functional addition and are hardy and quite long-lived (over 10 years) if given good conditions. Their one aquarium drawback is that they get large and, like any snail of that size, they may become "blundering remodelers." All cowries have an ovoid shell, similar in shape to an American football flattened on the bottom, with an elongate slit running down the middle of the flattened bottom surface. Shells are highly polished, and the animal often extends the mantle up over the shell. Typically the shell is gray or tan with dark black or brown spots.

CYPRAEA ANNULUS

Cypraea annulus, Cypraea moneta, Cypraea obvelata
Money cowries (ring cowries)

Maximum Size: Up to 1 in. (2.5 cm) long.
Range: Indo-Pacific.
Minimum Aquarium Size: Small tanks, 10 gal. (38 L) or larger.
Lighting: Must be sufficient to support healthy algal growth.
Foods & Feeding: Eat filamentous green algae, diatoms and small macroalgae.
Aquarium Suitability/Reef Aquarium Compatibility: Beneficial herbivores, harmless to other animals. May be at risk from hermit crabs.
Captive Care: The best cowries for reef tanks are the "money" or "ring" cowries and those animals related to them. These are the species listed above and several similar-appearing species. They are found on the shallow reef flats of the Indo-Pacific where they may be very abundant. Their habitat is one of extremes of temperature, making them very hardy and tolerant of both temperature and salinity extremes. They are active grazers and make excellent aquarium inhabitants. They are small, shells are white, light tan, or a pale dirty greenish-white, and are somewhat flattened with a more-or-less pronounced hump on the top. This hump is often surrounded by a gold or yellow line.

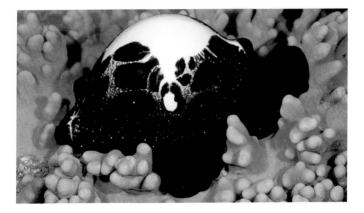

Ovula ovum
Egg cowrie (ovulid)

Maximum Size: Up to 3 in. (7.6 cm) long.
Range: Indo-Pacific.
Minimum Aquarium Size: Large tanks, 100 gal. (380 L) or larger.
Lighting: Immaterial.
Foods & Feeding: Prey on soft corals.
Aquarium Suitability/Reef Aquarium Compatibility: Dangerous predators; eat many types of soft corals.
Captive Care: *Ovula ovum*, and the other several similar species, should be avoided by most reef aquarists. They appear to be large cypraeid cowries (Family Cypraeidae), but are actually in a closely related but slightly different taxonomic group (Family Ovulidae), which contains a couple of dozen species, many of which are predators on various corals. If you are troubled by an excess of *Sarcophyton*, these are the animals for you. Otherwise, do not purchase or order them. Shells look rather like shiny eggs or glossy white, somewhat elongate cowries, with the aperture shifted to one side. The glassy white color is not found in any cypraeid cowrie. When the mantle is out they are extraordinarily beautiful: the mantle is jet black with white protuberances often tipped in gold.

CYPHOMA GIBBOSUM

Cyphoma gibbosum = **flamingo tongue** (leopard conch)
Cymbovula acicularis = **West Indian simnia**

Maximum Size: Up to 1.2 in. (3 cm) long.
Range: Caribbean.
Minimum Aquarium Size: Large tanks, 100 gal. (380 L) or larger.
Lighting: Must be sufficient to support healthy growth of its prey corals.
Foods & Feeding: Prey on gorgonians and other soft corals.
Aquarium Suitability/Reef Aquarium Compatibility: Not reef safe; difficult to feed.
Captive Care: These are beautiful predatory snails that eat the flesh off gorgonians and other soft corals, leaving only the harder skeletal parts. They cannot be maintained without a continual supply of live gorgonian foods. The elongate, highly polished shells range in color from white to salmon. *Cyphoma* is blunt-ended and has a ridge running equatorially across the animal. *Cymbovula* has tapered ends and lacks the ridge. A fleshy mantle, which is white or tan patterned with gold and black, covers the shell. On *Cyphoma*, the gold is in regular spots outlined in black; on *Cymbovula*, the gold and black form a pattern of intertwined, irregular lines. In both cases, the pattern acts to camouflage the snails on the gorgonians that they eat.

Lambis spp.
Spider conchs

Maximum Size: Up to 6 in. (15 cm) long.
Range: Indo-Pacific.
Minimum Aquarium Size: Large tanks, 100 gal. (380 L) or larger.
Lighting: Must be sufficient to support healthy algal growth.
Foods & Feeding: Herbivorous. Graze on all sorts of microalgae. May accept pelleted herbivore rations.
Aquarium Suitability/Reef Aquarium Compatibility: Good grazers. Harmless. Need a lot of open sand surface area.
Captive Care: As with the more common queen conchs (page 311), these interesting animals have large, prominent eyes and will often watch aquarists as avidly as they are being watched. They are totally herbivorous, relatively active snails. They need at least 4 ft.^{2} (0.4 m^2) of contiguous sand in a large patch. Eat diatoms and other fine algae, but will not usually attack hair algae. Need a lot of algae, and will not survive in tanks with only a few patches of algae or with many algae-eating competitors. Hermit crabs should not be put with these snails. The distinctive shell aperture flares widely; the outer edge of the aperture is 5 to 10 in. (13 to 25 cm) long; tubular, leglike extensions are often present, giving this conch its name.

Strombus alatus
Fighting conch

Maximum Size: Up to 4 in. (10 cm) long.
Range: Caribbean.
Minimum Aquarium Size: Large tanks, 100 gal. (380 L) or larger.
Lighting: Must be sufficient to support healthy algal growth.
Foods & Feeding: Herbivorous. Grazers on all sorts of microalgae. May accept pelleted herbivore rations.
Aquarium Suitability/Reef Aquarium Compatibility: Good grazer. Harmless. Needs a lot of open sand surface area.
Captive Care: The fighting conch is not aggressive. It moves with a lurching motion and may hop if threatened. With enough food, it will add up to an inch of shell length per month, reaching full size in about two years. It needs a lot of algae; only feed when on sand. Will not survive if there are other herbivores on the sand. Often buries in sand for a week or more. Hermit crabs will kill them. Individuals less than 0.75 in. (1.9 cm) long often climb on rocks and aquarium walls. The shell is brownish to chestnut inside; the outside is drab gray to brown, with small bumps on the rim of each whorl. The body is gray to pale drab green; a pair of large eyes with an evident iris and pupil are visible on tentacles at the front.

Strombus gigas
Queen conch

Maximum Size: Up to 16 in. (0.4 m) long.
Range: Caribbean.
Minimum Aquarium Size: Large tanks, 100 gal. (380 L) or larger.
Lighting: Must be sufficient to support healthy algal growth.
Foods & Feeding: Herbivorous. Grazer on all sorts of microalgae. May be fed pelleted herbivore foods.
Aquarium Suitability/Reef Aquarium Compatibility: Good grazer. Harmless. Needs a lot of open sand surface area.
Captive Care: Wild populations have been devastated by overfishing; specimens in the aquarium trade are aquacultured. Characterized by large eyes with an evident iris and pupil, it alertly surveys its surroundings. Will outgrow a small tank relatively rapidly. Needs a lot of algae; only feed when on sand. The shell inside is pink, peach, yellow, or orange; the outside is drab green or gray, with large bumps or low spines on the rim of each whorl. The shell aperture will flare widely at sexual maturity. The body is olive or pale drab green. Hermit crabs will kill them. Individuals less than 0.8 in. (2 cm) long often climb on rocks and aquarium walls, but larger, heavier conchs remain on the bottom substrate. Moves with a lurching motion.

Petaloconchus spp.
Caribbean worm snails

Maximum Size: Aggregations up to several feet; individuals 0.25 in. (6 mm) in diameter, 1.75 in. (4.5 cm) long.
Range: Caribbean.
Minimum Aquarium Size: Moderate tanks, 50 gal. (190 L) or larger.
Lighting: Immaterial.
Foods & Feeding: Feed on suspended particulate matter.
Aquarium Suitability/Reef Aquarium Compatibility: Uncommon reef aquarium animals; may hitchhike into tanks on live rock.
Captive Care: These are snails that fasten to rocks and send up a vertical tube. They look like a tube worm. Upon hatching, a juvenile snail crawls away from the parent's tube. Eventually, it glues itself to the substrate. It forms a loosely coiled shell mass and then sends up a more-or-less vertical tube. The end of the tube is plugged by an operculum when the animal withdraws. Feeds by extruding mucous strands from the tube's aperture. Particulate material adheres to the strands, and the animal then reels them in and eats them. These snails prefer moderate- and high-current areas. They will form moderate to large patch reefs in some areas. Similar, smaller species may become very common in reef aquariums.

Thyca crystallina
Linckia shell

Maximum Size: Up to 0.5 in. (1.3 cm) long.
Range: Indo-Pacific.
Minimum Aquarium Size: Large tanks, 100 gal. (380 L) or larger.
Lighting: Immaterial.
Foods & Feeding: Parasite on sea stars: *Linckia multifora, L. laevigata*.
Aquarium Suitability/Reef Aquarium Compatibility: Parasitic on *Linckia* sea stars and should be removed.
Captive Care: This hitchhiker is small and limpetlike, with a blue (on *Linckia laevigata*, see page 375) or occasionally tan (on *Linckia multifora*, see page 376) shell with a raised spire and prominent ridges. Lives on the surface of the sea star, and feeds by using its long, extensible proboscis to punch a hole in the echinoderm, often in the groove where the tube feet emerge, and sucking out fluids. Often, two shells are found on the star. If so, the larger is the female, the smaller the male. They generally do not kill their hosts, but they should be removed and disposed of. May be difficult to dislodge, but if jostled sufficiently by repeated small taps from some object, they may detach from their host. If this doesn't work, the aquarist may simply have to gently pull them off.

EPITONIUM BILLEEANUM

Epitonium spp. and related forms
Wentletraps

Maximum Size: Up to 2 in. (5 cm) long; most smaller.
Range: All seas.
Minimum Aquarium Size: Nano tanks, 1 gal. (3.8 L) or larger.
Lighting: Immaterial.
Foods & Feeding: Parasites; predators on cnidarians, such as corals, sea anemones, and soft corals.
Aquarium Suitability/Reef Aquarium Compatibility: Parasitic on corals, sea anemones, etc. Should be removed.
Captive Care: These attractive shelled animals typically arrive in an aquarium clinging to the side of their prey sea anemone or soft coral. The snails should be removed from the tank and disposed. They survive well under standard reef aquarium situations and can be quite voracious. To remove them from a valuable specimen, prodding with a rod or turkey baster will often cause them to detach. Shells are typically white, occasionally yellow or tan, and often have a series of ridges around the whorls. These ridges, parallel to the body's long axis, are almost paper-thin, and often very delicate. Ridges may flare out at the "corners" of the whorl. The aperture is oval, with no hint of a spout.

ARCHITECTONICA PERSPECTIVA

Architectonica spp., *Heliacus* spp.
Sundial shells

Maximum Size: Up to 2 in. (5 cm) in diameter; most about 0.4 in. (1 cm) in diameter.

Range: Tropical seas.

Minimum Aquarium Size: Small tanks, 10 gal. (38 L) or larger.

Lighting: Immaterial.

Foods & Feeding: Predatory on zoanthids.

Aquarium Suitability/Reef Aquarium Compatibility: Not suitable for reef aquariums.

Captive Care: Attractive and common, but cryptic and destructive; enter tanks on live rock or in zoanthid colonies. All zoanthids should be carefully inspected before being put into a tank. A light brushing with a soft toothbrush will often remove small snails. Sundials are nocturnal predators and may eat one or more zoanthid polyps in a night. If polyps are disappearing, examine the colonies at night for evidence of the snails. Shells are conical but appear discoidal. They are tan or beige and often have a series of brown markings on the top of the outer whorl that look like the markings on a sundial. The aperture is highly angular, with distinct corners; a small, pagoda-shaped plug closes the aperture when the animal withdraws.

CHARONIA VARIEGATA

Charonia spp.
Triton's trumpets

Maximum Size: Up to 24 in (0.6 m) long; most smaller.

Range: Tropical seas.

Minimum Aquarium Size: Large tanks, 100 gal. (380 L) or larger.

Lighting: Immaterial.

Foods & Feeding: Predators on live echinoderms: any large sea urchin or sea star. May eat "sleeping" fishes.

Aquarium Suitability/Reef Aquarium Compatibility: These ecologically important predators should not be collected, purchased, or kept. They have a very toxic and exceptionally acidic saliva. Significant quantities of this fizzy, poisonous slime are liberated during feeding. If you do happen to acquire one, the aquarium water should be largely changed after each meal.

Captive Care: These large snails have tan, gold, or peach shells with bands of brown or black lines and chevron markings. Predatory, their preferred prey are sea stars, including the crown-of-thorns, and sea urchins. Will resort to scavenging if no suitable prey are present. Small specimens are occasionally collected, but their potential large size and toxic saliva make them incompatible in most reef tanks. They should be left in the wild.

Pleuroploca gigantea
Horse conch

Maximum Size: Up to 24 in. (0.6 m) long; most smaller.
Range: Caribbean.
Minimum Aquarium Size: Large tanks, 100 gal. (380 L) or larger.
Lighting: Immaterial.
Foods & Feeding: Predators on live food; will eat almost anything.
Aquarium Suitability/Reef Aquarium Compatibility: Voracious predators not suitable for reef aquariums, but good for a "species" tank.
Captive Care: The horse conch is one of the largest snails known. An adult would wreak havoc in a reef tank, but juveniles may arrive uninvited on live rock. Juveniles have a bright orange or brilliant red body; shells are often black, occasionally red or orange. These small predators will attack and eat almost any smaller mobile animal, particularly smaller snails and clams. If well fed, they grow rapidly. They are hardy animals tolerant of temperature and salinity swings. Adults have a plain tan to pinkish shell, which may have a black or brownish proteinaceous layer on the outside. The aperture is almost triangular; the narrow apex of the triangle forms an extensive spout. Adult soft parts are tan, reddish, or brown. A plate of horny material plugs the aperture when the animal is withdrawn.

Nassarius spp.
Sand snails

Maximum Size: Up to 1 in. (2.5 cm) long; most smaller.
Range: All seas.
Minimum Aquarium Size: Small tanks, 10 gal. (38 L) or larger.
Lighting: Immaterial.
Foods & Feeding: Obligate scavengers on meaty foods. Will not eat detritus or attack healthy animals.
Aquarium Suitability/Reef Aquarium Compatibility: Good scavengers.
Captive Care: These small, whelklike snails may live decades in captivity, performing useful scavenging chores, if not overstocked and allowed to starve. Specialized to eat carrion, not live flesh, they will rapidly consume leftover food. If well fed, they lay small, circular egg masses on the aquarium walls, which develop for several days and then hatch, releasing planktonic larvae. They have a short, acutely bent spout or siphonal canal at the front end. A small groove around the front of the shell behind the curved spout is diagnostic and distinctive; no other small whelks have a similar structure. Typically gray, tan, or brown, but color is variable. The shell has low, longitudinal ridges running around it and often has spiral incised lines running around the body. Hermit crabs will kill and eat them.

Engina mendicaria
Bumblebee snail

Maximum Size: Up to 0.5 in. (1.3 cm) long; most smaller.
Range: Indo-Pacific.
Minimum Aquarium Size: Small tanks, 10 gal. (38 L) or larger.
Lighting: Immaterial.
Foods & Feeding: Predatory on other snails, worms.
Aquarium Suitability/Reef Aquarium Compatibility: Questionable addition to a reef tank. Will prey on beneficial animals in live sand and on live rock.
Captive Care: This small whelk has a shell that has spiraling yellow or white stripes resembling the yellow and black banding pattern of some wasps or bees. It is sold as and acts as a scavenger that will consume uneaten meaty food or carrion. However, an *Engina* individual will also prey on beneficial polychaetes and other snails in captivity. In tanks with sand beds, it is likely to eat sand-dwelling worms. This species is found in shallow water throughout the Indo-Pacific and is fairly hardy. Has a more-or-less rectangular aperture, with a thickened outer edge, which typically has several bumps extending into the aperture. In fully adult animals, the aperture may be quite narrow.

OLIVA RETICULARIS

***Oliva* spp.** (about 200 species)
Olive shells

Maximum Size: Up to 2 in. (5 cm) long.
Range: Tropical seas.
Minimum Aquarium Size: Moderate tanks, 50 gal. (190 L) or larger.
Lighting: Immaterial.
Foods & Feeding: Predatory. Feed on sediment infauna, such as worms and other animals.
Aquarium Suitability/Reef Aquarium Compatibility: Not suitable for reef aquariums.
Captive Care: These snails have highly polished olive-shaped shells. They live within and burrow through sediments and are seldom seen on the sediment surface. They occasionally enter marine aquariums in live sand and will live for a while in captivity, rapidly exhausting their food sources in the sand; after this they typically starve. Colors vary within and between species, from white to black, with many species tending toward earth tones or brown and tan mottling. Have a long slitlike aperture with flared front end found along most of the shell length. When moving, their large foot extends out of the aperture and completely covers the shell.

A cone snail, possibly *Conus eburneus*: aquarists need to recognize and respect these snails. Cone snails may sting, and some have killed humans.

Introduction to *Conus* Species

Important—**before you attempt to keep a cone snail, read the description of fish-eating *Conus* on page 325. Fish-eating species of *Conus* have a venomous sting and are capable of causing human fatalities.**

These are snails all marine aquarists should know and recognize. It is relatively easy to identify a snail as a cone snail. The genus name is quite fitting. They look like a cone, with the apex being the front of the animal. The broad base of the cone is often flat, but just as often it extends as a smaller conical projection. The aperture typically runs from the base of the cone to the apex, and is often quite slitlike. Cone shells are often robust and quite heavy. They range from small species the size of acorns to larger species the size of a clenched fist.

Conus is possibly the largest animal genus, with several thousand described species. Over the last few decades, it has become apparent that many of these so-called "species" are, in fact, simply color or

Conus textile: stings from individuals of this species have killed people. The stinging tooth is held in the proboscis (orange tube coming from the front of the snail).

shape variants of other species, so the total number of real species is probably somewhere on the order of 600. This is still an immense number of species, and *Conus* remains the largest genus, reflecting the ecological and evolutionary success of the group. It is impossible to try to identify many cone snails in the scope of this book, but shell collectors love this group and there are many excellent identification guides, often available in public libraries.

Cone snails are found almost exclusively in the Tropics and are distributed in all tropical seas. Most are found in shallow waters. These are truly animals of the reefs, reef flats, and reef sand beds. All cone snails are predatory, and they typically spear their prey with a tooth that looks like a harpoon and functions like a hypodermic needle. When the cone snail senses an appropriate prey species nearby, a tooth is released from an internal quiver, and is passed out of the mouth until it can be gripped by the tubular proboscis. The proboscis surrounds the mouth like a single long, tubular lip. Once the tooth is held in the proboscis, the proboscis extends so that the tooth is held some distance out from the apical end of the conical shell. When the food item comes close enough, or when the animal

Conus imperialis: cone snails possess neurotoxic venoms that are typically injected into their prey through a harpoon-shaped, hypodermic, needlelike tooth.

moves close to the food, internal muscles contract and fill the tooth and proboscis with a neurotoxic venom. The tooth is then rammed into the prey, which dies and is eaten. It is a measure of the effectiveness of this hunting method and the toxicity of the venoms that very few potential prey have evolved any escape or flight response to the *Conus* species.

Cone snails are often specialist predators, and they typically eat animals in one of three groups—worms, snails, or fishes. Most cones eat worms, a few species eat other snails, and fewer yet eat fishes. There are a couple of generalized *Conus* spp. that will eat a wide variety of foods, but these species are actually fairly uncommon in most reef situations.

Cone snails occasionally appear in reef aquariums, most often arriving on live rock or possibly in live sand. They should be treated with extreme caution, as the venoms from individuals of the fish-eating cones are some of the most lethal toxins known when injected into humans.

Most cones, however, are harmless to aquarists and will live well if maintained in normal reef aquarium conditions. Cone snails typi-

Conus sp.: the basic color pattern on this shell is found on several species, including some of the more dangerous cone snails. All should be treated with caution.

cally bury in the sand with just their tubular siphons extended like a snorkel above the sand surface. When they get hungry, they climb out of the sediment and begin to hunt.

Watching cone snails hunt definitely brings a new meaning to the phrase "the thrill of the chase." They are among the slowest-moving of all snails, moving at the rate of inches per day. However, when they do find a prey item, the action is fast and furious. The worm-eating cones make good aquarium specimens and do well in tanks with a good population of worms in a sand bed. Many worm-eating cones can be taught to eat earthworms, and will live well on this diet. They make interesting, if slow, pets and many of them have very attractive patterns on their shells.

Over the course of a few weeks, snail-eating cones can slowly track down, sting and remove all the grazing snails from a tank. These animals also make fascinating pets, but need a regular supply of snails to stay alive. If well cared for, any given cone snail may live a decade or more.

CONUS GEOGRAPHUS

Conus geographus, Conus striatus and several others
Fish-eating cone shells

Maximum Size: Up to 5 in. (13 cm) long.
Range: Tropical seas.
Minimum Aquarium Size: Moderate tanks, 50 gal. (190 L) or larger.
Lighting: Immaterial.
Foods & Feeding: Predatory on fishes.
Aquarium Suitability/Reef Aquarium Compatibility: *Exceptionally danger-ous; should never be kept by amateur aquarists.*
Captive Care: If you are stung by one of these snails, there is a very good chance you will die. The venom is fast-acting and there is no antivenin. If fish-eating cones are kept in an aquarium with a deep sand bed, it is all too easy to overlook their small proboscides extending from the sand. Luckily, these snails are easily recognized. Their shell apertures tend to flare relatively widely at the narrow end of the shell. Additionally, their shells are often colored with a mottled or fine chevron pattern, typically brown or chestnut on white or tan. This pattern is also found on some other nondeadly cones, but it is better to err on the side of caution. They may be picked up by using a pair of tongs or pliers to grasp the blunt end. Dispose of them humanely by freezing.

Chelidonura hirundinina (leech headshield slug): looking like a nudibranch, this species inhabits sandy areas and is carnivorous, feeding on other headshield slugs.

Introduction to Headshield Slugs and Bubble Shells

These animals generally appear in reef aquariums some time after adding a new piece of live rock. Among the headshield slugs there are both carnivorous and herbivorous species. Most of the bubble shells that we find in our systems are herbivores, but some of the more sluglike of the species are carnivores. All of them will do well at normal reef temperatures and salinity. Some are exceptionally attractive. If you are fortunate enough to get two of them in your system, they may reproduce. Successful aquarium reproduction has been documented in several species.

These snails belong to the group of opisthobranch snails referred to as the Cephalaspidacea. The species in this group can be placed in a series, from those with a strong and relatively robust external shell to those with a reduced internal shell. The latter animals look superficially like nudibranchs (like the *Chelidonura* shown above), but have a very different internal anatomy.

In those animals with a visible external shell, the shell is typically shaped like a barrel, sometimes appearing a bit inflated. The shell is generally colored white or tan and may have some patterning. The front end of the animal is typically expanded into a structure encompassing the head and about the first third to half of the body. This structure is called the "headshield," and gives the group their scientific name (*cephal* = head, *aspida* = shield). The headshield typically bears a pair of sensory tentacles rising vertically from the anterior end, and a large flap of tissue that is held near the substrate. This is called the oral veil, and is often elaborated out into a lateral flap on either side.

If the shell is interior, its presence may be discerned by noticing that the back is inflated to form a large hump. If this is gently touched, the shell may feel like a rigid structure within the tissue. These animals also bear a headshield and it extends back to the base of the internal bubble shell. The foot is often elaborated laterally into a flaplike extension called a parapodium, which is often folded onto the body surface above the shell.

HYDATINA PHYSIS

Bulla striata, Haminoea spp., *Hydatina* spp.
Bubble shells

Maximum Size: Up to 2 in. (5 cm) in diameter.

Range: Tropical seas.

Minimum Aquarium Size: Small tanks, 10 gal. (38 L) or larger.

Lighting: Immaterial.

Foods & Feeding: Feeding habits vary by genus. Primarily diatom grazers; may eat filamentous algae.

Aquarium Suitability/Reef Aquarium Compatibility: Good reef aquarium animals.

Captive Care: Bubble shells are typically nocturnal, hiding during the day and foraging on diatoms and algae. The large size of *Bulla* spp. often startles aquarists. They are tan with a mottled "diatom" color that matches the substrate. The internal shell is covered by tissues forming the body "hump." Animals bear a headshield that extends back to the base of the internal bubble shell. Occasionally, smaller bubble shells, probably *Haminoea* spp., are available to aquarists. They also feed on diatoms. They are mottled golden brown or tan and are small (less than 0.4 in. [1 cm] in length). Otherwise, they are similar to *Bulla*. Some *Hydatina* species, very seldom seen in aquariums, may eat polychaete worms.

Chelidonura varians
Blue-striped nudibranch (blue-striped sea slug)

Maximum Size: Up to 1 in. (2.5 cm) in diameter.
Range: Indo-Pacific.
Minimum Aquarium Size: Small tanks, 10 gal. (38 L) or larger.
Lighting: Immaterial.
Foods & Feeding: Predator on flatworms; will eat the red planarian flatworm *Convolutriloba retrogemma*.
Aquarium Suitability/Reef Aquarium Compatibility: Good reef aquarium animal if prey is present; otherwise, will starve in captivity.
Captive Care: These slugs are sold to control planarian flatworm pests, but such control is an illusion: they eat their prey as best they can, but the planaria are mobile and reproduce well. Generally, when the slugs are introduced into an aquarium with a flatworm plague, they thrive and eat many of them. Eventually, the flatworm numbers drop very low. At these low populations, the slugs can't find enough flatworms to eat and starve to death. Unfortunately, there are always a few flatworms left, and within a few days, the flatworm plague returns. These animals have an internal shell and look superficially like a nudibranch but are distinguished by the headshield and folded parapodia over the top of the body.

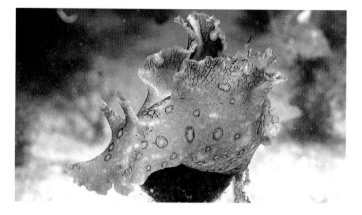

Aplysia dactylomela
Spotted sea hare (Caribbean sea hare)

Maximum Size: To about 5 in. (12.5 cm) in length; most smaller.
Range: Caribbean.
Minimum Aquarium Size: Small tanks, 10 gal. (38 L) or larger.
Lighting: Needs sufficient lighting to ensure rapid growth of algae.
Foods & Feeding: Macroalgae; typically noncalcareous algae. Generally will not eat *Caulerpa*.
Aquarium Suitability/Reef Aquarium Compatibility: Needs lots of food. Requires calm tanks and cannot withstand high currents.
Captive Care: Sea hares earn their common name because the anterior sensory tentacles look like rabbit ears; viewed from the side, the whole body looks somewhat rabbitlike. Requires substantial growths of tender macroalgae in a quiet lagoon-type biotope tank. It has a totally internal shell. Typically the body is light brown to green with small, irregular spots outlined in green, brown, or black. Will secrete a thick purple ink if stressed; the ink has not been shown to be toxic, but it is probably good to do a water change if a sea hare colors your tank. Hermaphroditic; if a pair is kept together, they may spawn and the larvae may survive in large systems. Bigger fishes and crustaceans will often attack and damage them.

Stylocheilus longicauda
Sea bunny

Maximum Size: Up to 3 in. (8 cm) in length.
Range: Indo-Pacific.
Minimum Aquarium Size: Small tanks, 10 gal. (38 L) or larger.
Lighting: Immaterial.
Foods & Feeding: Macroalgae; typically noncalcareous algae. Generally will not eat *Caulerpa*.
Aquarium Suitability/Reef Aquarium Compatibility: Needs lots of food. Requires a calm tank and cannot withstand high currents.
Captive Care: Like *Aplysia* (page 330) this sea hare has anterior sensory tentacles that remind one of rabbit ears when viewed from the side. Requires substantial growths of tender macroalgae in a quiet lagoon-type biotope tank. It has a totally internal shell. Typically the body is olive brown to tan with many thin brown lines and small blue rings or spots and a long tapering tail. Will secrete a bright red ink if stressed; the ink has not been shown to be toxic, but it is probably a good idea to do a water change if a sea hare colors your tank. Hermaphroditic; if a pair is kept together, they may spawn and the larvae may survive in large systems. Many fishes and virtually all crustaceans will attack, eat, or damage them.

Elysia crispata
Lettuce slug

Maximum Size: Up to 2 in. (5 cm) in length.
Range: Caribbean.
Minimum Aquarium Size: Small tanks, 10 gal. (38 L) or larger.
Lighting: Needs bright lighting.
Foods & Feeding: Feeds on algae: *Bryopsis*, *Derbesia*, possibly *Caulerpa*.
Aquarium Suitability/Reef Aquarium Compatibility: Good aquarium animal, but often has limited survival due to dietary needs.
Captive Care: This animal looks like a nudibranch, but it is a sacoglossan slug. It is characterized by the lettucelike appearance of the back frills and the pair of rolled, tubular sensory tentacles (rhinophores) on the head. It feeds by using a strawlike tooth to pierce algal cells and suck out the contents. Most of the contents are digested, but the chloroplasts are stored in the slug's tissues in functional condition and are capable of photosynthesis. These chloroplasts cause the slug's color to vary from a pale green to a vibrant deep green. Because of its restricted diet, *Elysia crispata* needs a lot of its specific algal prey to survive. Normally, an individual will live only a few days to a few weeks in a reef tank. (Formerly called *Tridachia crispata*.)

Elysia ornata
Ornate *Elysia*

Maximum Size: Up to 2 in. (5 cm) in length.
Range: Caribbean.
Minimum Aquarium Size: Small tanks, 10 gal. (38 L) or larger.
Lighting: Needs bright lighting.
Foods & Feeding: Feeds on algae: *Bryopsis*, *Caulerpa*.
Aquarium Suitability/Reef Aquarium Compatibility: Needs lots of food. Requires a calm tank; does not do well with surge.
Captive Care: This sea slug reportedly feeds on a few specific algae, such as *Bryopsis* spp. Its owes its green coloration to chloroplasts in the tissues. It lacks the frilly structures on the back seen in *Elysia crispata* (page 332) and has instead two linear tissue flaps arising from the sides of the foot and carried over the back. Appears as if dusted with fine, colored dots. The two flaps are edged in black, with a lighter strip of orange, yellow, or beige separating the black border from the green of the body. Has the characteristic rolled rhinophores seen on *Elysia crispata*. If starved, it will change color from green to tan as it digests the chloroplasts in its tissues, leaving only its basic coloration. Large, active fish may bother this species.

Berthelinia spp.
Bivalved snails

Maximum Size: Up to 0.25 in. (5 mm) in length.
Range: Caribbean and Indo-Pacific.
Minimum Aquarium Size: Small tanks, 10 gal. (38 L) or larger.
Lighting: Need bright lighting.
Foods & Feeding: *Caulerpa*, possibly other algae.
Aquarium Suitability/Reef Aquarium Compatibility: Good aquarium animals.
Captive Care: Attractive and interesting, these creatures arrive in tanks on live rock or *Caulerpa* and are seldom noticed in captivity, usually overlooked in the algae due to their small size. They are at risk from tank predators, such as hermit crabs and some fishes, and are likely to live less than a year. Unlike all other snails, these small sacoglossan slugs have a bivalved clamlike shell hinged at the top of the animal. The head and foot protrude out the bottom. The body and shell are greenish, often bright green. The head bears two tubular rhinophores, similar to other sacoglossans. First scientifically described from fossils and considered clams, they were quite a surprise to scientists when a living specimen crawled out of some *Caulerpa* in a lab and it was realized they were snails.

Janolus sp.: unlike most arminacean nudibranchs, this species displays colorful bulb-like cerata (fleshy dorsal structures).

Introduction to Nudibranchs

About a dozen marine snail lineages have developed into the shell-less form we call "sea slugs." Unfortunately, aquarists tend to call all of them "nudibranchs," resulting in great confusion because only a single one of these lineages actually contains the nudibranchs. The true nudibranchs are shell-less snails in the Order Nudibranchia, with four suborders based on differences in the animals' anatomy and physiology.

All nudibranchs are predators on sessile animals, and all have specific mouth and gut modifications that prevent them from eating a wide variety of prey. Because these structural modifications are used to classify the four suborders, each group has a defined set of potential foods, as well as specific appearances.

But being reasonably closely related, all nudibranchs do share several characteristics. They are all hermaphroditic and reproduce by depositing egg masses containing large numbers of eggs in a jelly-like mass. The eggs all develop and hatch to release planktonic larvae, and in most cases, these larvae feed on phytoplankton. Each

Chromodoris magnifica: among the visually appealing nudibranchs, the dorids have specialized feeding habits and poor aquarium survivability.

larva bears a small, typical snail shell, but these shells are shed during the larvae's metamorphosis to juvenile forms.

Nudibranchs lack eyes and instead have a pair of dorsal sensory tentacles located near the front end of the animal. These tentacles, called rhinophores, are sensitive to chemicals in the water, current flow, and touch. Many nudibranchs have fleshy extensions of their dorsal surface, called cerata (singular = ceras). The structure and function of these cerata varies between the groups. The four suborders of the nudibranchs are as follows:

Arminacea—Two distinctly different body forms are found in this group. Those most commonly seen in captivity are characterized by a smooth, unbroken dorsal surface, with parallel longitudinal ridges and two small rhinophores at the middle of the front of the dorsal surface. These species primarily eat sea pens or other soft corals. The remaining arminaceans have a body form similar to the dorids. These animals are largely bryozoan predators. The unifying characteristic of all arminaceans is the presence of a large tissue flap at the front end, called the oral veil. Most authorities consider this group to be in need of taxonomic revision.

Cerberilla ambonensis: aeolid nudibranchs have the ability to eat anemones and other cnidarians and transport stinging nematocysts into their cerata for defense.

Doridacea—Dorid nudibranchs are characterized by having their anuses dorsally on the midline in the posterior third of the animal. The anus is typically, but not always, surrounded by a tuft of gills. The dorsal surface may range from being smooth to being covered with small bumps to having large tissue extensions (see photo, page 336). Dorids typically eat sponges, tunicates, or bryozoans, but a few eat other soft-bodied snails. They often have the capability of modifying or utilizing chemicals secreted by their prey, and these chemicals are used for protection against their own predators. Most dorids are exceptionally toxic animals, and are often brightly colored to advertise this fact.

Aeolidacea—Aeolids are characterized by having the anus on the right side at "shoulder" level, and by possessing rows or groups of cerata. The cerata are noticeable as "frills" or "fringe" on the animal's back (see photo, above). A brown, tan, or red strand of the gut is often visible in each of the cerata, and each is often tipped with a bright white spot. Aeolids typically eat cnidarians, including sea anemones and corals, but a few temperate species have also been shown to eat tunicates, mussels, and some crustaceans. Aeolids have

Marionia sp.: dendronotid nudibranchs sometimes sport elaborate cerata and may resemble their prey animals, which include soft corals and other cnidarians.

the capability to sequester, unfired and usable, the nematocysts that they ingest when they eat. These nematocysts are sometimes stored in the bright white ceratal tips, where they are thought to provide some protection from predation.

Dendronotacea—Dendronotaceans are characterized by having the anus on the right, similar to aeolids, but unlike aeolids they typically have a smooth dorsal surface. The body is often "angular," or appears rather "brick-shaped," with a defined edge around the upper surface, where small, fleshy gills or tissue extensions are found (see photo, above). Many tropical species are small, but some temperate examples may be very large, up to several kilograms in mass. Dendronotaceans typically eat soft corals, such as sea pens, zoanthids, jellyfish polyps, or sea anemones.

DERMATOBRANCHUS SP.

Arminia spp., *Dermatobranchus* spp.
Arminid sea slugs

Maximum Size: To 6 in. (15 cm) in length; most smaller.
Range: Indo-Pacific.
Minimum Aquarium Size: Small tanks, 10 gal. (38 L) or larger.
Lighting: Immaterial.
Foods & Feeding: Eat stoloniferous soft corals, clove polyps, sea pens, possibly *Xenia*.
Aquarium Suitability/Reef Aquarium Compatibility: Predators on soft corals; need live food. Not suitable for reef aquariums.
Captive Care: Arminids are always predatory on soft corals. If their food were readily available, they could be kept well in captivity, but alternative food sources are not known. These do well under normal conditions of temperature and salinity. They burrow out of sight and emerge when hungry to hunt for food. When they find suitable prey, they will start feeding and completely consume it within a few days. They have a flattened back, lacking appendages, that is covered in longitudinal stripes or fine ridges; tapers to a point at the posterior end, while being "squared off" at the front. Two small, solid rhinophores extend out from under the dorsal covering at the middle of the front end.

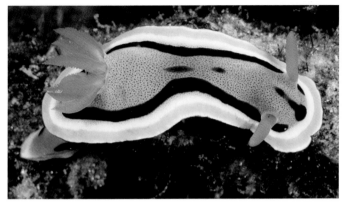

CHROMODORIS ANNAE

Chromodoris spp.
Chromodorid sea slugs

Maximum Size: Up to 6 in. (15 cm) in length.
Range: Tropical seas.
Minimum Aquarium Size: Small tanks, 10 gal. (38 L) or larger.
Lighting: Immaterial.
Foods & Feeding: Eat live prey, mostly sponges.
Aquarium Suitability/Reef Aquarium Compatibility: Predators that need live food. Very toxic. Short-lived, and when they die, they can poison everything in a tank. Not suitable for reef aquariums.
Captive Care: Chromodorids are some of the most beautiful and strikingly colored marine invertebrates, often bright blue with yellow, gold, white, or black highlights, but with other brilliant colors as well. These animals are bulky; large ones may exceed a pound (450 gm) in weight. They are imported either in the interstices of live rock, by occasional collection, or riding on corals or other animals. The diets of most species are unknown (most are presumed to eat specific sponges). Given sufficient and appropriate foods, many temperate dorids are hardy animals; tropical ones are likely similar. However, these dorids appear to have lifespans of only a few months and at best would be transitory in captivity.

Chromodoris sp.

Chromodoris leopardus

Chromodoris dianae

Chromodoris kunei

Chromodoris coi

Chromodoris sp.

With almost 2,000 known species, the nudibranchs are the most diverse group of sea slugs, many with vivid coloration and virtually all with highly specialized feeding habits. The chromodorids, shown above, prey on live sponges—severely limiting their lifespans in captivity.

NEMBROTHA CRISTATA

Nembrotha spp., *Okenia* spp.
Tunicate- or bryozoan-eating dorids

Maximum Size: Up to 3 in. (7.5 cm) in length.
Range: Indo-Pacific.
Minimum Aquarium Size: Small tanks, 10 gal. (38 L) or larger.
Lighting: Immaterial.
Foods & Feeding: Eat live prey, such as tunicates and bryozoans.
Aquarium Suitability/Reef Aquarium Compatibility: Predators on tunicates or bryozoans; need live food. May be poisonous. Not suitable for reef aquariums.
Captive Care: These are slender dorid nudibranchs, with gills that are not retractile and remain extended at all times. *Nembrotha* are often colored in earth tones or black, with brightly colored highlights of red, orange, green, or white, and are typically about 2 in. (5 cm) long and 0.5 in. (1.3 cm) wide. *Okenia* are small (less than 1 in. [2.5 cm] long, and ⅕ in. [5 mm] wide), have elongate cerata without gut strands or nematocyst pouches, and eat bryozoans from which they may derive some chemical protection. Unfortunately, most aquarists are unable to provide appropriate food. Harmless to most of our decorative species, they would do well under normal reef conditions, but they probably have a short life expectancy.

Dendrodoris spp.
Sponge-eating dorid nudibranchs

Maximum Size: Up to 4 in. (10 cm) in length.
Range: All seas.
Minimum Aquarium Size: Small tanks, 10 gal. (38 L) or larger.
Lighting: Immaterial.
Foods & Feeding: Eat live sponge prey.
Aquarium Suitability/Reef Aquarium Compatibility: Predators on sponges. Need live food. May be poisonous. Not suitable for reef aquariums.
Captive Care: These nonchromodorids are generally oval and relatively flattened. Their upper surfaces are typically smooth or covered with small papillae. They occur in several color patterns, often mottled or "blotchy"; common colors are white to brilliant reds or yellows. Sponge-eating dorids tend to lack the chromodorid "racing stripes." Because they sequester active chemicals from their prey and modify them to increase toxicity, when they die, their decomposing bodies may release some of the most toxic natural compounds known into the closed environment of an aquarium. This can wipe out an entire system. Sponge-eating dorids can do well under normal reef conditions if they have sufficient and proper food: a 4-in. (10-cm) dorid can easily consume a pound of live sponge per week.

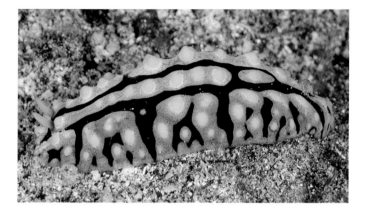

Phyllidia varicosa
Fish-killing nudibranch

Maximum Size: Up to 4.5 in. (11 cm) in length.
Range: Indo-Pacific.
Minimum Aquarium Size: Small tanks, 10 gal. (38 L) or larger.
Lighting: Immaterial.
Foods & Feeding: Eats live sponge.
Aquarium Suitability/Reef Aquarium Compatibility: Predator on sponges; needs live food. Poisonous. Not suitable for reef aquariums.
Captive Care: This visually striking species is one of the most lethal animals commonly encountered in reef tanks. In nature, if a fish bites a *Phyllidia*, the slug will probably be spat out with little consequence to either party: the nudibranch manufactures a chemical that is very poisonous to fishes, so a little of this chemical in the slime coat deters predation. In a reef aquarium, when the nudibranch dies of starvation (because there is never sufficient live sponge prey), the poison will affect the entire tank. This event has caused numerous fish kills. The bottom line: phyllidiids should not be kept. The color pattern consists of a light blue, white, or black background with starkly contrasting lines, circles or ovals of black, white, or yellow. It lacks the dorsal tuft of gills around the anus.

HEXABRANCHUS SANGUINEUS

Hexabranchus morsomus, Hexabranchus sanguineus
Spanish dancers

Maximum Size: Up to 24 in. (61 cm) in length.

Range: *Hexabranchus sanguineus*, Indo-Pacific; *Hexabranchus morsomus*, Caribbean.

Minimum Aquarium Size: Very big tanks, 200 gal. (760 L) or larger.

Lighting: Immaterial.

Foods & Feeding: Eat live sponges.

Aquarium Suitability/Reef Aquarium Compatibility: Predators on sponges; need live food. May be poisonous. Should not be collected or bought.

Captive Care: Spanish dancers are large, brilliant red nudibranchs capable of swimming in the water column. The Indo-Pacific species is the longest nudibranch, reaching to more than 24 in. (60 cm). They have six retractable gills, and a large flaplike edge to the foot, which provides swimming capability. Their red coloration and non-reclusive behavior are likely signals that they are toxic (reds or oranges are common colors on other toxic sponge-eating nudibranchs). Although this has not been investigated, there is every reason to conclude they are noxious. Although they could do well under normal reef conditions, a sufficient live food source cannot be offered and they will starve to death in captivity.

FLABELLINA SP.

Flabellina spp., *Phestilla* spp., *Phyllodesmium* spp.
Aeolid nudibranchs

Maximum Size: Up to 1.5 in. (3.8 cm) in length.
Range: All seas.
Minimum Aquarium Size: Small tanks, 10 gal. (38 L) or larger.
Lighting: Immaterial.
Foods & Feeding: Eat live prey.
Aquarium Suitability/Reef Aquarium Compatibility: Predators on corals, soft corals, sea anemones; need live food. Not suitable for reef tanks, as they will starve to death without the appropriate food.
Captive Care: Aeolids are typically small, slender hitchhikers that commonly appear in reef aquariums. Aeolid diversity is manifested in the patterns of cerata, basic size, and color. Many species tend to look superficially alike. and identification is actually quite difficult. Most live a year or less. They have several discrete tufts of often brightly colored cerata, used as gills and for protection, on the upper surface in groups on either side of the midline. Extensions of the gut may often be seen in the cerata, culminating at the tip in an area of contrasting color. They should not be considered reef-safe, as they have too much predatory potential and are often very adept at finding hiding places in tanks.

Aeolid Nudibranchs: Coral Predators

Phestilla sp.: members of this genus may feed on *Goniopora*.

Phyllodesmium kabiranum: this genus may harbor zooxanthellae.

Phyllodesmium sp.: feeding on the branches of a sea fan.

Phyllodesmium kabiranum: morph preying on a colony of *Xenia*.

Phyllodesmium longicirrum: attacking a leather coral.

Phyllodesmium sp.: mimics the bad-tasting *Xenia*, which it can eat.

TRITONIOPSIS SP.

Marionia spp., *Tritonia* spp., *Tritoniopsis* spp.
Dendronotid nudibranchs

Maximum Size: Up to 12 in. (30 cm) in length; most much smaller.
Range: All seas.
Minimum Aquarium Size: Small tanks, 10 gal. (38 L) or larger.
Lighting: Immaterial.
Foods & Feeding: Eat live prey: soft corals, sea pens, gorgonians.
Aquarium Suitability/Reef Aquarium Compatibility: They will starve to death in captivity without appropriate foods.
Captive Care: These nudibranchs have rectangular to oval elongate bodies with highly branched cerata at the edges of the dorsal surface. The cerata lack internal gut strands. Their bodies are generally white and often have contrasting color patterning, particularly on the cerata, consisting of narrow white, brown, or red lines. *Tritoniopsis* only reaches lengths of 2 in. (5 cm), *Marionia* are also small, but some *Tritonia* are large animals, up to 12 in. (30 cm) or more in length. All do well under normal reef tank conditions if the aquarist is able to provide appropriate and sufficient food. Although small species probably have short lifespans, some large *Tritonia* appear to live several years. They do not seem to be toxic and probably present no threat to fishes or invertebrates other than their prey items.

NAUTILUS POMPILIUS

Allonautilus spp., *Nautilus* spp.
Chambered nautiluses

Maximum Size: Up to 8 in. (20 cm) in diameter.
Range: Indo-Pacific.
Minimum Aquarium Size: Large tanks, 100 gal. (380 L) or larger.
Lighting: Immaterial.
Foods & Feeding: Prefer live prey (crustaceans, fishes); will eat carrion.
Aquarium Suitability/Reef Aquarium Compatibility: Predators on crustaceans, perhaps fishes. Unsuitable for reef aquariums, due to their depth, lighting, and temperature requirements.
Captive Care: Although captivating animals, nautiluses need specialized care and facilities, beyond the reach of most home aquarists, and their husbandry should not be attempted. Many *Nautilus* populations are threatened by overcollection. These half-dozen species in two genera have a planispirally coiled white or gray shell, radially banded with reddish stripes. The pink, white, or orange body has 60 to 90 tentacles, a large dorsal cap, and large, pinhole eyes. These animals have a short lifespan in captivity. Their optimal temperatures are considerably lower than surface reef temperatures, so they tolerate normal aquarium temperatures only for very short periods. Under reef aquarium lighting, they are effectively blinded.

SEPIA MESTUS (REAPER CUTTLEFISH)

Metasepia pfefferi **= Flamboyant cuttlefish**
***Sepia* spp. = Cuttlefishes**

Maximum Size: Up to 18 in. (46 cm) in length (*Sepia* spp.).
Range: Indo-Pacific, Mediterranean.
Minimum Aquarium Size: Large tanks, 300 gal. (1,140 L) or larger.
Lighting: Normal diurnal cycle. Bright lighting is best.
Foods & Feeding: Prefer live foods, primarily larger fishes.
Aquarium Suitability/Reef Aquarium Compatibility: Prey on crustaceans, perhaps fishes. Suitable for large tanks or specialized tanks only.
Captive Care: Cuttlefishes come from reef margins and seagrass beds, so they will need a large tank with a small rock island in a sand bed well planted with seagrass, but with sufficient open area for the animal to patrol. Match temperature to habitat of collection. Indo-Pacific specimens should not be kept at temperatures lower than 80°F (27°C). Because they are intolerant of fouled water and must be fed large food items, a heavy-duty skimmer and high-volume water circulation are required. May be trained to take substitutes for live foods, but most live less than three years in captivity. Try to get a small animal and raise it to maturity. Cuttlefish tend to be rather drab, but *Metasepia pfefferi* is brightly patterned with black, violet, and yellow. It has a pair of dorsal fins lacking in *Sepia* species.

Metasepia pfefferi (flamboyant cuttlefish): distinguished by bold colors, this cuttlefish feeds on small fishes, crustaceans, and snails.

Sepia latimanus (broadclub cuttlefish): an exceptionally large tropical cuttlefish, it may exceed half a meter (1.6 feet) in length.

Sepia sp.: all of the cuttlefishes have the ability to change colors rapidly for protection and in response to stress or predatory threats.

Sepia sp.: cuttlefishes are heavy feeders and require aquariums with excellent water circulation and filtration to removed dissolved organic wastes.

Sepia sp.: most cuttlefishes seen by aquarists hail from near-reef areas with shallow water, often over seagrass beds or open areas with sandy or soft bottoms.

Metasepia pfefferi (flamboyant cuttlefish): note two large dorsal fins at rear (left), not present in the more commonly seen *Sepia* spp.

Euprymna spp.
Bobtail squids

Maximum Size: Up to 2 in. (5 cm) in length.
Range: Indo-Pacific.
Minimum Aquarium Size: Moderate tanks, 50 gal. (190 L) or larger.
Lighting: Diurnal cycle necessary. Moderate to bright lighting.
Foods & Feeding: Prefer live foods (small fishes or shrimp). Very small _Euprymna_ may take live adult brine shrimp.
Aquarium Suitability/Reef Aquarium Compatibility: Predators on crustaceans, perhaps fishes. Not suitable for reef aquariums.
Captive Care: Bobtail squid are animals of sand flats, and they ought to be kept in a biotope-type aquarium with an open sand-bed and minimal aquascaping or rockwork. Often quite reclusive, they will bury in the sand with just their eyes showing, and will wait for prey to swim by. These squids are temperature sensitive and should not be kept at temperatures lower than 80°F (27°C). They are intolerant of fouled water; a good skimmer and high-volume water circulation is a necessity. Make captivating and easily trained pets. They have short life spans; most live less than two years in captivity. Try to get a small animal and raise it to maturity if you wish to keep it for the longest possible time.

Hapalochlaena lunulata: capable of biting through rubber gloves and dive suits, this animal can deliver a potent venom resulting in serious injury or even death.

Introduction to Octopuses

Highly intelligent and fully capable of becoming aquatic pets, octopuses can provide a reward experience for their keepers, but it can also be an exceptionally frustrating one. Several species of octopuses may be kept in the home aquarium, others are not advised.

One group of species *not* to attempt to keep is typified by the genus *Hapalochlaena*, the blue-ringed octopuses (there are a couple of similar appearing species in this genus, all masquerading under the single name *Hapalochlaena lunulata*). **The bite of *Hapalochlaena* is always very painful, may be fatal, and for all practical purposes there is no antivenin.** Octopuses are the ultimate escape artists. Imagine the possibilities of one of the blue-rings escaping and being encountered where it is unexpected. Bites and their logical outcome will be the result. Unfortunately, there will always be people foolhardy enough to want to keep deadly animals, and nothing anyone says seems enough to dissuade such behavior.

Many species in the genus *Octopus*, on the other hand, will make

Octopus marginatus (veined octopus): intelligent, strong and crafty, an octopus can and will escape any aquarium with a top not carefully and tightly secured.

good pets, but certain precautions are necessary. Most tropical species available in the hobby are Caribbean: *Octopus joubini* and *Octopus briareus* are probably the most common ones collected. *Octopus bimaculatus* is also available, collected from the Eastern Pacific. (Some taxonomists doubt that *Octopus joubini* is a valid species.) These species probably live about two years in the wild, so you should attempt to purchase a small one if you want a pet for the longest possible time.

Special care is needed to set up an octopus tank. To repeat, octopuses are amazing escape artists. They can squeeze through a hole no larger than one of their beaks, which means, for these species, a hole about 2 to 3 millimeters on a side. So the tank needs to be sealed—well sealed. A tight-fitting lid is a must, and as the animals can exert a surprisingly large amount of force with their tentacles, the lid needs to be fastened or weighted down. When I kept small octopuses for my invertebrate zoology classes, I generally used 10 to 15 pounds of lead scuba weights to hold down the lid.

The animal will have to have at least one rocky cave, hiding place, or den. Octopuses are nocturnal and generally will not be

Octopus marginatus (veined octopus): hiding in a shell, this small specimen illustrates the octopus's need to find sheltering nooks where they can feel secure.

visible during the day. They *need* their privacy and will become very stressed without it. This stress can kill them. Don't be surprised if the animal rearranges its rockwork to suit its purposes. Octopuses need some additional space, but not a lot: a small octopus may be kept well in a 10- to 20-gallon (38 to 76 L) aquarium with room to spare. One important caveat: almost any other animal housed with an octopus will be eaten, including most fishes.

Octopuses prefer dimly lit situations, which will help with the control of algae. This is a fortunate circumstance, because any animal you put into the tank to graze on the algae will become octopus food.

They need *very* pure and *very* highly oxygenated water. Good skimming is a must, and supplemental aeration or circulation helps. The temperature should be 80 to 82°F (27 to 28°C). Frequent water changes are probably a good idea for most octopus tanks.

Octopuses have an exceptionally high metabolic rate and cannot go very long without food. They will generally not eat dead foods, so you must have a source of live food. An octopus tank is a good way to get rid of those excess blue-leg hermit crabs you bought by

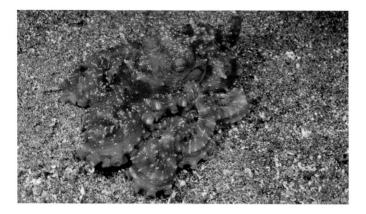

Octopus luteus (starry octopus): although not long-lived, even in the wild, an octopus can make a fascinating aquarium pet, learning to interact with its keeper.

mistake. Small tropical fishes will often be acceptable foods, but do not feed them freshwater fishes. If you live near a seashore, live shrimps or small shore crabs are good foods as well. Having a discriminating palate, octopuses *do not* consider brine shrimp to be acceptable prey.

Octopuses are messy feeders and will foul the water significantly during feeding. After feeding, they will excrete a lot of urine, which is high in ammonia and other nitrogenous compounds. Uneaten foods should be rapidly removed.

These animals can become wonderfully interactive pets. They will rapidly learn to identify the source of their food (the aquarist) and can be taught tricks or other responses. Although they may seem endearing, do not give in to the temptation to handle them. Their epidermis is thin, fragile, and prone to tearing, and this kind of injury can become infected and rapidly cause their death.

OCTOPUS SP.

Octopus bimaculatus, Octopus briareus, Octopus joubini
Octopuses

Maximum Size: Up to 8 in. (20 cm) in diameter.
Range: Caribbean (*O. briareus, O. joubini*); Eastern Pacific (*O. bimaculatus*).
Minimum Aquarium Size: Small tanks, 20 gal. (76 L) or larger.
Lighting: Diurnal cycle necessary. Dim to moderate lighting.
Foods & Feeding: Prefer live foods (small marine fishes or shrimps).
Aquarium Suitability/Reef Aquarium Compatibility: Predators on crustaceans, perhaps fishes. Not suitable for reef tanks.
Captive Care: Octopuses need at least one hiding space or den; large barnacle shells or pieces of PVC pipe work well. Nocturnal. Must have very pure, highly oxygenated water. Cannot go very long without live food: do not attempt to keep one unless you have a ready supply of live crabs or small bait fish. These messy feeders liberate a lot of urine after feeding, so a good skimmer is a must. They are crafty, strong escape artists and need a tight-fitting lid. These three species are the most common in the hobby. *Octopus bimaculatus* is distinguished from *O. briareus* by the presence of two large, whitish "eyespots" on the web at the base of the arms, in front of and below the eyes.

Hapalochlaena lunulata
Blue-ringed octopus

Maximum Size: Up to 10 in. (25 cm) in diameter.
Range: Indo-Pacific.
Minimum Aquarium Size: Small tanks, 10 gal. (38 L) or larger.
Lighting: Diurnal cycle necessary. Dim to moderate lighting.
Foods & Feeding: Prefers live foods (small fishes or shrimps).
Aquarium Suitability/Reef Aquarium Compatibility: *Venomous. Potentially deadly. No antivenin currently available. Should not be kept by any amateur aquarist.*
Captive Care: The rewards of octopus husbandry can be had without selecting one that can kill you. The blue-ringed octopus has bitten and killed many people, mostly fisherfolk in tropical countries, and deserves utmost respect. This smallish species is characterized by having a light tan to white body covered with rings or "eyespots" of a bright or iridescent blue that flash when the animal is under stress. It can turn aggressive and is prone to bite, injecting maculotoxin into its victim; this can lead to rapid paralysis and may even be fatal as there is no antivenin. Keeping a small octopus is probably the best way to have an interactive marine pet, but keeping a small blue-ringed octopus is simply inviting a tragedy to happen.

Unidentified crinoid (feather star): part of the tremendously diverse Phylum Echinodermata, including sea urchins, sea stars, sea cucumbers, and others.

Introduction to the Echinoderms

For many of us, one of the most enjoyable aspects of keeping coral reef tanks is the opportunity to maintain and observe a few truly odd or bizarre creatures. And there are very few animals more utterly strange than the echinoderms. These are animals with no heads, no front or back ends, no left or right sides. For that matter, they don't have anything that corresponds to what we call a "side" in other animals. While they have no brain, they may have quite complicated behaviors. They are without a heart or circulatory system, yet they have an internal hydraulic system of many thousands of valves and pipes.

Echinoderm means "spiny skin," a most reasonable name, considering that most have some types of spines sticking out of their body surfaces. Placed by taxonomists in the Phylum Echinodermata, there are about 5,000 described species. The living forms are grouped into five taxonomic classes: The Crinoidea (feather stars), the Asteroidea (sea stars), the Ophiuroidea (brittle, serpent, and basket stars), the Holothuroidea (sea cucumbers), and the

A deposit-feeding sea cucumber. Similar animals are common in all soft sediment marine communities, from reefs to the abyss.

Echinoidea (sea urchins, sand dollars, and sea biscuits).

The organ system that defines echinoderms is a hydraulic network used in food capture and locomotion. This system is known by several synonymous names—the hydrovascular system, the water vascular system or the ambulacral system—and is a high-pressure (higher than ambient seawater pressure, anyway) plumbing maze, with an exceptionally complex interworking of valves and muscles. The obvious external manifestations of the system are the "tube feet," or podia, that most echinoderms use to move or to catch food.

The success of the echinoderm group is a property of this unique hydrovascular system, and their limitations are due to its limitations. The system uses intracellular chemical pumps to alter the ionic concentrations in the water-vascular fluid, and this physiological process appears to have a narrow capability of controlling differences in salinity. Consequently, echinoderms are predominantly animals found in full strength salinity (35 ppt or greater).

In estuarine environments, there is often a gradient of echinoderm species, which parallels the increases in salinity of the embayments, with very few species in the upper brackish reaches and a rich

Asthenosoma varium (fire urchin): sea urchins must be handled with respect, and some venomous species such as this one can deliver painful puncture wounds.

assemblage near the mouth in areas of full-strength seawater.

It is easy to see, therefore, that the first absolutely critical factor in echinoderm aquarium husbandry is the maintenance of the salinity of the system within the appropriate range. If echinoderms are transferred from tank to tank, extreme care must be taken to ensure that the salinities of the various systems match, or that the animal is acclimated very slowly. Most of the internal tissues of echinoderms are very thin and diaphanous, and changes in salinity or ionic balances can rupture these membranes, resulting in the death of the animals in just a few days.

Other factors contributing to water condition are important for echinoderms as well. In general, they need good, clean, well-aerated water. Proper skimming, filtration, and water circulation or aeration are a necessity. Lighting is generally unimportant, but many echinoderms appear to prefer dimmer areas or lower-light regimes.

Unidentified crinoid (feather star): lovely animals that depend on filter feeding for survival, making them very poor candidates for life in home aquariums.

Introduction to the Crinoids or Feather Stars

Undoubtedly, the most beautiful of the echinoderms are the feather stars and their deeper-water relatives, the sea lilies. These are the animals known as crinoids. They all have a relatively small central body surrounded by 10 to 200 arms, which have fine lateral branches that give the arms the appearance of fine feathers. The central body, or calyx, has a few tendril-like cirri on the underside, which the animal uses to grasp the substrate. Feather stars are common reef inhabitants, and are particularly diverse in the Indo-Pacific, where they are found in relatively high densities. They are also commonly seen in the Caribbean, although there are only a few species there.

Coral-reef crinoids are generally moderate in size, with a span across the extended arms that ranges from 12 to 24 inches (30 to 60 cm). They hang onto various reef substrates with their cirri and extend their arms out into the current to catch plankton. They possess all the characteristics of the echinoderm phylum, including tube feet. Unlike most other echinoderms, however, they do not use the

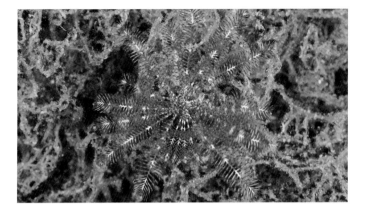

Crinoid juvenile: able to move slowly over the reef with cirri, tendril-like clasping organs that also allow them to cling to hard substrates and resist strong currents.

tube feet for locomotion. If they need to move, they generally do so slowly, by the deliberate grasping of the substrate by the cirri. If they need to move more rapidly, perhaps to escape a predator, they release the grip of the cirri, and using a particularly graceful undulatory motion of the arms, they propel themselves up into the water, swimming for short distances.

Crinoids use their tube feet in a unique feeding method, where individual tube feet differentially respond to touching potential food particles in the water. Their responses vary, based on the particle's characteristics. Such an active feeding method is significantly different from most other suspension-feeding organisms, which passively filter food from the water and then sort it somehow after it is collected. Crinoids actively choose to feed, or not to feed, on each particle that touches a tube foot. Presumably, these choices are made based on the particle size, density, and chemical composition or flavor. In any case, it means that these animals can be exceptionally discriminating in their choice of food.

The selectivity of the feeding process ensures that the animal gets the maximum benefit for the minimum expenditure of energy.

Crinoid (feather star): until new and acceptable substitute suspension foods are available, aquarists should consider these animals unkeepable and avoid them.

However, it also means that an aquarist who wishes to maintain these beautiful animals has to provide a food that passes all of the crinoid's criteria. Sadly, in most cases, it appears that this is presently impossible. Unlike the other suspension-feeders, which can make use of substitute foods, crinoids do not even seem to recognize the substitutes as food.

As a consequence, if we put crinoids in our systems, we can do nothing for the most part to encourage their feeding, and the animals simply starve to death. Such a death is particularly difficult to observe in these beautiful animals, as the animals slowly fall to pieces, while all the time trying to feed.

Crinoids should not be kept until we make more strides in understanding how we can provide the right kind of food to these lovely, delicate creatures.

MAIN PHOTO: ADULT; INSET: JUVENILE

Acanthaster planci
Crown-of-thorns

Maximum Size: Up to about 18 in. (46 cm) in diameter.
Range: Indo-Pacific.
Minimum Aquarium Size: Large tanks, 100 gal. (380 L) or larger.
Lighting: Immaterial.
Foods & Feeding: Feeds on living corals.
Aquarium Suitability/Reef Aquarium Compatibility: Not suitable for a coral reef aquarium. Spines can inflict a painful wound.
Captive Care: Infamous for its ability to eat corals, this species is occasionally imported and purchased by aquarists. Although it reaches diameters of 18 in. (46 cm), most in the reef hobby are much smaller, typically only a few inches across. The basic color is gray to green, occasionally orange, and the spines may be red, gray, green, or orange. It may have a dozen or more arms or rays. The long, up to 4 in. (10 cm) spines on the upper surface, appear to be poisonous; if they pierce the skin they can leave a painful wound. They need a large tank stocked with the appropriate corals for them to feed on and require standard reef conditions of temperature and salinity. Triton's trumpet snails (*Charonia* spp., page 316) will eat this species, but as adults they are likely to have no other enemies.

Choriaster granulatus
Doughboy star (Kenya star)

Maximum Size: Up to about 20 in. (0.5 m) in diameter.
Range: Indo-Pacific.
Minimum Aquarium Size: Large tanks, 200 gal. (760 L) or larger.
Lighting: Immaterial.
Foods & Feeding: Prefers live corals, but will scavenge carrion/detritus.
Aquarium Suitability/Reef Aquarium Compatibility: Will readily eat corals. Hardy, but not safe in most coral reef aquariums.
Captive Care: This attention-getting—somehow comical—sea star has five arms and a thick, puffy, inflated appearance. The arms are actually very stiff and turgid. The body is pink to gray, with plates on the body being orange, black, or reddish. This facultative coral predator eats some corals, but is also capable of being a scavenger. It may be kept in reef tanks, provided the tank is large enough and stocked with the appropriate corals for it to feed on. It requires standard reef conditions of temperature and salinity. Triton's trumpet snails (*Charonia* spp., page 313) will eat this species, but as an adult the Doughboy is likely to have no other enemies. As long as salinity is kept at full strength and it has has plenty of food, it will be quite hardy.

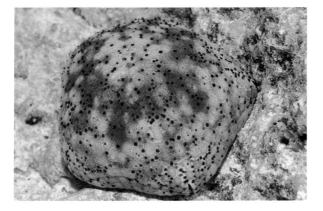

Culcita novaeguineae
Cushion star

Maximum Size: Up to 12 in. (30 cm) in diameter.
Range: Indo-Pacific.
Minimum Aquarium Size: Large tanks, 100 gal. (380 L) or larger.
Lighting: Immaterial.
Foods & Feeding: Feeds on live corals; may scavenge a bit.
Aquarium Suitability/Reef Aquarium Compatibility: Not safe in a coral reef aquarium.
Captive Care: This coral-eating sea star hardly looks like a sea star when full grown, because large individuals become almost spherical with only a hint of having arms. Only when the animal is turned over do the central mouth and five star-shaped rows of tube feet reveal its identity. Smaller individuals are star-shaped; as they grow, the inter-ray areas fill in and expand relative to the tube-foot rows. This star is seen in shades of red, brown, black, or green and may have patches of yellow highlighting. It may be kept in large reef tanks with appropriate corals as food. It requires standard reef temperatures and salinity. Triton's trumpet snails will eat this species, but as an adult it is likely to have no other enemies. With full-strength salinity and plenty of food, it will be quite hardy.

Fromia monilis
Elegant sea star (marble star)

Maximum Size: Up to 6 in. (15 cm) in diameter.
Range: Indo-Pacific.
Minimum Aquarium Size: Large tanks, 100 gal. (380 L) or larger.
Lighting: Immaterial.
Foods & Feeding: Possibly feeds on sponges; will not eat most meaty foods.
Aquarium Suitability/Reef Aquarium Compatibility: Not suitable for most tanks; will often live for a year or so and then die of malnutrition.
Captive Care: *Fromia monilis* has a brilliant orange to red central disc with numerous evident pores and cream to whitish plates on the arms. The outer portion of each arm is brilliant red or orange. May eat low-growing sponges or perhaps other animals growing in the surface films. An established tank with sponges and small sessile animals for grazing will probably provide the best chance for survival. Water conditions, particularly salinity, are paramount in their care. Acclimate slowly, adding water from its new system to its shipping water in small increments over a period of hours.

Fromia milleporella
Porous sea star (marble star, elegant sea star)

Maximum Size: Up to 6 in. (15 cm) in diameter.
Range: Indo-Pacific.
Minimum Aquarium Size: Large tanks, 100 gal. (380 L) or larger.
Lighting: Immaterial.
Foods & Feeding: Primarily feed on live sponges; may scavenge a bit. May eat frozen sponge rations.
Aquarium Suitability/Reef Aquarium Compatibility: Not suitable for most tanks; will often live for a year or so and then die of malnutrition.
Captive Care: These boldly patterned species do best in established tanks with sponges and small sessile animals for them to eat. Water conditions, particularly salinity, are paramount in their care. Acclimate slowly, adding water from its new system to its shipping water in small increments over a period of hours. It may eat low-growing sponges or perhaps other animals growing in the surface films. An established tank with sponges and small sessile animals for grazing will probably provide the best chance for survival.

Fromia ghardaqana
Ghardaqana sea star (Red Sea marble star)

Maximum Size: Up to about 3 in. (7.5 cm) in diameter.
Range: Red Sea, Mauritius.
Minimum Aquarium Size: Large tanks, 100 gal. (380 L) or larger.
Lighting: Immaterial.
Foods & Feeding: Diet unknown. Possibly eats sponges.
Aquarium Suitability/Reef Aquarium Compatibility: Not suitable for most tanks; will often live for a year or so and then die of malnutrition.
Captive Care: Endemic to the Red Sea, this species typically is red or orange with white or yellow contrasting large beadlike plates on the upper surface. It will likely do best in a large, well-established tank with a lot of sponge and epifaunal growth. Needs higher salinities and temperatures than most sea stars. The salinity should be in the range of 37 to 38 ppt, with temperatures of 82 to 84°F (27 to 29 °C). As with all echinoderms, it should be acclimated very slowly, over a period of hours, to new water conditions.

Fromia nodosa
Nodous sea star (marble star)

Maximum Size: Up to 6 in. (15 cm) in diameter.
Range: Indo-Pacific.
Minimum Aquarium Size: Large tanks, 100 gal. (380 L) or larger.
Lighting: Immaterial.
Foods & Feeding: Primarily feed on live sponges; may scavenge a bit. May eat frozen sponge rations.
Aquarium Suitability/Reef Aquarium Compatibility: Not suitable for most tanks; will often live for a year or so and then die of malnutrition.
Captive Care: *Fromia nodosa* is dark red to blackish orange, with scattered plates on the arms and no distinct coloration to the ends of the rays. A row of tubercles extends from the central disc out along the midline of each arm. This boldly patterned species does best in established tanks with sponges and small sessile animals for grazing. Found on reef rubble and larger unconsolidated material, it is unlikely that this species will eat larger sessile animals. Target feeding is likely to be unsuccessful but should be attempted. Water conditions, particularly salinity, are paramount in its care. Acclimate slowly, adding water from its new system to its shipping water in small increments over a period of hours.

Iconaster longimanus
Double star

Maximum Size: Up to 3.5 in. (9 cm) in diameter.
Range: Indo-Pacific.
Minimum Aquarium Size: Large tanks, 100 gal. (380 L) or larger.
Lighting: Immaterial.
Foods & Feeding: Natural diet unknown; may be an omnivorous scavenger.
Aquarium Suitability/Reef Aquarium Compatibility: Not suitable for most tanks; often lives a few months and then dies of malnutrition.
Captive Care: This strikingly patterned species has large marginal plates around the disc and rays. The plates delimit an area on the central disc covered with other plates of contrasting colors, forming a star. This star-within-a-star gives the species its common name. The five arms are relatively narrow. The large marginal plates are of contrasting colors, often reds, oranges, tan, gray, cream, or yellow. The random pattern of the colored plates gives the edges of the arms a characteristic mottled pattern. This species natural diet is unknown, but it may be a scavenger. It will survive under normal reef tank conditions, but good water parameters, especially maintenance of full-strength salinity, are a must.

Linckia laevigata
Blue *Linckia*

Maximum Size: Up to about 16 in. (40 cm) in diameter.

Range: Indo-Pacific.

Minimum Aquarium Size: Large tanks, 100 gal. (380 L) or larger.

Lighting: Good illumination will support algal growth on live rock, providing grazing opportunities.

Foods & Feeding: Natural and necessary diet unknown. Appears to eat and may accept meaty foods, but seldom survives more than 18 months. Appears to die of malnutrition.

Aquarium Suitability/Reef Aquarium Compatibility: Able to live at least a year in a reef aquarium if properly acclimated and provided with sufficient food.

Captive Care: With bright colors that range from aqua to almost violet, this is one of the most popular sea stars, and one of the few that may persist in reef aquariums. It reproduces asexually when one arm or ray pulls itself away from the central disc and walks away; the disc heals and grows a new ray, while the ray grows a new body and arms. *Important:* acclimate very slowly to new water, over a period of several hours or more. May be attacked by hermit crabs and several species of parasitic snails that need to be removed with forceps.

Linckia multifora
Spotted *Linckia* (multicolored *Linckia*)

Maximum Size: Up to 4 in. (10 cm) in diameter.
Range: Indo-Pacific.
Minimum Aquarium Size: Large tanks, 100 gal. (380 L) or larger.
Lighting: Immaterial.
Foods & Feeding: Natural diet unknown.
Aquarium Suitability/Reef Aquarium Compatibility: Suitable for most tanks, as they generally seem to be able to persist indefinitely.
Captive Care: *Linckia multifora* is much smaller than other *Linckia*, seldom exceeding 4 in. across and is among the most hardy of the starfishes available to aquarists. Typically mottled red, white, orange, and sometimes blue, it appears to reproduce asexually far more often than the larger *Linckia*, probably due to its smaller adult size. During such reproduction, one ray pulls itself away from the central disc and moves away. The disc heals and grows a new ray. The detached ray grows a new central disc that then buds and grows four new arms. This sea star needs to be acclimated very slowly. Once established, it generally does well and is quite hardy. May be attacked by hermit crabs, true crabs, and some fishes.

ASTROPECTEN SP.

Astropecten spp., *Luidia* spp.
Sand-sifting stars

Maximum Size: Up to 12 in. (30 cm) in diameter.
Range: Tropical seas.
Minimum Aquarium Size: Large tanks, 100 gal. (380 L) or larger.
Lighting: Immaterial.
Foods & Feeding: Feed on sediment infauna.
Aquarium Suitability/Reef Aquarium Compatibility: Not suitable for most tanks, as they remove all edible life from the sand bed and then starve.
Captive Care: Sold as scavengers, these stars move across the sediment surface until they decide to submerge into the substrate. While burrowing, they ingest any potential food items, then move to a new location. They eat brittle stars, worms, snails, sea cucumbers, and smaller organisms. These sea stars need a lot of food: once the animals in the sediment are eaten, the sea stars often starve to death. These stars are brown, gray, off-white, or black. Along the edges of each ray are large, shieldlike plates; these plates and their spines are larger in *Astropecten* than in *Luidia*, giving the sides of *Astropecten* arms a comblike appearance. *Luidia* often have limper, more flexible arms. *Astropecten* typically have five rays, as do most, but not all, *Luidia*. Some are active nocturnally.

Oreaster reticulatus
Caribbean cushion star

Maximum Size: Up to 12 in. (30 cm) in diameter.
Range: Caribbean.
Minimum Aquarium Size: Large tanks, 100 gal. (380 L) or larger.
Lighting: Immaterial.
Foods & Feeding: Its natural diet is sponges. Confined in an aquarium, it will eat sponges and other echinoderms, but these foods do not provide complete nutrition and the stars typically starve.
Aquarium Suitability/Reef Aquarium Compatibility: Not suitable for reef tanks. Lacks the flexibility to crawl on rockwork.
Captive Care: This very stiff, rugged star, with little flexibility, is sometimes offered for sale. It cannot maneuver in a crowded reef tank, and needs an aquarium with an open expanse of sand resembling its seagrass bed native habitat. It must have full-strength salinity and normal reef temperatures to do well. The upper surface of its body is covered with short, blunt spines arranged in a reticulated (netlike) pattern that gives this species its scientific name. Its basic color is typically orange, tan, or brown, with the spines being darker. Relatively few fishes or invertebrates will harm this species.

Pentagonaster duebeni
Red spot star

Maximum Size: Up to 6 in. (15 cm) in diameter.
Range: Indo-Pacific.
Minimum Aquarium Size: Large tanks, 100 gal. (380 L) or larger.
Lighting: Immaterial.
Foods & Feeding: Feeds on encrusting sponges and bryozoans.
Aquarium Suitability/Reef Aquarium Compatibility: Not suitable for reef tanks, which are too warm and probably lack the appropriate foods.
Captive Care: This cooler-water star is found in subtropical and cooler tropical regions but is occasionally imported for the reef aquarium hobby. Its basic color is white, but large reddish plates are imbedded in this skin. The five arms are rather thick and merge with a large central area, giving the impression of blunt arms. This star eats encrusting organisms, such as bryozoans, and perhaps sponges. It will do best in cooler water from about 70 to 77°F (21 to 25°C), and may be a good star for hobbyists with cooler-water tanks. Salinity should be kept at 35 to 37 ppt. The dietary habits of this star are poorly known, and it is possible that it may eat small-polyped corals or low soft corals in addition to its regular diet. Reef fishes are unlikely to harm these stars.

PROTOREASTER NODOSUS

Protoreaster lincki = Red-spined star
Protoreaster nodosus = Chocolate-chip star

Maximum Size: *Protoreaster nodosus* to 5 in. (13 cm) across; *P. lincki* to 12 in. (30 cm) across.
Range: Indo-Pacific.
Minimum Aquarium Size: Large tanks, 100 gal. (380 L) or larger.
Lighting: Immaterial.
Foods & Feeding: Reported to feed on sponges in nature.
Aquarium Suitability/Reef Aquarium Compatibility: Not suitable for reef tanks. May eat sessile invertebrates, including soft corals, stony corals, and sea anemones.
Captive Care: These species often do poorly in the aquarium; some don't eat at all or eat inappropriate foods that do not provide complete nutrition. Most die of malnutrition. Their stiff, spinous bodies prevent them from getting into the rockwork in search of food. Both species have five relatively stiff rays with a smooth, almost featureless epidermis from which rises a series of large, evident spines. Chocolate-chip stars are tan or light brown with large, blunt, dark brown spines. The spines of the orange to pale green red-spined stars are brilliant red, sharp, and have a network of low red ridges connecting them. Few other aquarium animals will bother them.

Protoreaster lincki (red-spined star): most often found in sandy, shallow areas and seagrass beds, it should have a relatively flat, open aquarium aquascape.

Protoreaster nodosus (chocolate-chip star): color variant. Believed to feed on sponges in the wild, it is not a great candidate for the marine aquarium.

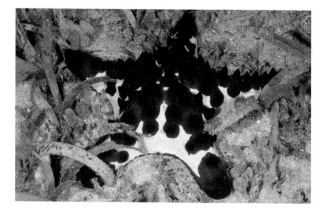

Protoreaster nodosus (chocolate-chip star): dark color variant. Note its typical habitat, a sandy seagrass bed.

Protoreaster nodosus (chocolate-chip star): orange color variant. May accept sponge-containing frozen marine rations.

Ophiomastix variabilis (black brittle star): often cryptic, staying hidden in the dark recesses of the reef during daylight, this can be a useful aquarium scavenger.

Introduction to the Ophiuroids
(Basket Stars, Brittle Stars, Serpent Stars)

The 1,600 or so species of ophiuroids, Class Ophiuroidea, are both remarkable and odd. Although they have the same sensitivity to salinity changes as the sea stars, they differ from them in a number of ways. All ophiuroids have a well-defined central disc, with the rays or arms set off by discrete notches or grooves. Most of them are fairly small, but some do get quite large. The largest are found in very deep waters in the Gulf of Mexico and reach almost 10 ft. (3 m) across. As a whole, the class is strongly pentamerous (having body parts in multiples of five), with relatively few animals having appendages or other body parts in numbers not divisible by five.

They move by the articulation of rays, and the rays move by articulation of ossicles rather than by the action of tube feet. Additionally, their digestive system is much reduced. The mouth opens directly into a capacious stomach, which can have several sections. They have no intestine or anus.

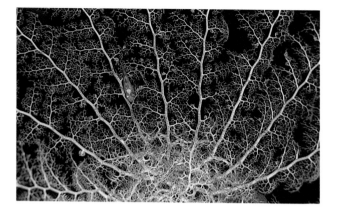

Astroboa nuda (night-feeding basket star): although spectacular to behold, these filter feeders are extremely difficult to keep well-nourished in the aquarium.

The feeding of ophiuroids has largely been investigated with temperate or cold-water species, although the feeding methods of some tropical species are also known. Many more types of feeding modes are found in ophiuroids than in asteroids (sea stars). The variety of feeding methods is illustrated by the behaviors of one North Atlantic species *Ophiocomina nigra*, which:

• May use their tube feet to pick up small particles of food, which are then mixed with mucus, rolled into little spheres, and transported to the mouth by being passed from one tube foot to another.

• May use their jaws (pointed ossicles beside the mouth) to graze on dead animals and algae.

• May loop one of the arms off the bottom and use that loop to grasp a small animal or piece of detritus.

• May trap small microplankton by suspension feeding: the arms lift off the bottom and strands of mucus are produced, which hang off the arms and spines. The tube feet pick the mucus strands from between the spines, wrap them into small balls and convey them to the mouth.

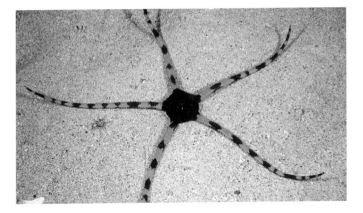

Ophiolepis sp. (serpent star): once introduced into a reef aquarium, these scavengers will often go unnoticed unless viewed at night with a red or very dim light.

• May trail their arms at the water's surface to collect the thin surface layer of organic material that is present.

Perhaps the oddest method of feeding by brittle stars was demonstrated by Mike LaBarbera in 1978. He showed that a North Pacific suspension-feeding brittle star, *Ophiopholis aculeata*, is able to collect material from the plankton without the use of a sticky mucus net. The animal extends its arms off the bottom into a water current. Its arms are then able to pick up an electrostatic charge from the water flow, which is then capable of attracting charged particles, such as small organic particulate material, from the plankton. This particular brittle star species may be found in many aquariums.

Ophiocoma wendtii, from the Caribbean, uses its tube feet to collect small particulate matter that adheres to its spines after extending its arms up into the water current. This may indicate that this species is also making use of an electrostatic feeding method.

What all this means to the average marine aquarist is that these animals are exceptionally good at scavenging within the nooks, crannies, and interstices of a reef, eating waste food, dead animals and other detritus.

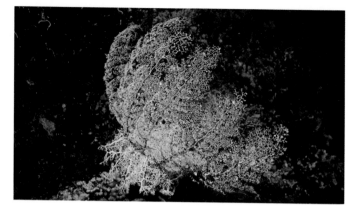

ASTROBOA NUDA

Astroboa nuda, Astrophyton muricatum
Basket stars

Maximum Size: To about 24 in. (60 cm) in diameter.
Range: *Astrophyton muricatum*, Caribbean; *Astroboa nuda*, Indo-Pacific.
Minimum Aquarium Size: Very large tanks, 300 gal. (1,140 L) or larger.
Lighting: Dim lighting is best.
Foods & Feeding: Need a continuous supply of zooplankton at night.
Aquarium Suitability/Reef Aquarium Compatibility: Suitable for only the largest reef tanks. Typically starve in captivity. Should not be kept with most reef fishes.
Captive Care: These are large, hard-to-keep stars with five arms that branch repeatedly, giving rise to many terminal prehensile tendrils that catch small planktonic food items. They hide during the day, crawling into a safe spot and tightly coiling their arms about them to protect them from fish predation. After dusk, they crawl to high areas and unfurl to feed. Need a very large tank to fully expand. Require good current flow completely across their entire width. Small particulate food should be tried for acceptability. If malnutrition is recognizable by the terminal erosion of the arm branches, a shift in foods is imperative. Require normal reef tank conditions of temperature and salinity. Colors are cream to tan to yellow.

Ophiactis spp.
Spiny brittle stars

Maximum Size: Up to 6 in. (15 cm) in diameter.
Range: Tropical seas.
Minimum Aquarium Size: Moderate tanks, 50 gal. (190 L) or larger.
Lighting: Immaterial.
Foods & Feeding: Scavengers on detritus; predatory on some bottom-dwelling animals.
Aquarium Suitability/Reef Aquarium Compatibility: Good aquarium animals. Generally beneficial scavengers.
Captive Care: These brittle stars can be a valuable addition to a reef aquarium "cleanup" crew, but need to be well nourished. In under-fed tanks, they will not receive sufficient food, the arm tips will start to "erode," and eventually they will starve to death. They have a small central disc; the five arms look too big for the central disc. Arms have large, narrow, sharp spines on their sides. Typically gray, tan or mottled combinations of gray, tan, brown and black. They live under rocks during the day and forage at night. They often remain in a crevice or cave and collect food with their arms, which extend out over the aquarium surfaces. May occasionally capture and eat an unwary or "sleeping" fish. Crustaceans may attack them.

Ophiarachna incrassata
Green brittle star ("The Green Death")

Maximum Size: Up to 20 in. (50 cm) in diameter.
Range: Indo-Pacific.
Minimum Aquarium Size: Large tanks, 100 gal. (380 L) or larger.
Lighting: Immaterial.
Foods & Feeding: Predatory on many types of animals.
Aquarium Suitability/Reef Aquarium Compatibility: One of the most voracious invertebrates found in captivity; not suitable for reef tanks.
Captive Care: This predatory brittle star forages for food at night and has been documented to eat firefishes, damselfishes, mandarinfishes, blennies, small gobies, cleaner wrasses, cleaner shrimps, and crabs. However, if maintained in a tank dedicated to its care, it will be an excellent pet. Needs a cave or place out of bright light in which to lurk. Its base color is light green to olive, with a fine patterning of light white or yellow spots and dark black or dark green bands on the surface. Central disc may be up to 2 in. (5 cm) across and relatively thick in a mature specimen. When ingesting a large meal, the disc may assume the proportions of a large marble or golf ball. Arms are relatively stout and highly muscular with rows of spines running down the length of each arm.

Ophiocoma **spp.**
Spiny black brittle stars

Maximum Size: Up to 8 in. (20 cm) in diameter.
Range: Caribbean.
Minimum Aquarium Size: Moderate tanks, 50 gal. (190 L) or larger.
Lighting: Immaterial.
Foods & Feeding: Adventitious predators, scavengers.
Aquarium Suitability/Reef Aquarium Compatibility: Good scavengers.
Captive Care: These brittle stars, as with many ophiuroids, are very good at avoiding light and escaping detection. Will often hide in aquariums under rocks or within the rockwork during the day and forage for food at night. They seldom harm other animals during their food foraging, although stationary or "sleeping" fishes may be too much of a temptation. They require normal reef conditions of temperature (80 to 84°F [27 to 29°C]) and salinity (36 ppt) and need a cave or place out of the bright light in which to lurk. They are black or deep chocolate brown with large, blunt spines in rows on either side of the arms. The arms are relatively short for the disc size, generally only about 5 to 8 disc diameters in length. Their planktonic larval stages preclude successful reproduction in hobbyist tanks.

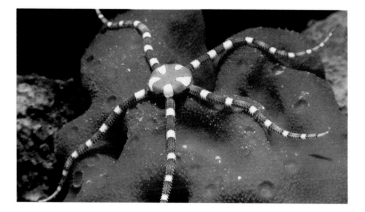

Ophioderma spp.
Short-spined brittle stars

Maximum Size: Up to 12 in. (30 cm) in diameter.
Range: Caribbean.
Minimum Aquarium Size: Moderate tanks, 50 gal. (190 L) or larger.
Lighting: Immaterial.
Foods & Feeding: Adventitious predators, scavengers.
Aquarium Suitability/Reef Aquarium Compatibility: Good scavengers.
Captive Care: These cryptic foragers often hide during the day and search for food at night, but their diet in nature is unknown. Some species have been seen to climb up on soft corals or gorgonians, indicating they may be feeding on the polyps or, more likely, climbing to get into the area of swift currents for suspension feeding. In captivity, they seem to be scavengers. Need a place to hide during the day, and may remain unseen for long periods unless special effort is made to hunt for them. Require normal reef conditions of temperature (80 to 84°F [27 to 29°C]) and salinity (36 ppt). Smooth-appearing arms actually have one or more rows of small spines down their sides. The central discs are relatively large. Some species are drab, brown to gray and black, others, such as *Ophioderma rubicundum*, are brilliant red or mottled red and white.

Ophiothrix spp.
Needle-spined brittle stars

Maximum Size: Up to 12 in. (30 cm) in diameter.
Range: Tropical seas.
Minimum Aquarium Size: Moderate tanks, 50 gal. (190 L) or larger.
Lighting: Immaterial.
Foods & Feeding: Symbiotic or commensal with large sponges or other large suspension feeders. Natural diets are unknown.
Aquarium Suitability/Reef Aquarium Compatibility: Poor survival rate in captivity, presumably due to inappropriate substrate and food.
Captive Care: These long-spined brittle stars generally live a few weeks to a few months and then start to die from the arm tips in toward the disc, a pattern typical of malnutrition. In the wild, they are found living on the surfaces of large sponges; may be getting food from the surface of the sponge or may be filtering in their own right or grazing on the sponge. They do not seem to require a hiding space and often seem to remain exposed for long periods, probably the result of having totally inappropriate habitats in captivity. They have moderately sized central discs and long arms that bear lateral rows of long, needle-like spines. Tend to be solid black, violet or gray; some have armbands of contrasting colors.

Diadema setosum (long-spined sea urchin): these beneficial herbivores can help control various types of algae in spacious aquariums.

Introduction to the Sea Urchins

The presence of spines really characterizes all members of the Class Echinoidea, but in sea urchins it is the anatomical feature that can't be ignored. Sea urchins generally have long, thin spines, and many are the divers, snorkelers and aquarists who have discovered the pain they can deliver. In some cases, the spines may be hollow (and thus they easily break off in a potential predator). Some have a venom gland (basically a bag of venom) at the tip of exceptionally sharp spines, while others have venom-filled spines. Most sea urchin spines, however, are solid, rugged, and without venom. The spines are modified ossicles, and as such they are generally under a layer of epidermis. The only exceptions to this rule are the pencil urchins, which have exposed spines with no epidermal covering.

Beneath the spines, the standard-issue sea urchin is essentially a hollow sphere made by a rigid body wall surrounding a body cavity that contains the gut, gonads, and other internal organs. The skeleton and spines of sea urchins (and all other echinoderms) are

Asthenosoma ijimai (fire urchin): the memorably bright colors should serve as a warning—members of this Indo-Pacific genus bristle with venom-tipped spines.

composed of ossicles of calcium-magnesium carbonate, and are produced within the body wall. Each ossicle (and spine, as the spines are modified ossicles) is a single crystal of the calcium salt. First, an organic matrix is laid down and then the calcitic material is deposited around it. These ossicles are amazing. Their maximum strength per unit weight is close to the theoretical maximum for calcium carbonate materials. In some sea urchins, these crystals may reach a foot (30 cm) or more in length. Crystals can be embedded in the dermis, free of attachment, or they may be very tightly fastened to another crystal with protein secretions, such as collagen fibers, forming the rigid body of the sea urchin.

Most sea urchins have a more-or-less spherical body, large evident spines and do not burrow through sediments. These are referred to as "regular" sea urchins. "Irregular" sea urchins are those modified to live within sediments, and include sand dollars and heart urchins.

The mouth is located on the oral or bottom surface of most sea urchins and has five sharp, biting teeth. There are special chemosensory tube feet around the mouth. The anus is at the other pole, and

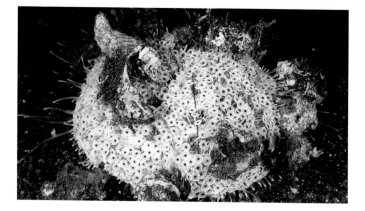

Toxopneustes pileoleus (flower urchin): although quite attractive, this curious-looking species delivers a venom-laced sting that is capable of causing death.

is surrounded by five plates, each of which contains an opening to a gonad. Light-sensitive plates are found in these plates, as well.

Sea urchins may also have spines modified into pinching structures, called pedicellariae. Two of the basic forms are tridentate pedicellariae, which have three elongate jaws used for food transfer and pinching defense, and globiferous pedicellariae, which contain venom glands at their bases.

Many sea urchins are imported into marine aquariums only to die there from either malnourishment or salinity stress. When a sea urchin begins to die, it will generally start to "drop" spines. The aquarist should consider that these spines are a fundamental part of the body wall, and when they are lost, large areas of epidermis are also lost, opening the animal up to infection and death. By the time large numbers of spines start to be dropped, it is too late to help the animal recover.

If spine dropping is noted, the aquarist might do well to isolate the sea urchin in a hospital tank with plenty of algal food, such as nori or rock covered in coralline algae. If the cause was malnourishment, this treatment may arrest the problem.

Diadema spp.
Long-spined urchins

Maximum Size: Up to 24 in. (60 cm) in diameter; most smaller.
Range: Tropical seas.
Minimum Aquarium Size: Moderate tanks, 50 gal. (190 L) or larger.
Lighting: Immaterial.
Foods & Feeding: Primarily herbivorous; will take meaty foods.
Aquarium Suitability/Reef Aquarium Compatibility: Good reef inhabitants, if they have enough food and proper water conditions.
Captive Care: Several species are encountered in the hobby. May be black, violet, blue-black, or gray. Spines may be solid colors or banded. The spherical body is surrounded by long, thin, sharp spines. Spines are longer on the upper surface than on the lower, allowing the mouth to get down to the substrate to feed. Use care when handling: the spines are not venomous, but are capable of inflicting painful puncture wounds. The spines, covered with epithelial tissues and bacteria, break easily into barbed segments that work deeper into wounds. *Diadema* eat all kinds of algae, including coralline algae, but are also excellent grazers on filamentous or "hair" algae. They need water with a salinity of 36 to 37 ppt and normal reef temperatures to do well.

ECHINOMETRA LACUNTER

Echinometra lacunter, Echinometra mathei
Short-spined urchin (rock urchin)

Maximum Size: Up to 3 in. (7.6 cm) in diameter; most smaller.

Range: *Echinometra lacunter*, Caribbean, *E. mathei*, Indo-Pacific.

Minimum Aquarium Size: Moderate tanks, 50 gal. (190 L) or larger.

Lighting: Immaterial.

Foods & Feeding: Primarily herbivorous; will take meaty foods.

Aquarium Suitability/Reef Aquarium Compatibility: Good reef inhabitants, if they have enough food and proper water conditions.

Captive Care: In nature, these animals may bore holes in reef rock and live in them, foraging near the holes after dark for algae. Three *Echinometra* species are common in the hobby, but *E. lacunter* is probably the most common, hitchhiking in on aquacultured Caribbean live rock. They are good at controlling hair algae in aquariums. Colors are black or dark purple, sometimes with a reddish cast, and the color is uniformly distributed over the animal and spines. *Echinometra mathei*, found on Indo-Pacific rock, is effectively identical. Spines are shorter, about 1 in. (2.5 cm) long in adults, blunter and significantly less dangerous than on *Diadema* urchins. The spines project completely around the animal. Salinity should remain at or slightly above 36 ppt, with temperatures around 82°F (28°C).

Mespilia globulus
Blue tuxedo urchin

Maximum Size: Up to 2 in. (5 cm) in diameter; most smaller.
Range: Indo-Pacific.
Minimum Aquarium Size: Moderate tanks, 50 gal. (190 L) or larger.
Lighting: Immaterial.
Foods & Feeding: Primarily herbivorous; will take meaty foods.
Aquarium Suitability/Reef Aquarium Compatibility: Good reef inhabitant, if it has enough food and proper water conditions.
Captive Care: A beautiful animal, the blue tuxedo urchin is easily distinguished from all other sea urchins by its thick, straight rows of short, silver or gray spines separated by a velvety body surface that may range from brilliant blue to dull green. The spines are very sharp, but only about 0.25 in. (6 mm) long. The animal carries bits of debris, shells, algal fragments, and such on its surface, presumably as either visual camouflage from visual predators, such as fishes, or as tactile camouflage from non-visual predators, such as sea stars. As long as the urchin is carrying its bits of rock and debris, it is in good health; one without its covering material is not healthy and remedial action needs to be taken. Salinity should remain at or slightly above 36 ppt, with temperatures around 82°F (28°C).

Microcyphus rousseaui
Red tuxedo urchin

Maximum Size: Up to 24 in. (61 cm) in diameter; most smaller.
Range: Indo-Pacific.
Minimum Aquarium Size: Moderate tanks, 50 gal. (190 L) or larger.
Lighting: Immaterial.
Foods & Feeding: Primarily herbivorous; will take meaty foods.
Aquarium Suitability/Reef Aquarium Compatibility: Good reef inhabitant, if it has enough food and proper water conditions.
Captive Care: Easily distinguished from all other sea urchins by its thick rows of short (about 0.25 in. [6 mm] long) very sharp gray or tan spines. The spine rows have bars that alternate from side to side, giving the bare orange-red to pinkish inter-row areas a meandering appearance. The animal carries bits of debris, shells, algal fragments and such on its surface, presumably as either visual camouflage from visual predators, such as fishes, or as tactile camouflage from non-visual predators, such as sea stars. As long as the urchin carries bits of rock and debris, it is very likely in good health; one without its covering material may be unhealthy or dying. Salinity should remain at or slightly above 36 ppt, with temperatures around 82°F (28°C).

TOXOPNEUSTES ROSEUS

Toxopneustes spp.
Flower urchins

Maximum Size: Up to 6 in. (15 cm) in diameter.
Range: Indo-Pacific.
Minimum Aquarium Size: Large tanks, 100 gal. (380 L) or larger.
Lighting: Immaterial.
Foods & Feeding: Herbivorous; need an occasional "meat meal."
Aquarium Suitability/Reef Aquarium Compatibility: *They are venomous, possibly deadly, and potentially pose a great threat to the aquarist.*
Captive Care: The vividly colored surface of these urchins is covered with small, circular structures about 0.25 in. (6 mm) across, looking much like little pink or red flowers with a white rim. These are modified spines, called pedicellariae, that have the potential of killing humans; at least one fatality has been documented. The pretty pedicellariae function as pinching jaws. These spines have a stalk supporting three jaws, each of which has sharp, recurved teeth and a basal venom gland. When the jaws close, they inject venom through the holes cut into the outer tissue layers by the teeth. They are harmless once in a reef aquarium, but transferring them to another tank or inadvertently touching them during maintenance could be *very* dangerous.

TRIPNEUSTES GRATILLA

Tripneustes spp.
Sea eggs (collector sea urchins)

Maximum Size: Up to 4 in. (10 cm) in diameter.
Range: Caribbean.
Minimum Aquarium Size: Large tanks, 100 gal. (380 L) or larger.
Lighting: Immaterial.
Foods & Feeding: Primarily herbivorous; forage on detritus and will take meaty foods.
Aquarium Suitability/Reef Aquarium Compatibility: Not suitable for reef tanks. Need seagrass debris and a sand bed for good health.
Captive Care: These are creatures of seagrass beds, and will do well in a aquarium with a large expanse of open sand and planted seagrasses. In a crowded reef tank, they may be destructive, as they are large and capable of significantly remodeling the landscape. They may be predatory on sessile animals. They have a flattened spherical shape. The spines are relatively small, compared to the size of the body, about 0.4 in. (1 cm) long. They carry bits of debris, detritus, and shells over their surface, probably as camouflage. Care needs to be taken to ensure the proper, full-strength (36 ppt) salinity and normal reef temperatures of 82°F (28°C).

Tripneustes gratilla (sea egg): using bits of rubble and other debris, these urchins seem to camouflage themselves to escape detection by predators.

Tripneustes gratilla (sea egg): barely visible beneath an accumulated cloak of seagrass, this urchin is a curiosity, but can be destructive in reef aquariums.

ASTHENOSOMA IJIMAI

Asthenosoma spp.
Fire urchins

Maximum Size: Up to 6 in. (15 cm) in diameter.
Range: Indo-Pacific.
Minimum Aquarium Size: Large tanks, 100 gal. (380 L) or larger.
Lighting: Immaterial.
Foods & Feeding: Herbivorous; need an occasional meaty meal.
Aquarium Suitability/Reef Aquarium Compatibility: *Not suitable for a reef aquarium; capable of inflicting a painful, dangerous sting.*
Captive Care: Vividly colored, these stinging urchins have a flexible, rather than rigid, body. Long, fragile spines are visible, but small, comblike groups of shorter spines are found between them. These smaller spines have repetitive swellings that look like beads, and they have bulbous poison sacs just below the tips. The venom sacs are colored bright blue in some species, bright white in others. If the spines pierce the skin, the pain is often sharp and immediate, but it also often seems to increase in intensity over the next few hours. Once in a reef tank the urchins would be harmless, but transferring them or inadvertently touching them during maintenance could be dangerous. Careless aquarists can be seriously injured, and these animals ought not to be collected from the reef.

EUCIDARIS TRIBULOIDES

Eucidaris tribuloides, Heterocentrotus mammillatus
Slate pencil urchins

Maximum Size: *Eucidaris tribuloides* up to 6 in. (15 cm) in diameter; *Heterocentrotus mammillatus* up to 12 in. (30 cm); most smaller.

Range: *Eucidaris tribuloides*, Caribbean; *Heterocentrotus mammillatus*, Indo-Pacific.

Minimum Aquarium Size: Large tanks, 100 gal. (380 L) or larger.

Lighting: Immaterial.

Foods & Feeding: Omnivorous, with a tendency toward carnivory.

Aquarium Suitability/Reef Aquarium Compatibility: Will eat sessile animals, and can catch mobile ones as well.

Captive Care: These are fascinating animals with blunt spines, not appropriate for typical reef aquariums, but good for the "species" tank with open spaces. They normally are red or red with white highlights, but both species are variable in coloration. They live in burrows during the day and forage at night. Somewhat territorial, they return to the same hole each night using their large, heavy spines to wedge themselves in the rocks. Will eat and do well on standard fresh or fresh-frozen foods, such as diced fish or krill that are offered as fish food. Provide them a place to hide from the light of day. Need proper salinity and normal reef temperatures as well.

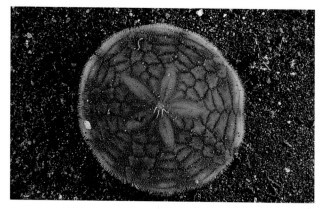

CF. *PERONELLA* SP.

Clypeaster spp., *Encope* spp., *Mellita* spp., and others
Sand dollars

Maximum Size: Up to 6 in. (15 cm) in diameter; most smaller.
Range: Caribbean, Indo-Pacific.
Minimum Aquarium Size: Moderate tanks, 50 gal. (190 L) or larger.
Lighting: Immaterial.
Foods & Feeding: Herbivores. Ingest sediments and eat diatoms, other microalgae, and bacteria. May feed on algae in suspension.
Aquarium Suitability/Reef Aquarium Compatibility: Good reef community animals. Need sand beds that are at least 4 in. (10 cm) deep.
Captive Care: Sand dollars make very interesting aquarium specimens, but they need a lot of sand to thrive, at least 10 ft.^{2} (1.0 m^2) of surface for an individual 4 in. (10 cm) in diameter. They cannot tolerate and may suffocate in fine sediment, such as aragonitic sandy muds. Shapes vary from almost circular to broad arrowhead; generally discoidal. Colors range from dark purple to green to tan or gray. Live either just exposed or slightly below the sediment surface; may burrow considerably deeper. The top surface has a series of modified tube feet arranged in a structure looking vaguely like a flower, called a petaloid. They require proper salinity. Verify origin before purchase: subtropical animals die in normal reef temperatures.

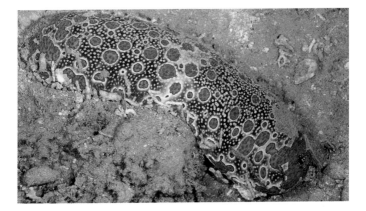

Bohadschia argus (leopard sea cucumber): these animals can eject their viscera as a survival mechanism, potentially poisoning everything in an aquarium.

Introduction to Sea Cucumbers

Repulsive to many, fascinating to anyone with a bent for biology and, once in a while, simply beautiful, sea cucumbers are for marine aquarists who love the unusual or even bizarre.

As a start, these are animals that may, in a defensive reaction, or in response to severe stress, expel part of their internal organs (viscera) through the anus. The ejected viscera are sloughed, and if the animal had been in prior good health and the eviscerating stress is removed, the animal will grow a new set of internal organs. If this happens in a well-aerated or well-skimmed aquarium, and the eviscerated guts are removed from the tank, generally nothing drastic will occur. On the other hand, if the eviscerating cucumber is of the wrong species, some of the animals may be poisoned and die.

Some tropical bottom-feeding sea cucumber species have defensive structures, called Cuvierian tubules or Cuvierian organs. If these animals are stressed, they may expel these tubules from the anus during a partial evisceration. The Cuvierian tubules are sticky and, in some species, contain a vertebrate-specific toxin called holothurin.

Thelenota rubralineata (candy-stripe sea cucumber): an Indo-Pacific species too large for most tanks. Smaller sea cucumbers can perform sand-stirring services.

In nature, this reaction probably just distracts, irritates, and sickens a potential predator. It is unlikely that it would be lethal. However, the predator is probably deterred from that particular cucumber, which will live to regenerate its lost parts. In the enclosed volume of an aquarium, however, the evisceration response, followed by the holothurin liberation, may result in contamination that could rapidly kill all the fishes and perhaps some of the invertebrates.

A few other holothuroids, particularly the sea apple (*Pseudo-colochirus axiologus*) commonly sold to aquarists, have high concentrations of holothurin in their tissues. If stressed, they tend to release this substance into the tank water, and it may be as fatal as the evisceration of the Cuvierian tubules.

All of this aside, some species of sea cucumbers will perform quiet scavenging services, burrowing in the substrate of the aquarium and keeping deep sand beds healthy. Chosen wisely, a sea cucumber can be a positive addition to the aquarium. An unwise choice, however, may be a time bomb that can cause a lot of problems.

Holothuria thomasi
Tiger tail sea cucumber

Maximum Size: Up to 6.5 ft. (2 m) long; most smaller.
Range: Caribbean.
Minimum Aquarium Size: Large tanks, 100 gal. (380 L) or larger.
Lighting: Immaterial.
Foods & Feeding: Herbivore. Ingests sediments and eats diatoms, other microalgae, and bacteria. A deep sand bed is necessary for good health.
Aquarium Suitability/Reef Aquarium Compatibility: Good reef tank animal.
Captive Care: Seldom seem at full length, this sea cucumber moves slowly, daubing the surface with its mucus-laden oral tentacles to collect and eat small detritus particles and bacterial aggregates. When small it will wander around in search of food, but as it grows, it will find a place to hide and only the front end will extend out to feed. It may release the toxin holothurin if bothered by hermit crabs, which should be removed. Colored with alternating bands of light yellowish gray or gray, and black or dark gray. May periodically shed a cuticular layer that covers the body. May reproduce asexually by fission; during this period of fission, the animal becomes reclusive for a week or two, only to emerge as two individuals.

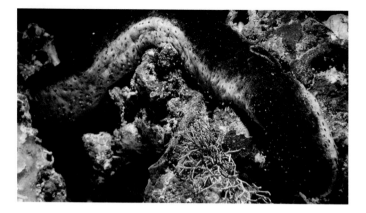

Holothuria edulis
Black sand-mopping cucumber

Maximum Size: Up to 16 in. (40 cm) long; most smaller.
Range: Indo-Pacific.
Minimum Aquarium Size: Moderate tanks, 50 gal. (190 L) or larger.
Lighting: Immaterial.
Foods & Feeding: Herbivore. Ingests sediments and eats diatoms, other microalgae and bacteria. A deep sand bed is necessary for good health.
Aquarium Suitability/Reef Aquarium Compatibility: Good reef tank animal.
Captive Care: True to its name, this sausage-shaped sea cucumber moves slowly over the sediments, "mopping" up its dinner. It is not reclusive and has tube feet confined to the bottom of the animal and warts or short fleshy spines on the top and sides. Colors are typically shades of black, gray, or dark brown, often with a black dorsal surface and a pink, rose, or tan ventral surface. May release holothurin toxin if stressed by abnormal physical conditions or if bothered or irritated by hermit crabs, which should be removed. May help clean the substrate. May shed a cuticular layer that covers the body. May reproduce asexually by fission; during this period, the animal becomes reclusive for a week or two, only to emerge as two individuals.

Pseudocolochirus **spp.** (*P. axiologus, P. tricolor, P violaceus*)
Sea apples

Maximum Size: Up to 6 in. (15 cm) long; most smaller.
Range: Indo-Pacific.
Minimum Aquarium Size: Moderate tanks, 50 gal. (190 L) or larger.
Lighting: Immaterial.
Foods & Feeding: Suspension feeders; need lots of fine particulate foods. Phytoplankton supplementation or rotifers are necessary.
Aquarium Suitability/Reef Aquarium Compatibility: Hard to feed. They may poison an entire tank if stressed.
Captive Care: These three species (perhaps color forms of the same species) seem irresistible to some aquarists despite many disastrous episodes caused by their defenses. Body walls and internal structures contain high concentrations of poisons that can be deadly in a reef tank if the animals are stressed. Rows of tubercles (modified tube feet) are found on each of the upper sides of the tough body. Body color is red, blue, or violet; tube feet and tubercles are red or yellow (sometimes on stripes of contrasting color); feeding tentacles are red, white, or blue. Needs cooler temperatures of 76 to 79°F (24 to 26°C) and normal reef salinities. Slowly starves in most systems and should not be purchased unless the aquarist can feed it properly.

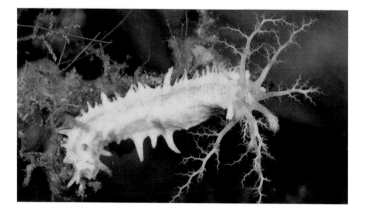

Colochirus robustus
Yellow cucumber

Maximum Size: Up to 2 in. (5 cm) long; most smaller.
Range: Indo-Pacific.
Minimum Aquarium Size: Small tanks, 10 gal. (38 L) or larger.
Lighting: Immaterial.
Foods & Feeding: Suspension feeder; needs lots of fine particulate foods. Phytoplankton supplementation or rotifers are necessary.
Aquarium Suitability/Reef Aquarium Compatibility: Good aquarium animal.
Captive Care: Small, bright yellow and with numerous relatively large bumps distributed over the upper body surfaces, this little "cuke" is unmistakable. Naturally found in large and dense aggregations on rock walls in nature, it tends to like vertical surfaces. Requires strong currents. Regularly asexually reproduces in captivity, dividing in two by splitting at about the midpoint of the body. The front half appears to grow a new rear end, and the converse occurs for the other half. Care should be taken to ensure the proper salinity and temperature. Hermit crabs, particularly the aggressive blue-legged hermits, need to be kept at minimum for this cucumber to survive. No reports of tank crashes or mortalities are linked to this species.

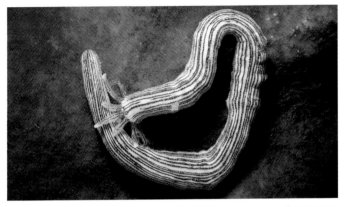

SYNAPTULA SP.

Euapta spp., *Opheodesoma* spp., *Synaptula* spp.
Medusa worms

Maximum Size: Up to 5 ft. (1.5 m) long; most smaller.

Range: Tropical seas.

Minimum Aquarium Size: Large tanks, 100 gal. (380 L) or larger.

Lighting: No special illumination required.

Foods & Feeding: Bottom-moppers, or gleaners. Occasionally some species appear to feed on suspended material.

Aquarium Suitability/Reef Aquarium Compatibility: Generally good aquarium animals. Have the potential to cause tank "wipeouts."

Captive Care: These translucent wormlike sea cucumbers crawl and twine their way across the substrate and are often capable of extensive inflation. They lack tube feet, but adhere to the substrate by means of small, anchor-shaped ossicles that protrude from the body surface; ossicles make them sticky and hard to handle. Characteristics like tentacle structure, ossicle structure, and shape separate the genera, but all are sold as "medusa" worms. Large specimens are seldom found in the trade. Care should be taken to ensure the proper salinity and temperature. Hermit crabs, particularly the aggressive blue-legged hermits, need to be kept at a minimum for these cucumbers to survive.

Didemnum molle (green barrel colonial tunicate): superficially spongelike in appearance but much more complicated, with a rapid retraction response when touched.

Introduction to the Tunicates (Ascidiaceans)

Superficially simple-seeming, the tunicates are complicated animals closely related to fishes. During their larval stages, they possess a backbonelike structure, linking them to the vertebrates. Additionally, the pharynx of ascidians is perforated, as in the gills of fishes. They are highly derived animals with life stages similar to those of fishes and invertebrates.

There are about 1,200 species of ascidiaceans, otherwise known as tunicates or sea squirts. The adults are all sessile, benthic-dwelling, ciliary-mucous suspension-feeding animals. Although there are a great many completely solitary species, many others are typified by individuals budded from a parent to form a colony of clones. Some of these clonal species have more-or-less separate individuals, or zooids (these are called social or gregarious tunicates), whereas in others many thousands of zooids share a common tunic (these are called compound or colonial tunicates). All tunicates live fastened to the substrate by their cellulose tunic.

There are two tunic openings, the incurrent (branchial) and the

Clavelina robusta (colonial tunicate): a very common Indo-Pacific species that may arrive on live rock. Feeds on fine, suspended particulate matter.

excurrent (atrial) siphons. Water enters the animal through the incurrent siphon and passes through a large filtering region, called the branchial basket. Here, small slits in the tissues allow the water to pass through while food is strained out. Water is pumped through the basket by the action of cilia lining the edges of the gill slits. Very fine particulate material, mostly bacterioplankton, is filtered from the water and is caught on the mucous layer lining the branchial basket. Tunicates are impressively effective suspension-feeders. Even small ones can filter hundreds of liters of water per day and remove well over 95 percent of the bacteria.

The number, shape, and position of these slits are some of the major taxonomic characteristics, but much of the currently existing taxonomy of tunicates, particularly of compound tunicates, is simply outdated and unreliable. Recent work indicates that many species remain undescribed or poorly described. As a general rule, it is simply impossible to identify most tunicates to the species level by visual examination. Microscopic examination of the internal structures is an absolute necessity, particularly in compound tunicates.

Polycarpa aurata
Giant Pacific tunicate

Maximum Size: Up to 8 in. (20 cm) in diameter; most much smaller.
Range: Indo-Pacific.
Minimum Aquarium Size: Large tanks, 100 gal. (380 L) or larger.
Lighting: Immaterial.
Foods & Feeding: Suspension feeder; needs lots of fine particulate foods. Bacterial aggregate supplementation necessary.
Aquarium Suitability/Reef Aquarium Compatibility: Poor survivor in captivity. Most die of malnutrition due to lack of planktonic foods.
Captive Care: This animal is a prize for any true lover of invertebrates, but it needs dedicated care and feeding to survive. Orange, tan, or gold, with violet or maroon patches or bands. In nature, it will filter thousands of liters of water in a day to remove its food; in captivity, we generally do not have enough bacteria or nanoplankton to keep this species alive. Phytoplankton supplementation may help, but it normally does not eat this type of food. Most tunicates secrete antifouling agents that may be toxic, so this large animal may create problems in tanks. If well maintained and fed properly, it may produce gametes, and it is possible that smaller individuals will appear in the aquarium. For advanced aquarists only.

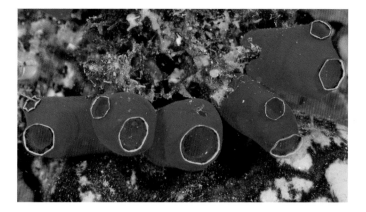

Rhopalaea spp.
Cobalt tunicates

Maximum Size: Up to 3 in. (7.6 cm) in diameter; most much smaller.
Range: Tropical seas.
Minimum Aquarium Size: Large tanks, 100 gal. (380 L) or larger.
Lighting: Immaterial.
Foods & Feeding: Suspension feeders; need lots of fine particulate foods. Bacterial aggregate supplementation necessary.
Aquarium Suitability/Reef Aquarium Compatibility: Poor survival. Most die of malnutrition due to lack of planktonic foods.
Captive Care: Stunningly beautiful, these tunicates can be quite hardy in captivity, but only if given sufficient foods. They require normal reef temperatures and salinities, but need expert feeding of fine particulate foods. Phytoplankton supplementation may be tried, but this may potentially hinder the animals by fouling the filter apparatus. A large, long-established reef tank with minimal skimming may suit them best. These species are often vivid blue with contrasting color bands around the siphonal edges and running in a band down the side. Transparent or translucent tunics, shaded by blues or yellows, are also often seen. Highly toxic, but probably won't be bothered by any organisms in the tank.

CLAVELINA MOLUCCENSIS

Clavelina diminuta = Orange social tunicate
Clavelina moluccensis = Blue social tunicate
Symplegma viride = Encrusting social tunicate

Maximum Size: Up to 6 in. (15 cm) in diameter.
Range: Tropical seas.
Minimum Aquarium Size: Moderate tanks, 50 gal. (190 L) or larger.
Lighting: Immaterial.
Foods & Feeding: Suspension feeders; need lots of fine particulate foods. Bacterial aggregate supplementation necessary.
Aquarium Suitability/Reef Aquarium Compatibility: Poor survival. Most die of malnutrition due to lack of large amounts of microplanktonic foods.
Captive Care: These pretty, delicate-looking colonial tunicates sometimes are collected on live rock, but they normally live only a few weeks or months in the aquarium. A small colony may get enough bacteria out of the water to survive, particularly in tanks with a good sand bed. If they have sufficient food, they will reproduce. Small but distinct individuals grow from a common spreading base. Form cylindrical zooids rising from the bottom, and have two siphons visible at the top of the cylinder. Siphons often surrounded by thin lines of highly contrasting color. Bottom connections often obscure. Must be collected on a piece of substrate to survive.

Clavelina detorta: in this genus of tunicates, the body is divided into two regions, an upper region containing the feeding apparatus and a lower region containing the remainder of the body organs.

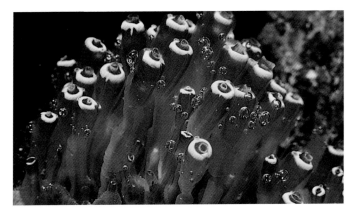

Clavelina robusta: distinguished by the rings of contrasting color around the siphons, this species is one of the most common *Clavelina* species in the Indo-Pacific. It often hitchhikes into aquariums on live rock.

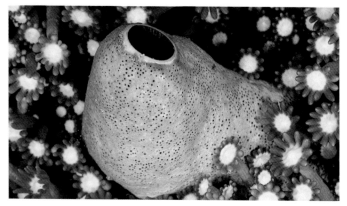

DIDEMNUM MOLLE

Atriolum robustum, Didemnum molle
Indo-Pacific green barrel colonial tunicates

Maximum Size: Colonies up to 2 in. (5 cm) in diameter; rarely larger.
Range: Indo-Pacific.
Minimum Aquarium Size: Small tanks, 10 gal. (38 L) or larger.
Lighting: Bright illumination will be beneficial.
Foods & Feeding: Suspension feeders; need lots of fine particulate foods. Bacterial aggregate supplementation necessary.
Aquarium Suitability/Reef Aquarium Compatibility: Poor survival; most die of malnutrition due to lack of large amounts of planktonic foods.
Captive Care: These sea squirts form cylindrical, barrellike colonies with a single large cloacal or excurrent opening. Incurrent siphons are found on the outer surface of the barrel and tend to be minute in *Didemnum;* larger in *Atriolum. Didemnum* colonies grow to several inches in diameter, *Atriolum* are typically less than 1.2 in. (3 cm) in height. Both are drab green due to the presence of a symbiotic cyanobacterium, *Prochloron,* which supplies some of the colony's nutritional needs. They are, surprisingly, relatively mobile and move across substrates probably in search of better conditions. Should do well in a well-lit tank where the symbiont can assist the colony in obtaining nutrition.

ABDOMEN: The posterior or last section of a crustacean body.

ANTENNAE: Either of the two anterior appendages (the "feelers") of a crustacean, or the most anterior appendages on the head of a polychaete annelid worm.

APERTURE: The opening of a snail's shell or of a tubeworm's tube.

APOSEMATIC COLOR: Warning coloration; "striking" color pattern designed to attract attention to warn a predator that the animal bearing the pattern is distasteful or poisonous.

ASEXUAL PLANULAE: Larvae of cnidarians (sea anemones, corals, or hydrozoans) produced by clonal means (such as budding) rather than by sexual reproduction.

AUTOTOMY: The process of voluntarily severing, or "dropping," an appendage or body part. Common in crabs and some other crustaceans; also occurs in some snails, such as *Stomatella varia*, which will autotomize part of its foot.

BIOLUMINESCENT: Shining with light produced from within a living organism by chemical means.

BROOD POUCH: Also called a marsupium, this is a structure located ventrally in amphipods, isopods, and mysids; eggs are brooded inside this structure until they hatch.

BYSSUS: The proteinaceous threads produced from the foot of several different types of clams.

CALCAREOUS SPONGE: A sponge in the taxonomic Class Calcarea in the Phylum Porifera; the spicules constituting the internal skeleton of these animals are made of calcium carbonate.

CARAPACE: The "shell" or covering of the anterior portion of crabs, shrimps, and lobsters.

CARNIVORY: The act of eating meat.

CEPHALOTHORAX: In the advanced crustaceans, the anterior body region resulting from the fusion of the anterior two body regions, the head and thorax.

CERATA (SINGULAR = CERAS): The frills on the back of a nudibranch.

GLOSSARY

CHAETAE (SINGULAR = CHAETA): The bristles of a polychaete annelid composed, in most cases, of solid rods of chitin.

CHELAE: In crustaceans, pincers or claws formed from the last two segments of a stenopodial appendage.

CHELICERATA: Arthropods lacking antennae or jaws; with four pairs of walking legs; with a body divided into two main regions, an anterior prosoma, and posterior opisthosoma. Examples are horseshoe crabs, scorpions, spiders, mites, and sea spiders.

CHELIPEDS: In crustaceans, appendages bearing claws; in crabs these are generally just the first pair of thoracic legs; in shrimps, any of the first three pairs of thoracic legs may be chelipeds.

CLOACA: A body chamber containing the openings of the digestive tract and urogenital systems; found in fishes, sea cucumbers, echiurids, and a few other groups.

CNIDARIA: The animal group or phylum containing sea anemones, hydroids, jellyfishes, and corals.

COLUMELLA: The central shell axis of coiling in gastropods; forms the inner edge of the aperture.

CORALLITES: The depressions or skeletal pockets that coral animals secrete around themselves.

CTENOPHORE: A member of the taxonomic Phylum Ctenophora; characterized by fringed feeding tentacles and rows of locomotory structures called ctenes.

DICHOTOMOUS BRANCHING: A pattern of branching where branch formation results in two branches identical in size; found in many algae, hydrocorals, and some primitive plants.

EPITOKE: A swimming reproductive stage found in several types of polychaete annelids; the posterior portion of the worm changes so the gut degenerates, and the body cavity becomes filled with gametes. Given the right cues, this portion of the worm will break off from the rest of the body and will swim up in the water column, disintegrating and releasing gametes. The rest of the worm, safe in its burrow, regenerates a new posterior body.

FOOT: In mollusks, the locomotory structure located on the ventral surface; in clams, it may contain a byssal gland to secrete byssal threads; in gastropods it may be more-or-less elaborated for swimming, burrowing, or other locomotion.

GIRDLE: In chitons, the tough tissue surrounding the eight shells.

HEADSHIELD SLUG: A type of snail with a reduced or absent shell (varies with the species). The front part of the body is characterized by a rectangular region delineated by grooves or folds (the headshield); may also have flaps extending up over each side of the body. Some headshield slugs appear to be nudibranchs, but they are internally quite different.

HERBIVORY: The act of eating food of plant or algal origin.

HERMAPHRODITE: Possessing functional reproductive organs of both male and female systems; may be simultaneous or sequential.

HOLOTHURIN: A poison found in some types of sea cucumbers; when liberated into the water it specifically affects fishes.

INTROVERT: A body region, found in sipunculans, which can be withdrawn into itself and pulled into the body by the action of the retractor muscles; similar in structure to some types of gastropod proboscides.

LOBULATE: Being formed with or by lobes.

MANTLE: That part of a mollusk, brachiopod, or tunicate that secretes the external covering (shell or tunic).

MARGINAL PLATES: Large ossicles in the body wall of a sea star or brittle star that lie on the sides of the rays.

MEDUSAE (SINGULAR = MEDUSA): Jellyfishes.

NEMATOCYST: The stinging capsule of cnidarians; often venom-filled, used in prey capture.

OMNIVORE: An animal that eats a wide variety of foods, including both animal and plant material.

OPERCULUM: The plug to the aperture of a snail, calcareous tubeworm, or bryozoan hole.

OPISTHOSOMA: The posterior, or second, portion of the body of a horseshoe crab or other chelicerate animal.

OSSICLES: Calcareous plates found in the tissues of the echinoderms; may be fused (as in sea urchins) or free; may be modified to form spines or pedicellariae.

PALPS: Tentaculate appendages that are found on the most anterior segments of several types of polychaete annelid worms.

PAPILLATE: Covered with small bumps or pimples.

PARAPODIA: The small appendages found on both sides of each segment of polychaete annelid worms. In some polychaetes these may be very reduced and hard to see; in others, like the fireworms, they may look like small legs.

PEDAL LACERATION: The production of small clonal individuals by the fragmentation of the foot of anemones and mushroom polyps. As the animal moves, a small blob of tissue is shed from the foot. This differentiates over a few days and changes into a complete small anemone.

PEDICELLARIAE (SINGULAR = PEDICELLARIA): These are modified spines found on some sea stars and sea urchins. The spines are modified into biting two- or three-jawed pinching structures at the ends of long, flexible stalks.

PETALOID: The flowerlike, five-rayed pattern seen on the back of a sand dollar.

PHYTOPLANKTON: Unicellular algae that live in the water column.

PINHOLE EYE: Simple image-forming eye found in nautiloids; instead of going through a lens, the light enters the eye through a small opening (the pinhole) in the outer surface of the eye.

PINNATE TENTACLES: Tentacles with small branches found on both sides of the central axis; characteristic of the tentacles of all soft corals and of many feather duster worms.

PLANISPIRAL: A mollusk shell that is coiled in one plane, such as in the chambered nautilus.

PLANKTIVORE: An animal that eats plankton.

PROBOSCIS: An anterior extension of the gut of many animals, generally it is extensible with the mouth at the tip.

PROSOMA: The anterior, or first portion, of the body of a horseshoe crab or other chelicerate animal.

PSEUDOPODIA: The extension of the body of an amoeba or amoebalike animal used for food gathering or locomotion.

RADULA: A tonguelike projection, found in the mouth of most mollusks, which is covered with teeth and used to rasp up food.

ROSTRUM: The projection extending forward from between the eyes of some shrimps and crabs.

SEGMENT: A repeated portion of an animal's body. Segmented animals are generally comprised of many similar segments; characteristic of annelid worms, arthropods, tapeworms, and vertebrates.

SETAE: Hairlike projections covering crustaceans; although they look like hairs, they are hollow and contain nerves. They have a sensory function.

SIPHONAL CANAL: The calcareous tube or spout on whelks, conchs, and some other snails; the flexible breathing tube or siphon extends out from this canal.

SIPHONOZOID: One of the types of colonial "individuals" constituting a soft coral; these are modified polyps lacking tentacles whose function is to pump water into the colony.

SPICULES: Mineralized deposits found in the tissues of many animals. Depending upon the animal, they may be formed from calcium carbonate, calcium phosphate, or silica.

STOLONIFEROUS SOFT CORALS: Soft corals in which all the individual polyps arise from runners sent out from a single ancestral polyp.

STOLONS: Extensions of the body of some animals, such as some soft corals and some tunicates, that function as "runners" and which can give rise to other clonal individuals.

SWEEPER TENTACLES: Tentacles produced by many corals as an aggressive response. Often packed with virulent nematocysts, they are used to sting and kill potential competitors or aggressors.

TEST: Shell or casing. The sea urchin skeleton is called a test, as is the shell of a foraminiferan.

TUBE FEET: The locomotory or feeding appendages of echinoderms, and the "business end" of their water vascular system. They are often tipped with an adhesive pad and may extend long distances, in some cases over 3 feet (91 cm), from their base.

TUNIC: The covering of a tunicate or sea squirt, animals in the taxonomic Class Ascidiacea of the Phylum Urochordata; composed of cellulose and some other materials.

VERRUCAE: Bumps or tubercles found on the columns of sea anemones, these are adhesive and help stabilize the animal in sediments.

ZOOID: An "individual" of a colonial animal, such as a compound ascidiacean, bryozoan, siphonophore, or soft coral.

ZOOPLANKTON: Small animals found living in the water column.

ZOOXANTHELLAE: Symbiotic unicellular dinoflagellate algae, in the genus *Symbiodinium*, that live in the tissues of many tropical animals, such as corals, sea anemones, soft corals, tridacnid clams, some sponges, and some foraminiferans.

The following links will get you started if you have questions about the various groups in this volume. These in turn will lead you to many more of the thousands of websites available.

REEF AQUARIUM ANIMALS

http://www.rshimek.com/animal_identifications1.htm

SPONGES

http://www.ucmp.berkeley.edu/porifera/porifera.html
http://www.palaeos.com/Invertebrates/Porifera/Porifera.htm

CNIDARIANS

http://www.ucihs.uci.edu/biochem/steele/default.html

SEA ANEMONES/CORALS

http://www.kgs.ukans.edu/Hexacoral/

HYDROZOANS

http://www.ucmp.berkeley.edu/cnidaria/hydrozoa.html

SCYPHOZOANS

http://www.ucmp.berkeley.edu/cnidaria/scyphozoa.html

CTENOPHORES

http://www.ucmp.berkeley.edu/cnidaria/ctenophora.html
http://faculty.washington.edu/cemills/Ctenophores.html

FLATWORMS

http://www.rzuser.uni-heidelberg.de/~bu6/

ANNELIDS

http://www.ucmp.berkeley.edu/annelida/annelida.html
http://www.discoverlife.org/nh/tx/Annelida/

ARTHROPODS/CRUSTACEA

http://www.crustacea.net/crustace/

MOLLUSCA: BIVALVES

http://animaldiversity.ummz.umich.edu/site/accounts/information/
    Bivalvia.html

MOLLUSCA: GASTROPODS
> **SHELLED SNAILS:** http://www.gastropods.com/
> **SEA SLUGS:** http://www.seaslugforum.net/

MOLLUSCA: CEPHALOPODS
http://www.dal.ca/~ceph/TCP/

BRYOZOANS
http://www.civgeo.rmit.edu.au/bryozoa/default.html

PHORONIDS
http://www.earthlife.net/inverts/phoronida.html

ECHINODERMS
http://www.palaeos.com/Invertebrates/Echinoderms/echinodermata.htm

CRINOIDS
http://www.nova.edu/ocean/messing/crinoids/w1title.html

ASTEROIDS
http://www.ucmp.berkeley.edu/echinodermata/asteroidea.html

BRITTLE STARS
http://www.ucmp.berkeley.edu/echinodermata/ophiuroidea.html
http://home.att.net/~ophiuroid/

SEA URCHINS
http://www.ucmp.berkeley.edu/echinodermata/echinoidea.html
http://www.nhm.ac.uk/palaeontology/echinoids/

SEA CUCUMBERS
http://tolweb.org/tree?group=Holothuroidea&contgroup=Echinodermata

TUNICATES
http://www.guiamarina.com/ascidiacea/list.php?i=allspccies&p=1
http://www.earthlife.net/inverts/ascidiacea.html

Abbott, R.T. 1974. *American Seashells*. Van Nostrand Reinhold Company, New York. Pp. 663.

Abbott, R.T. and S.P. Dance. 1982. *Compendium of Sea Shells. A Color Guide to More than 4,200 of the World's Marine Shells*. E.P. Dutton, Inc., New York. Pp. 410.

Ambariyanto and O. Hoegh-Guldberg. 1999. Net Uptake of dissolved free amino acids by the giant clam *Tridacna maximua*: alternative sources of energy and nitrogen. *Coral Reefs* 18:91-96.

Anderson, R.C. and J.A. Mather. 1996. Escape responses of *Euprymna scolopes* Berry, 1991 (Cephalopoda: Sepiolidae). *J Molluscan Stud* 62:543-545.

Bell, L.J. 1992. Reproduction and larval development of the West Indian topshell, *Cittarium pica* (Trochidae), in the Bahamas. *Bull Marine Sci* 51:250-266.

Birkeland, C. 1974. Interactions between a sea pen and seven of its predators. *Ecol Monogr* 44:211-232.

Bloom, S.A. 1981. Specialization and noncompetitive resource partitioning among sponge-eating dorid nudibranchs. *Oecologia* 49:305-315.

Borneman, E.H. 2001. *Aquarium Corals. Selection, Husbandry and Natural History*. Microcosm Ltd./T.F.H. Pubs., Neptune City, NJ. Pp. 463.

Britton, J.C. and B. Morton. 1993. Are there obligate marine scavengers? In: *The Marine Biology of the South China Sea*, Morton, B. (Ed.). Hong Kong University Press, Hong Kong:357-391.

Britton, J.C. and B. Morton. 1994. Marine carrion and scavengers. *Oceanogr Mar Biol Ann Rev* 32:369-404.

Bruce, A.J. 1992. Two new species of *Periclimenes* (Crustacea: Decapoda: Palaemonidae) from Lizard Island, Queensland, with notes on some related taxa. *Rec Austr Mus*: 44:45-84.

Caso, M.E. 1979. Descripcion de una nueva especie de ofiuroideo de la Laguna de Terminos, *Amphiodia guillermosoberoni* sp. nov. *Anales del Centro de Ciencias del Mar Y Limnologia Universidad Nacional Autonoma de Mexico* 6:161-184.

Cherbonnier, G. and A. Guille. 1978. Echinodermes: ophiurides. *Faune De Madagascar* 48:1-272.

Chess, J.R., E.S. Hobson, and D.F. Howard. 1997. Interactions between *Acanthaster planci* (Echinodermata, Asteroidea) and Scleractinian Corals at Kona, Hawaii. *Pac Sci* 51:121-133.

Colin, P.L. 1978. *Caribbean Reef Invertebrates and Plants*. T.F.H. Pubs., Neptune City, NJ. Pp. 478.

Colin, P.L. and C. Arneson. 1995. *Tropical Pacific Invertebrates. A Field Guide to the Marine Invertebrates Occurring on Tropical Pacific Coral Reefs, Seagrass Beds, and Mangroves*. Coral Reef Press, Beverly Hills, CA. Pp. 296.

Deheyn, D., V. Alva, and M. Jangoux. 1996. Fine structure of the photogenous areas in the bioluminescent ophiuroid *Amphipholis squamata* (Echinodermata, Ophiuridea). *Zoomorph* (Berlin) 116:195-204.

Dunn, D.F. 1981. The clownfish sea anemones: Stichodactylidae (Coelenterata: Actinaria) and other sea anemones symbiotic with pomacentrid fishes. *Trans Am Philosoph Soc* 71:1-115.

Ernisse, D.J. and P.D. Reynolds. 1994. Polyplacophora. In: *Microscopic Anatomy of Invertebrates*, Harrison, F.W. and A.J. Kohn (Eds.). Mollusca I. Wiley-Liss. New York:55-110.

Fauchald, K. 1977. *The Polychaete Worms; Definitions and Keys to the Orders, Families, and Genera. Science Series 28*. Natural History Museum of Los Angeles County, Los Angeles, CA. Pp. 188.

Fautin, D.G. and G. Allen. 1992. *Field Guide to Anemonefishes and Their Host Sea Anemones*. Western Australian Museum, Perth, Australia. Pp. 160.

Fautin, D.G., C.-C. Guo, and J.-S. Hwang. 1995. Costs and benefits of the symbiosis between the anemone shrimp *Periclimenes brevicarpalis* and its host *Entacmaea quadricolor*. *Mar Ecol Prog Ser* 129:77-84.

Fiedler, G.C. 1998. Functional, simultaneous hermaphroditism in female-phase *Lysmata amboinensis* (Decapoda: Caridea: Hippolytidae). *Pac Sci* 52:161-169.

Fletcher, D.J., I. Kotter, M. Wunsch, and I. Yasir. 1995. Preliminary observations on the reproductive biology of ornamental cleaner prawns *Stenopus hispidus*, *Lysmata amboinensis* and *Lysmata debelius*. *Int Zoo Yearbk* 34:73-77.

Fuhrman, F.A., G.J. Fuhrman, and K. DeRiemer. 1979. Toxicity and pharmacology of extracts from dorid nudibranchs. *Biol Bull* 156:289-299.

Ghyoot, M., P. Dubois, and M. Jangoux. 1994. The venom apparatus of the globiferous pedicellariae of the toxopneustid *Sphaerechinus granularis* (Echinodermata, Echinoida): Fine structure and mechanism of venom discharge. *Zoomorph* 114:73-82.

Gibbs, P.E. and E.B. Cutler. 1987. A classification of the Phylum Sipuncula. *Bull Brit Mus Nat Hist (Zool)* 52:43-58.

Gosliner, T.M., D.W. Behrens, and G.C. Williams. 1996. *Coral Reef Animals of the Indo-Pacific. Animal Life from Africa to Hawaii Exclusive of the Vertebrates*. Sea Challengers, Monterey, CA. Pp. 314.

Green, J.L. and A.J. Kohn. 1989. Functional morphology of the *Conus proboscis* (Mollusca: Gastropoda). *J Zool, London* 219:487-493.

Griffiths, C.L. and D.W. Klumpp. 1996. Relationships between size, mantle area and zooxanthellae numbers in five species of giant clam (Tridacnidae). *Mar Ecol Prog Ser* 137:139-147.

Guo, C.-C., J.-S. Hwang, and D.G. Fautin. 1996. Host selection by shrimps symbiotic with sea anemones: A field survey and experimental laboratory analysis. *J Exp Mar Biol Ecol* 202:165-176.

Gwaltney, C.L. and W.R. Brooks. 1994. Host specificity of the anemone shrimp *Periclimenes pedersoni* and *P. yucatanicus* in the Florida Keys. *Symbiosis* 16:83-93.

Hickman, C.S. and J.H. Lipps. 1983. Foraminiferivory: selective ingestion of foraminifera and test alterations produced by the neogastropod Olivella. *J Foram Res* 13:108-114.

Hickman, C.S. and J.H. McLean. 1990. Suprageneric classification of Trochacean gastropods. *Nat Hist Mus Los Angeles County, Sci Ser* 35:vi + 169.

Hoegh-Guldberg, O. 1996. Nutrient enrichment and the ultrastructure of zooxanthellae from the giant clam *Tridacna maxima*. *Mar Biol* 125:359-363.

Holland, N.D., A.B. Leonard, and D.L. Meyer. 1991. Digestive mechanics and gluttonous feeding in the feather star *Oligometra serripinna* (Echinodermata: Crinoidea). *Mar Biol* (Berlin) 111:112-120.

Humann, P. 1992. *Reef Creature Identification. Florida-Caribbean-Bahamas.* New World Pubs., Jacksonville, FL. Pp. 344.

Humann, P. 1993. *Reef Coral Identification. Florida-Caribbean-Bahamas.* New World Pubs., Jacksonville, FL. Pp. 252.

Hyman, L.H. 1940. *The Invertebrates. Volume 1. Protozoa through Ctenophora.* McGraw-Hill Book Co., NY. Pp. 726.

Hyman, L.H. 1951. *The Invertebrates. Volume 2. Platyhelminthes and Rhynchocoela, the Acoelomate Bilateria.* McGraw-Hill Book Co., NY. Pp. 550.

Hyman, L.H. 1951. *The Invertebrates. Volume 3. Acanthocephala, Aschelminthes, and Entoprocta, the Pseudocoelomate Bilateria.* McGraw-Hill Book Co., NY. Pp. 572.

Hyman, L.H. 1955. *The Invertebrates. Volume 4. Echinodermata, the Coelomate Bilateria.* McGraw-Hill Book Co. NY. Pp. 763.

Hyman, L.H. 1959. *The Invertebrates. Volume 5. Smaller Coelomate Groups.* McGraw-Hill Book Co., NY. Pp. 783.

Hyman, L.H. 1967. *The Invertebrates. Volume 6. Mollusca I*. McGraw-Hill Book Co. Pp. 792.

Jensen, K.R. 1991. Comparison of alimentary systems in shelled and non-shelled Sacoglossa (Mollusca, Opisthobranchia). *Acta Zool (Stockholm)* 72:143-150.

Jensen, K.R. 1996. Phylogenetic systematics and classification of the Sacoglossa (Mollusca, Gastropoda, Opisthobranchia). *Philosoph Trans Royal Soc London B Biol Sci* 351:91-122.

Jensen, K.R. 1997. Evolution of the Sacoglossa (Mollusca, Opisthobranchia) and the ecological associations with their food plants. *Evol Ecol* 11:301-335.

Keen, A.M. 1971. *Sea Shells of Tropical West America*. Stanford University Press, Palo Alto, CA. Pp. 1064.

Kerth, K. 1983. Radulaapparat und Radulabildung der Mollusken. I. Vergleichende Morphologie und Ultrastruktur. *Zool Jb Anat* 110:205-237.

Kerth, K. 1983. Radulaapparat und Radulabildung der Mollusken. II. Zahnbildung, Abbau und Radulawachstum. *Zool Jb Anat* 110:239-269.

Kohn, A.J. 1959. The ecology of *Conus* in Hawaii. *Ecol* 29:47-90.

Kohn, A.J. 1961. Chemoreception in Gastropod Molluscs. *Am Zool* :291-308.

Kohn, A.J. 1970. Food habits of the gastropod *Mitra litterata* Lamarck: Relation to trophic structure of the intertidal marine bench community in Hawaii. *Pac Sci* 24:483-486.

Kohn, A.J. 1972. Radula tooth structure in the Gastoropod *Conus imperialis* elucidated by scanning electron microscopy. *Sci* 176:49-51.

Kohn, A.J. 1983. Feeding biology of Gastropods. In: *Physiology (2)*, Wilbur, K.M. (Ed.). Academic Press, New York:1-63.

Kohn, A.J. and M.E. Rice. 1971. Biology of Sipuncula and Echiura. *Biosci* 21:583-584.

Klumpp, D.W. and C.L. Griffiths. 1994. Contributions of phototrophic and heterotrophic nutrition to the metabolic and growth requirements of four species of giant clan (Tridacnidae). *Mar Ecol Prog Ser* 115:103-115.

Klumpp, D.W. and J.S. Lucas. 1994. Nutritional ecology of the giant clams *Tridacna tevoroa* and *T. derasa* from Tonga: influence of light on filter-feeding and photosynthesis. *Mar Ecol Prog Ser* 107:147-156.

Kott, P. 1980. Algal-bearing didemnid ascidians in the Indo-West Pacific. *Mem Queensland Mus* 20:1-48.

LaBarbera, M. 1978. Particle capture by a Pacific brittle star: Experimental test of the aerosol suspension feeding method. *Sci* 201:1147-1149.

Lares, M.T. and J.B. McClintock. 1991. The effects of temperature on the survival, organismal activity, nutrition, growth and reproduction of the carnivorous tropical sea urchin *Eucidaris tribuloides*. *Mar Behav Physiol* 19:75-96.

Leclair, E.E. 1996. Arm joint articulations in the ophiuran brittlestars (Echinodermata: Ophiuroidea): A morphometric analysis of ontogenetic, serial, and interspecific variation. *J Zool London* 240:245-275.

Lindquist, N., M.E. Hay and W. Fenical. 1992. Defense of ascidians and their conspicuous larvae: Adult vs. larval chemical defenses. *Ecol Monogr* 62:547-568.

Littler, M.M. and D.S. Littler. 1999. Castles built by a chiton from the Great Astrolabe Reef, Fiji. *Coral Reefs* 18:158.

Loo, L.O., P.R. Jonsson, M. Skold, and O. Karlsson. 1996. Passive suspension feeding in *Amphiura filiformis* (Echinodermata: Ophiuroidea): Feeding behaviour in flume flow and potential feeding rate of field populations. *Mar Ecol Prog Ser* 139:143-155.

Mather, J.A. and R.C. Anderson. 1999. Exploration, Play, and Habituation in Octopuses (*Octopus dolfleini*). *J Comp Psychol* 113:333-338.

McGehee, M.A. 1992. Distribution and abundance of two species of Echinometra (Echinoidea) on coral reefs near Puerto Rico. *Carib J Sci* 28:173-183.

Monniot, C., F. Monniot, and P. Laboute. 1991. *Coral Reef Ascidians of New Caledonia*. Editions de L'ORSTOM, Paris. Pp. 248.

Nizinski, M.S. 1989. Ecological distribution, demography and behavioral observations on *Periclimenes anthophilus*, an atypical cleaner shrimp. *Bull Mar Sci* 45:174-188.

Okuno, J. and M. Takeda. 1992. Description of a new hinge-beak shrimp, *Rhynchocinetes conspiciocellus*, from southern Japan, with designation of the lectotype of *Rhynchocinetes uritai* KUBO, 1942. *Bull Nat Sci Mus Ser (Zoology)* 18:63-72.

Perron, F.E. and A.J. Kohn. 1985. Larval dispersal and geographic distribution in coral reef gastropods of the genus *Conus*. *Proc Fifth Int Coral Reef Cong* 4:95-100.

Proksch, P. 1994. Defensive Role for secondary metabolites from marine sponges and sponge-feeding nudibranchs. *Toxicon* 32:639-655.

Rice, M. 1993. Sipuncula. In: *Onychophora, Chilopoda, and Lesser Protostomes*, Harrison, F.W. and M.E. Rice (Eds.). Wiley-Liss, NY: 237-325.

Rinkevich, B. 1993. Major preliminary stages of biomineralization in radular teeth of the limpet *Lottia gigantea*. *Mar Biol* 117:269-277.

Robertson, R. 1963. Wentletraps (Epitoniidae) feeding on sea anemones and corals. *Proc Malacol Soc London* 35:51-63.

Rudman, W.B. 1991. Further studies on the taxonomy and biology of the octocoral-feeding genus *Phyllodesmium* Ehrenberg, 1831 (Nudibranchia: Aeolidoidea). *J Molluscan Stud* 57:167-204.

Rufino, M.M. and D.A. Jones. 2001. Binary individual recognition in *Lysmata debelius* (Decapoda: Hippolytidae) under laboratory conditions. *J Crust Biol* 21:388-392.

Ruppert, E.E, R.S. Fox, and R.D. Barnes. 2003. *Invertebrate Zoology, A Functional Evolutionary Approach. 7th Ed.* Brooks/Cole-Thomson Learning. Belmont, CA. xvii +963 pp.+ I1-I26pp.

Seed, R. and R.N. Hughes. 1995. Criteria for prey size-selection in molluscivorous crabs with contrasting claw morphologies. *J Exp Mar Biol Ecol* 193:177-195.

Shimek, R.L. 2001. *Host Sea Anemone Secrets. A Guide to the Successful Husbandry of Indo-Pacific Clownfish Host Sea Anemones.* Marc Weiss Companies, Inc., FL. Pp. 24.

Spotte, S., R.W. Heard, P.M. Bubucis, R.R. Manstan, and J.A. McLelland. 1991. Pattern and coloration of *Periclimenes rathbunae* from the Turks and Caicos Islands (British West Indies), with comments on host associations in other anemone shrimps of the West Indies and Bermuda (North Atlantic Ocean). *Gulf Res Rep* 8:301-312.

Stoner, A.W. and V.J. Sandt. 1992. Population structure, seasonal movements and feeding of queen conch, *Strombus gigas*, in deep-water habitats of the Bahamas. *Bull Mar Sci* 51:287-300.

Tan, K.S. and B. Morton. 1998. The ecology of *Engina armillata* (Gastropoda: Buccinidae) in the Cape d'Aguilar Marine Reserve, Hong Kong, with particular reference to its preferred prey (Polychaeta: Serpulidae). *J Zool London* 244:391-403.

Telford, M. and R. Mooi. 1996. Podial particle picking in *Cassidulus caribbearum* (Echinodermata: Echinoidea) and the phylogeny of sea urchin feeding mechanisms. *Biol Bull* (Woods Hole) 191:209-223.

Thomas, F.I.M. and A.J. Kohn. 1990. Trophic roles of co-occurring species of Drupa (Gastropoda: Muricidae) at Enewetok Atoll. *J Molluscan Stud* 56:57-62.

Voltzow, J. 1990. The functional morphology of the pedal musculature of the marine gastropods *Busycon contrarium* and *Haliotis kamtschatkana*. *Veliger* 33:1-19.

Voltzow, J. 1994. Gastropoda: Prosobranchia. In: *Microscopic Anatomy of Invertebrates, Mollusca I*, Harrison, F.W. and A.J. Kohn (Eds.). Wiley-Liss:111-252.

Ward, P.D. 1987. *The Natural History of Nautilus*. Routledge, NY. Pp. 192.

Warner, G. 1977. *The Biology of Crabs*. Van Nostrand Reinhold Co., NY. Pp. 202.

West, T.L. 1991. Functional morphology of the proboscis of *Mitra catalinae* Dall, 1920 (Mollusca: Gastropoda: Mitridae) and the evolution of the mitrid epiproboscis. *Bull Mar Sci* 48:702-718.

Williams, S.T. 1999. Species boundaries in the starfish genus *Linckia*. *Mar Biol* 135:137-148.

Wulff, J.L. 1995. Sponge-feeding by the Caribbean starfish *Oreaster reticulatus*. *Mar Biol* (Berlin) 123:313-325.

Zhang, D. and J. Lin. 1998. Ingestion rate and feeding behavior of the peppermint shrimp *Lysmata wurdemanni* on *Artemia nauplii*. *J World Aquacult Soc* 29:97-103.

PHOTOGRAPHY CREDITS

All photographs by Scott W. Michael, except as follows:

Janine Cairns-Michael

24, 38, 39, 43, 62, 72(T, B), 73(B), 74, 77, 81(B), 83, 87(T), 89, 90, 91, 93, 95, 98, 109, 114(BL, BR), 121, 122, 126, 127, 128, 133, 139, 142(T), 143, 144, 145(T), 148, 149, 152(T, BR), 155(BL, BR), 158(BR), 160, 162, 163(T), 164, 165, 168, 173, 175, 176, 183(T), 184, 185(T), 189, 190, 191(inset), 192, 194, 195, 196, 198, 213, 214, 215, 246, 248, 249, 253, 259, 268, 283, 308, 313, 337, 338, 341(TL), 346, 351(B), 357, 359, 361, 364, 365, 366, 367, 370, 371, 372, 375, 380, 382(T, B), 392, 393, 394, 395, 396, 402, 411, 416, Back cover(T)

Paul Humann

11, 12, 34, 35, 37, 42, 45, 46, 49, 50, 52, 53, 54, 85, 96, 97, 101, 105, 107, 115, 116, 124, 138, 140, 141, 153, 158(T), 183(B), 202, 209, 225, 244, 262, 298(T), 304, 310, 311, 316, 317, 320, 330, 331, 378, 403, 407

Bioquatic Photo — A.J. Nilsen (www.biophoto.net)

20, 21, 23, 28, 29, 41, 44, 51, 55, 58, 61, 63, 64, 70, 102, 108, 136, 158(BL), 221, 230, 245, 257, 263, 269, 274, 298(B), 306, 312, 389, 417(B)

Ron Shimek

33, 103, 197, 198(inset), 223, 224, 226, 227, 232, 234, 272, 299, 339

Denise Nielsen Tackett

8, 16, 32, 56, 99, 205, 206, 208, 238, 275, 301, 325, 336, 384, 397, 401(B), 417(T)

Larry Tackett

203, 207, 222, 231, 233, 258, 261, 315, 328, 387, 404

PHOTOGRAPHY CREDITS

Svein A. Fosså
26, 78, 254, 264, 267, 273, 409

Robert Fenner
88, 300, 314, 389

John Goodman
14

J.F. Hamel
228

Sally Jo Headlee
114(CR)

John P. Hoover
92, 323

Jun Imamoto
334

Larry Jackson
145(B)

Alan Kohn
322

Michael Paletta
81(T)

Wayne Shang
161

Roger Steene
295

INDEX

443

PHOTO BY ROXIE FREDRICKSON

DR. RONALD SHIMEK IS AN INVERTEBRATE ZOOLOGIST with over 30 years of experience in teaching about and working with marine and freshwater invertebrates. He has taught invertebrate zoology with an emphasis on understanding the organism's role in its environment and how that role is related to the functional morphology of the organism. His research specialty is predator-prey interactions in unconsolidated sediments, particularly the interactions involving turrid gastropods, and scaphopod mollusks. He has published numerous scientific articles and been an invited speaker at ten international or national symposia.

He has been Chairman of the Biology Department of the University of Alaska, Anchorage, and Assistant Director of the Bamfield Marine Sciences Centre on Vancouver Island, British Columbia. He has also taught at the University of Washington, the Oregon State University, and Montana State University.

Awarded the 2001 MASNA Award for Outstanding Contributions to the Marine Aquarium Hobby at MACNA XIII, he has published over 75 articles in aquarium magazines published in the United States. He has been an invited speaker at national, regional, and society meetings, where he has discussed and promoted reef-keeping based on knowledge of natural systems, and rationality.

He resides in Wilsall, Montana, where he is actively investigating the suitability of different organisms for the aquarium hobby.